FREEDOM FROM FEAR,
FREEDOM FROM WANT

D1600853

FREEDOM FROM FEAR, FREEDOM FROM WANT

An Introduction to Human Security

Robert J. Hanlon
Kenneth Christie

UNIVERSITY OF TORONTO PRESS

Copyright © University of Toronto Press 2016
Higher Education Division

www.utppublishing.com

Library and Archives Canada Cataloguing in Publication

Hanlon, Robert J., 1977–, author

       Freedom from fear, freedom from want : an introduction to human security / Robert J. Hanlon, Kenneth Christie.

Includes bibliographical references and index.

Issued in print and electronic formats.

ISBN 978-1-4426-0957-0 (paperback).—ISBN 978-1-4426-0958-7 (hardback).— ISBN 978-1-4426-0959-4 (pdf).—ISBN 978-1-4426-0960-0 (html).

    1. Human security. I. Christie, Kenneth, 1960–, author II. Title.

JC571.H37 2016   355.033   C2015-907494-0   C2015-907495-9

We welcome comments and suggestions regarding any aspect of our publications—please feel free to

contact us at news@utphighereducation.com or visit our Internet site at www.utppublishing.com.

North America
5201 Dufferin Street
North York, Ontario, Canada, M3H 5T8

2250 Military Road
Tonawanda, New York, USA, 14150

ORDERS PHONE: 1-800-565-9523
ORDERS FAX: 1-800-221-9985
ORDERS E-MAIL: utpbooks@utpress.utoronto.ca

UK, Ireland, and continental Europe
NBN International
Estover Road, Plymouth, PL6 7PY, UK
ORDERS PHONE: 44 (0) 1752 202301
ORDERS FAX: 44 (0) 1752 202333
ORDERS E-MAIL: enquiries@nbninternational.com

The University of Toronto Press acknowledges the financial support for its publishing activities of the Government of Canada through the Canada Book Fund.

Printed in the United States of America.

Dedicated to
Audrey, Taylor, and Jackie

CONTENTS

ACKNOWLEDGMENTS

This book would not have been possible without the support of many people in our lives who continue to inspire. We especially would like to thank the anonymous reviewers who offered exceptional advice and guidance on how to improve our work and develop the many themes running throughout this text. We thank our colleagues at Thompson Rivers University and Royal Roads University who have provided encouragement over the years, including our editor at University of Toronto Press, Mark Thompson, who has offered outstanding support and direction since we began this project. We would also like to extend thanks to our copyeditor, Leanne Rancourt, for her help, and a special thanks to John Ravenhill at the Balsillie School of International Affairs in Waterloo for providing a quiet place to write during the final stages of this text's production. We are also grateful for the invaluable assistance provided by Bryan and Shannon Robinson, as well as Lisa Hanlon. Finally, it would not be possible to write such a book without the inspiration we have gained over the years from our graduate students in the Human Security and Peacebuilding Program at Royal Roads University. The motivation and brilliance that they bring to the classroom is an everyday reminder that there are many of us who care deeply about what happens to the marginalized and vulnerable people on our planet. We wrote this book with our students in mind, and hope that this small contribution may offer some helpful thoughts on how we believe the world can become a little more secure.

PREFACE

Human security is a fairly well researched and documented subject within the disciplines of international relations, political science, and development. It's also been tackled by scholars in geography and anthropology, among other disciplines. Extensive scholarship has been developed by many of the world's leading political science and international relations theorists, including Aiden Hehir (2013), Michael Barnett, and Christoph Zürcher (2009); Alex Bellamy and Paul Williams (2009); Mary Kaldor (2007); Brian Job (2004); David Chandler (2004); Richard Falk (2005); Oliver Ramsbotham, Hugh Miall, and Tom Woodhouse (2011); Steve Smith (2005); Ramesh Thakur (2006); Roland Paris (2001); Paul Evans (2004); Taylor Owen (2004); Amitav Acharya (2001); Fen Osler Hampson and Jean Daudelin (2002); as well as Caroline Thomas (2001). While these authors are among the many who have contributed to the burgeoning field of human security, most of these important works remain at the highly theoretical level, are not of an interdisciplinary nature, and are inaccessible to undergraduates and the lay reader. As far as we are aware, no attempt has been made to compile such arguments in a book designed for students and educators alike. The fact is that human security is an interdisciplinary concept and framework that poses an alternative form of reality/social construction to traditional theories and practices of security.

This book aims to provide undergraduates and instructors with a practical resource for studying human security, conflict, and development from an interdisciplinary perspective. Unlike traditional security models, human security argues that *protection* and *empowerment* at the individual and collective levels are critical to achieving sustainable development and security. The text will provide students with necessary skills to analyze contemporary human security issues, such as climate change, crimes against humanity, failed states, humanitarian intervention, good governance, international law, poverty, terrorism and transnational crime, and others. While the book's primary target audience is undergraduates from a wide range of disciplines and subdisciplines of development, it will provide an interdisciplinary perspective. We also hope to enable students to critically assess emerging threats while at the same time evaluating potential mechanisms of deterrence, such as conflict resolution, economic development, diplomacy, peacekeeping, international law, and restorative justice.

This text also provides the theoretical foundations for individuals pursuing careers in areas related to human security, peacebuilding, and international development. While focused on human security, this book will also present debates from across the social sciences and humanities in a coherent and fluid framework. Indeed, by leveraging expert points of view from across academia, we hope to provide a model for interdisciplinary approaches to security studies.

This text, moreover, attempts to balance a rigorous theoretical overview of human security while offering instructors and students real-world case studies that are imperative for analyzing conflict and security in the post–Cold War era. The authors—who have many years of global experience having lived, taught, and researched all over the world—are now firmly based in Canada, and we hope that we have been able to provide much material drawn from the context of the global approach to human security. Within the context of the book, we also provide recommended links and direction to websites and readings designed to "show" students cases in human security. Here we are making an effort to bring the world of human security to the classroom through visual imagery and advanced scholarly debate. In short, we hope you (the student and the instructor) will find the book to be a unique contribution that enhances learning in the field of human security, conflict, and development and provides the student with a thought-provoking experience.

The book is divided into three sections. The first section begins with three chapters that explore the contending theoretical perspectives to human security, conflict, and development. The second section will compare the "top-down" and "bottom-up" approaches to resolving conflict through governance and intervention. The final section will discuss the relationship between development, globalization, and human security.

We realize that human security is a fairly new conceptual framework for understanding nontraditional security threats that came to prominence following the end of the Cold War. Nevertheless, we hope the text will be an important resource for students and educators alike within the world of human security, conflict, and development and the often complex relationships that surround them.

ROBERT HANLON AND KENNETH CHRISTIE
Vancouver and Victoria, British Columbia, Canada

PART ONE

Chapter 1

HUMAN SECURITY, CONFLICT, AND DEVELOPMENT

We have learned that we cannot live alone, at peace; that our own well-being is dependent on the well-being of other nations, far away. We have learned that we must live as men, and not as ostriches, nor as dogs in the manger. We have learned to be citizens of the world, members of the human community.

Franklin D. Roosevelt, fourth inaugural address, January 20, 1945
(quoted in Annan 2000a, 130)

INTRODUCTION

We are living in an age of insecurity. Political violence, resource depletion, and economic instability are only a few of the challenges facing the planet in the post–Cold War era. Nearly 900 million people live in absolute poverty, while another 663 million are without access to drinking water. Over 16,000 children die each day from pneumonia, diarrhea, and malaria (S. Jones 2015). While these numbers may seem appalling, they are an improvement over previous times. Multilateral efforts involving a range of actors, including the United Nations, government agencies, civil society groups, businesses, and grassroots activists, are working to improve human security. Globalization has brought new technology that beams human insecurity into our living rooms and Twitter feeds on an almost instantaneous basis. The continuous coverage of victims of war and humanitarian disasters allows us to immediately assess human crises, yet understanding why billions of people face such appalling struggles is complex and requires a serious study of vulnerable and marginalized populations.

In this introductory chapter, we address these challenges and introduce the key thematic areas of human security, conflict, and **development** in the post–Cold War world and how and why they relate to one another. From a conceptual and practical viewpoint we trace the historical emergence of human security as a new **interdisciplinary** framework that draws on nontraditional understandings of how and why human security relates to the state, conflict, peace, and development. An in-depth discussion of two of the key tenets of human security will be presented—namely the emphasis on "freedom from fear" and "freedom from want"—as well as the concepts of protection and empowerment. Stressing the importance of cooperation, peace, and empathy, human security will be considered as an extension of traditional security within a value-based framework that endorses conflict resolution and peacebuilding. This relates not only to vulnerable individuals, but also to aggregates and groups who have social development goals. We analyze key concepts as they pertain to safeguarding human lives; protecting fundamental human rights to survival, livelihood, and basic dignity; and "people-centered" versus state-centric approaches to security. Beginning with the 1994 UNDP (United Nations Development Programme) *Human Development Report*, we will examine the policy implications of human security doctrine for bilateral and multilateral actors as well as for nongovernment organizations (NGOs), particularly in the fields of good governance, rule of law, and human rights sectors.

The chapter also illustrates how human security has become globalized following the end of the Cold War using two cases that highlight different and similar kinds of conflict: Syria's ongoing civil war and Pakistan's conflict over religion and ethnicity. In all of these conflicts, the real casualties have been civilians on the receiving end of violence and intimidation and the consequences of human insecurity.

HUMAN SECURITY AND WHAT IT MEANS

Human Security, in its broadest sense, embraces far more than the absence of violent conflict. It encompasses human rights, good governance, access to education and health care and ensuring that each individual has opportunities and choices to fulfill his or her potential.

Kofi Annan, former secretary-general of
the United Nations, 1997–2007 (Annan 2001)

Why is human security and peacebuilding important in the twenty-first century, and what does it mean? First, **human security** is the protection of vulnerable individuals to threats and dangers posed by their environment. The concept is interdisciplinary, holistic, and has a normative bias in favor of the individual in a similar way as human rights. It has two main components: an expansive concept, "freedom from want," refers to basic needs such as food, shelter, and development, while a narrow version, "freedom from fear," includes identity needs and physical and personal safety. Both components are interrelated. Amartya Sen, the Nobel Prize–winning economist, discussed the notion of "development as freedom," reinforcing the connection between freedom from fear and freedom from want.

One of the critiques of the idea is that human security is a relatively new concept. It is a "contested" concept, not without controversy in academic and policy circles, and as such has had some difficulty gaining credibility in the academic world. The conceptual framework first emerged as a term in the 1980s as a riposte to "national" security, but it was not until 1994 that it really gained credence. The main difference seemed to be over a variance in definition: freedom from fear as different than a broader, expanded view, freedom from want. Both of these were developed in the UNDP's *Human Development Report of 1994* (UNDP 1994). According to the report the two components were explained as follows:

- Freedom from fear: The narrower of the two seeks to understand human security as protecting individuals from violent conflicts while at the same time seeing these threats as strongly associated with poverty, lack of state capacity, and other forms of inequities.
- Freedom from want: On the other hand, this view argues that threats involved in human security should be expanded to include hunger, poverty, disease, and natural environmental disasters because they are inseparable concepts in addressing the root of insecurity and they also typically kill far more people than war, genocide, and terrorism combined. This develops the focus beyond violence against individuals to emphasize human social and economic development as the optimum way to protect individual security.

In other words, the latter concept views the linkages in a more holistic way. Our argument is that human security encompasses both concepts as complementary and reinforcing—they are structurally linked together. The second term, freedom from want, is more broadly related to development, an umbrella that takes in all sorts of issues, including terrorism, refugees, democracy, peacekeeping, development, and many other types of security agendas. This continues despite the criticism that this framework is too general, unspecific in nature, and therefore problematic in its view of dealing with the issues and problem.

Individual human beings are entitled to security within the states they live in, so human security challenges the realist paradigm of **national security**. While states have typically defined security in a way where their interests are paramount, human security argues that it is individuals who need to be protected, especially when they are usually on the receiving end of state violence. By protecting human security, state security is also protected. And good governance means protecting human security, making people feel safe, and allowing them to pursue their goals. States, while still the main exponents of the monopoly of violence that defines them, have had to react to extra-state actors who threaten them (such as guerillas, terrorists, and social movements, among others) or who may also use violence in their repertoire.

It is also when people feel that their human rights are protected and they are secure that we are exercising good human security and good governance. And some states have adopted tenets of this. Canada and Japan, for instance, both strong proponents of human security, have incorporated features of the UN versions of human security into their foreign policy agendas.

Freedom from Fear

Conceptually, the notion of "freedom from fear" has some history in the human rights literature and is seen as one of the fundamental human rights defined in the Universal Declaration of Human Rights of 1948. In 1941, US President Franklin D. Roosevelt referred to it as one of the Four Freedoms in his State of the Union address. The other three freedoms—freedom of speech and expression, freedom of every person to worship God in his or her own way, and freedom from want—have become standard elements in the idea and practice of universal human rights. Roosevelt (1941) argued in realist, state-centered terms from the point of view of the nation-state that the idea meant "a world-wide reduction of armaments to such a point and in such a thorough fashion that no nation will be in a position to commit an act of physical aggression against any neighbor anywhere in the world." In one sense, this was a peacebuilding measure, but not one necessarily evoked along the lines of the people-centric notion of human security in current use.

Roosevelt's Four Freedoms formed an important pillar of the Universal Declaration of Human Rights adopted on December 10, 1948, by the UN General Assembly. The concept has been expanded over time and defined, perhaps inadvertently, in human security terms most notably by the Burmese freedom fighter and human rights activist Aung San Suu Kyi, who published a book on the view in 1991 with the title *Freedom from Fear* (Suu Kyi 2010). Aung San Suu Kyi, the leader of Burma's National League for Democracy, was detained in 1989 by the SLORC (now renamed), the ruling military junta at the time. She was freed from house arrest in November 2010. The Burmese opposition leader and human rights activist also discussed this in a 1995 speech she delivered in Beijing, China, at the NGO forum on Women in Beijing where she spelled out the connection with human security:

And where there is no security there can be no lasting peace. In its "Human Development Report" for last year the UNDP noted that human security "is not a concern with weapons—it is a concern with human life and dignity." The struggle for democracy and human rights in Burma is a struggle for life and dignity. It is a struggle that encompasses our political, social and economic aspirations. The people of my country want the two freedoms that spell security: freedom from want and freedom from fear. (Suu Kyi 1995)

It is the empathetic, people-driven need for dignity, rights, and life that we see at the core of the human security doctrine.

Throughout this book we will argue that changes in attitudes need to drive concerns for human security since many of the problems that drive human insecurity are structural and engrained in economic underdevelopment along with poverty. Individuals and society need to collectively bring about changes in human security through positive reinforcement of protection and empowerment, but they can only really do this when they are free of poverty and economic deprivation.

Freedom from Want

When we discuss the concept of "freedom from want" as part of human security we are really talking about the idea and process of economic and social security and how societies develop from economic, social, and political perspectives. Furthermore, we break human security down into individual categories that are separate but overlapping areas and fit side by side:

- *Economic security* means that individuals should be assured a basic income typically from productive and remunerative work or, as a last resort, from a government/state–financed safety net. Only about 25 percent of the world's population have this kind of security. Following the economic crisis of 2008–09, this has become a global problem, creating impoverishment and hardship for millions of people. Economic insecurity is one of the drivers of political and social insecurity, creating the conditions for violence and unrest on a global scale.
- *Food security* means that all people should have physical and economic access to basic food. The real problem is not shortages of food but how food is distributed. Food security is a growing area within the global agenda as famine, severe hunger, environmental degradation, and natural disasters create increasing problems in this area on a global scale.
- *Health security* is about minimum protection from diseases and unhealthy lifestyles. In most of the developing world, a leading cause of death is disease. For instance, on a global scale between 68 and 70 percent of people who died in 2012 died of noncommunicable disease, which was up nearly 10 percent from the

previous 10 years. These threats are lethal for poor people, especially children in poverty who represent the most vulnerable.

- *Environmental security* is centered on the effort to protect people from the long-term effects of human-made and natural disasters. Global warming and climate change represent two of the most significant threats to people. The **Millennium Development Project** defines environmental security as meeting three areas:

  o Preventing or repairing damage to the environment
  o Preventing or responding to environmentally caused conflicts
  o Protecting the environment because of its inherent moral value

- *Personal security* focuses on protecting people from physical violence, whether from the state or external states, from violent individuals and sub-state actors, or (in the case of children) from violent abuse from predatory adults. Violent crime is a component of personal insecurity, for instance.
- *Community security* aims to protect people from the loss of traditional values and from sectarian and ethnic violence. It focuses in particular on ethnic minorities who are under threat.
- *Political security* is concerned with whether people live in a society that honors their basic human rights and freedoms and allows them to pursue their aspirations and desires. Human rights constitute an important element in political security. Torture, ill treatment, and disappearance have become commonplace in many dictatorships and increased in intensity following 9/11, with secret prisons that violated basic human rights.

We argue that the two concepts of human security—freedom from want and freedom from fear—are complementary to one another. They are, in fact, both mutually reinforcing and supported by a culture of human rights developed through the Universal Declaration of Human Rights.

Interestingly, much of the innovative work on human security in the UNDP report came from an Asian scholar, Mahbub-ul-Haq, who was intimately familiar with the needs of the developing world. At the time this was criticized by the Canadian version of human security, which was based on the narrow "freedom from fear" version. The Japanese government was instrumental in pushing for the second "freedom from want" version, which relates to development. Most Asian governments supported this broader notion of human security, especially after the regional economic crisis in 1997 and more recently after the devastating earthquake that affected Japan in 2011. The 1997 recession undermined many decades of development—the so-called East Asian Miracle. Regional leaders at the time suggested more social safety nets were needed for the poor and the vulnerable. In Thailand it was certainly not seen as mutually exclusive—both complemented one another. Human security as freedom from fear was viewed as suspicious by many Asian governments, because it looked like yet another attempt to foist liberal human rights agendas by the West. Therefore, these governments adopted the broader view of human security, and hoped that human rights would come later by applying gentle pressure.

Moreover, many Asian societies claim that they come from a long-standing tradition of communitarianism, rather than a Western liberal democratic and individual ethos. Though this may have been disingenuous on the part of some Asian governments, there is nothing incompatible with the idea and practice of human security and communitarian values. The **Asian values** argument, which emanated from the fast-growing Southeast Asian states in the early 1990s, is considered within a later chapter.

We will, moreover, argue that human security means promoting human rights and vice versa, as well as national security. Extending human rights and human security enhances national security to the degree that both sets of interests are seen as parallel: that is, threats to national security are also threats to the well-being of individuals and communities. If human rights and human security abuses overseas can lead to security threats at home, it could be argued that the national interest justifies encouraging or pressuring foreign governments to clean up their records and by acting through regional mechanisms.

MECHANISMS OF HUMAN SECURITY

There are elements of human security that have been adopted completely into foreign policy, although this has varied from government to government and is subject to political change over time. The influence of the UNDP report of 1994 had a major impact on Canadian foreign policy at the time it was released. Lloyd Axworthy, who was Canada's foreign affairs minister between 1996 and 2000, made major efforts to shift the focus from state security to a more human-centered approach. In 1998, the Human Security Network was developed in Canada and Norway, among other nations as an effort to develop different political and legal mechanisms that would give states and NGOs the ability to further human security goals. Through this network Canada was influential in getting other states to sign on to the **Ottawa Treaty** (known more popularly as the Mine Ban Treaty), which was a crucial step forward in attempting to end human suffering caused by anti-personnel land mines. States were persuaded to sign the treaty, eliminate their stocks of mines, and carry out de-mining activities. By the end of 2009 nearly 158 states had signed the treaty, a significant success story in the human security field. Lloyd Axworthy did not stop there, however; he was also instrumental in achieving the establishment of the International Criminal Court, which provided a permanent institution to prosecute war criminals accused of genocide and crimes against humanity.

The International Criminal Court

The **International Criminal Court (ICC)** has some precedent in terms of how it developed, since such views were important at the time of the birth of the United Nations in 1945. The Nuremburg and Tokyo war trials conducted in the aftermath of World War II emerged as tribunals designed to try war criminals for **crimes against humanity** in the post-conflict period. In the 1990s, ad hoc tribunals were developed by the UN Security Council for crimes and genocide in former Yugoslavia and Rwanda. However, it was only with the end of the Cold War that the impetus for the ICC began to emerge. A conference held in Rome in 1998 by the UN International Law Commission cleared the way to move forward. The statute necessary to create the court was agreed on, and by 2002 there were enough signatories to the statute that the court came into being (by 2010, 110 parties had signed the statute). Seven countries refused to sign, including the United States, Israel, China, Iraq, Sudan, Yemen, and Libya. This may seem like an unusual mix of superpower democracies with some very undemocratic states, but the United States feared its military could be prosecuted because of the various wars the country was engaged in.

HUMAN SECURITY AND GOOD GOVERNANCE IN THE TWENTY-FIRST CENTURY

One of the arguments throughout this text is that the changing nature of conflict in the post–Cold War era requires that we focus on threats to the individual as opposed to the state. This is because it is highly vulnerable individuals who are most often at threat. Today we are faced with far more **intrastate conflicts**—in effect, **civil wars**, more often than not with an ethnic dimension. In contemporary times these internecine conflicts are often violent and brutal and support the English philosopher Thomas Hobbes's assertion that life for most people is nasty, brutish, and short, a point he made during the seventeenth-century English Civil War. Unlike Hobbes, however, who had the luxury of escaping to France during this conflict, the inhabitants of countries who face such present-day violent conflict are often unable to get out of their situations. Examples include the horrors in Darfur, Rwanda, the Congo, and Syria, which is still embroiled in a civil war as we write this book. In all of these atrocities one can see the desperate levels of fear and insecurity in the most vulnerable sections of the community. During the Olympic Games held in London in 2012, more than a few African athletes decided to stay in the United Kingdom rather than return home to civil strife and insecurity. Civil wars in Africa and much of the developing world will continue because ethnic and communal-based groups in these areas continue to challenge the state and its representatives for one reason or another. The recent sad case of migrants fleeing parts of North Africa and the Middle East for Western Europe is another example of how desperate people are to leave severe conflict zones and start a new life. Millions are leaving their country either as refugees or migrants, becoming internally displaced, refugees in another country, or managing to cross borders to seek a new life. The human security consequences of this are enormous, with thousands dying in their attempts to flee and resettle. Moreover they are subject to human smuggling criminal networks that take advantage of their dire situation to make a profit. Resources, autonomy, politics, and demands for a better life are not going to go away.

International relations, on the other hand, is used to dealing with states, often in terms of a **realist** doctrine, but we now face sub-state, communal conflict where groups are trying to win resources from the state, other groups, or in some cases overthrow the state itself. More often than not we are dealing with networks of **nonstate actors** who are trying to change policy through acts of terror and violence. This is not necessarily a new landscape, but it seems to have intensified and become exacerbated since the end of the Cold War. We argue that human security can offer better ideas and solutions, grounded as it is in interdisciplinary work. These types of conflict generate refugees, migrants, terrorism, guerrilla war, poverty, severe violations of human rights, and levels of acute political violence among others. Human security offers a better conceptual framework through which to understand and try to prevent these types of conflict because it is more realistic and nuanced in terms of its interdisciplinary approach. It can draw on different disciplines to attempt solutions, offer respite, and create efforts at securing development and human security.

We doubt in a realistic way whether the human security dilemma can ever be fully resolved and whether people will ever feel totally secure in their environments. Conflict appears to be a permanent feature of human society. So the demand for human security will never disappear—it is a basic need and as old as time itself. However, the need to make people more secure, to improve their lives and help them achieve their aspirations with the starting point as human security, is an old one as well, and we need to develop good governance to achieve this.

ANOTHER VIEW ...

There are several critiques of human security. Roland Paris, a prominent human security commentator and professor at the University of Ottawa, argues that human security is a neologism that encompasses such a wide array of concerns in virtually all domains of public welfare that it serves as a poor guide both for academic research and policy formulation. Its novelty as a concept/framework means that it has not had time to establish itself in credible theoretical terms. Paris sees the concept as too broad and undefined to be meaningful in a practical and pragmatic sense in the current reality.

For him, the expansion of the term into the field of development has further increased this difficulty and led to what might be described as "conceptual overstretch." If we define human security as encompassing everything, then effectively it might come to represent nothing. From a policy perspective, and for institutions like the UN and international humanitarian NGOs who are most likely to design policies based on the concept, this makes it problematic to say the least.

Another concern arises over human security's normative basis. It's clear that human security is based in **empathy** and morality and that one of its most important values is the desire to prevent and address human suffering. This also makes it difficult to work with in terms of how nation-states still perceive their national interests, which may often conflict with the broad version of human security. This is why we argue throughout this text that the interests of the nation-state are not necessarily incompatible with both narrow and broad versions of human security. Promoting human security would maximize the traditional notion of security precisely because having a developed, well-fed, community-oriented society that enjoys basic human rights and security would ensure stability and peace at all levels. The traditional views of security promoted by realism offer only a state-centric security emphasis to conflict; human security offers a new and global opportunity to emphasize peace and development at the individual, community, and state levels.

The United Nations Development Programme and Human Security

The UNDP is one institution that might be viewed as the heart of human security. Founded in 1965, the organization works with governments to promote multidimensional development strategies throughout the world. The agency's flagship publication, the *Human Development Report*, is considered "an independent intellectual exercise" that is protected under a UN resolution to guarantee the organization autonomy in carrying out its mandate to raise awareness about development throughout the world. Many of the agency's goals and focus are concerned with key areas of the human security agenda:

- Giving support to states to develop policies and actions that lead to poverty reduction
- Providing advice and technical support to sustain democratic governance
- Designing activities that attempt to prevent the outbreak of violence and aid in the rebuilding and reconstruction of those societies in post-conflict situations; the organization also provides assistance in natural disasters (earthquakes, etc.)
- Emphasizing sustainable development, which is at the core of many of the UNDP's activities, through long-terms solutions rather than short-term stopgaps
- Reducing the spread/impact of global diseases like AIDS, HN1, or Ebola

The UNDP was at the core of the human security agendas adopted by several countries, and many of the ideas and practices instituted throughout the world emerged from policies that the UNDP initiated. Today, the organization operates in 177 countries and chairs the United Nations Development Group, making it one of the most important intergovernmental institutions working to improve human security (UNDP 2015).

Rhoda Howard-Hassmann (2012) has also questioned the human security paradigm by asking if the concept has the potential to undermine human rights given its broad view. She notes a risk that it can "undermine the primacy of civil and political rights as a strategic tool for citizens to fight for their rights against their own states" (88). She sees a narrow view of human security as beneficial for human rights in that it has the ability to identify new approaches for thinking about rights victims, especially in a legal context.

Mark Duffield (2007) is another scholar who questions themes linked with human security, including humanitarianism. He sees such intervention as deeply linked to the Western world's post–Cold War expansion. For Duffield, humanitarianism is masked behind **liberal imperialism**, a paradox within the international order that allows for advanced countries to enjoy democratic governance models and strong human rights while at the same time fully accepting illiberal regimes as legitimate business partners. He argues these racist worldviews situate the developing world within a "permanent emergency" that needs to be solved by the West.

Vanessa Pupavac (2005) has also been critical of the concept. Focusing on the influence of social psychology in international development as a remedy for the mental well-being of communities, she has argued that the psychological well-being of a society should be a measure of good governance, one that is often overlooked by the human security field given its effort to securitize development. She argues that "human security essentially represents an attempt to salvage a demoralised development agenda by harnessing itself directly to the security field." Indeed, for Pupavac, human security is a problematic policy approach to development and human well-being.

A final critique worth exploring is by Des Gasper (2005), who provides an especially powerful observation and writes "[t]he danger arises that a human security agenda could be hijacked by the fears of the rich." Human security places the victim at the center of the security debate, one that is easily manipulated by states since they are often the arbiters of justice. Events involving human rights violations, poverty, conflict, and natural disasters all require states to respond for victims to achieve security. At the same time, there is a serious risk that governments are capturing the debate around human security to achieve their own gains. That is, human security can serve as political theater. A telling example is the Canadian government's retreat from the human security concept within its own foreign policy strategy. When the Conservative Party took office in 2006, there was a rollback in human security–led initiatives, especially surrounding peacekeeping and climate change (Kinsman 2015). For former Prime Minister Stephen Harper's government, human security as foreign policy was perceived as a Liberal Party initiative that had no room in the Conservative government's policy planning, raising serious concerns over the legitimacy of politically driven human security initiatives. Each of these concerns is valid, and none should be dismissed by those looking to develop an expansive understanding of human security. However, the Liberal Party's resounding defeat of the Conservatives on October 19, 2015, has seen a change in policy back to the human security agendas of the 1990s, with Prime Minister Justin Trudeau declaring a plan to resettle 25,000 Syrian refugees. It appears that foreign policy agendas are shifting once again with the new, and widely perceived as more progressive, government.

HUMAN SECURITY AND GLOBALIZATION

Much has been written on the process and phenomenon of **globalization** over the past two decades, but what impact has it had on human security? We have seen that human security is viewed as a conceptual framework that offers an alternative to the traditional state security–centric version of the world. The argument is that this non-traditional version of security is about much more than military force and conflict between states as the prime mover in global relationships. Globalization has allowed us to discover so much more about the world through several mechanisms, and these have all had an effect on human security. Here, we borrow Manfred Steger's (2013, 13) definition of globalization as "a multidimensional set of social processes that create, multiply, stretch, and intensify worldwide social interdependencies and exchanges while at the same time fostering in people a growing awareness of deepening connections between the local and the distant." This perspective offers a valuable framework for thinking about the ever-increasing interconnectedness between societies, which has a significant impact on human security. As will be argued throughout this book, human security must be considered within the context of globalization if we are to fully understand the connection between socioeconomic interdependency and human development.

Globalization: The Good, the Bad, and the Ugly

Proponents of globalization argue that it has produced positive results by opening up the global economy to new actors, increasing the levels of trade, and generally connecting different countries through trade and commerce. This has increased the global wealth of nations according to this view and provided massive economic benefits, enabling people to be lifted out of poverty and difficult economic circumstances. People who push for globalization think this is sustainable.

A different perspective sees globalization in a much more negative light. Globalization, according to this version, has simply exacerbated and increased overall global poverty and misery by creating massive inequalities between and within nation-states and within populations therein. Weak, failed, and underdeveloped states have in effect been further marginalized and are unable to play by the rules of the game, which are dictated by the major advanced Western industrial nations and their institutions (like the International Monetary Fund, for instance). The economic development of these states has been dictated by what is called "a race to the bottom." At the social level, we have seen a major increase in drug trafficking and the global phenomenon of human trafficking. Disease (HIV, for instance), terrorism, demographic pressures, global environmental problems, and economic crises are all seen as negative impacts of the globalization process. It's unsurprising that it was the UNDP's *Human Development Report* in 1994 that drew attention to these problems in human security; this argument will be further developed in the chapter on poverty.

Sakiko Fukuda-Parr (2004) has also shown that globalization operates within an environment of rapid change, an attribute that is far more pronounced in an emerging economy. This is compounded by negative impacts that could result in an unstable and insecure economic and social situation where human security issues are no longer within a country's capacities to control. The Greek crisis of 2015 provides a good example, where levels of debt threatened to overwhelm the Greek economy and might have led to an impoverishment of the Greek people. Human security interests that relate to globalization range from human rights abuses to income discrimination to food insecurity and beyond. Arguably one of the most discussed human security issues is the human rights abuse cases of exploited workers in the developing world that have resulted from multinational companies externalizing production processes to save money, as well as countries in the Arabian Gulf and elsewhere seeking to exploit the migrant labor force of the poorer countries around them. These places may not have adequate social and political infrastructure to prevent or even uncover human rights violations like labor exploitation and have little political will to stop them. More importantly, they simply might not care if the case is profit before people. Violations may be even more prevalent and likely to occur in countries that are ethnically diverse, particularly where ethnicity is tied to social class.

Globalization has also been cited as a factor compounding and contributing to the rate of violent conflicts in developing countries. Internal conflict in impoverished countries has been linked to economic disparity, government corruption, and ethnic discrimination. Theories have been put forward on either side of the equation within this debate. Some argue, for instance, that globalization decreases the likelihood of conflict, whereas others say it will increase as a result of the process. Some have argued that despite conventional wisdom that the severity of conflict would diminish with the spread of globalization because of its expected impact on social welfare, death rates from internal conflict, especially in countries that are ethnically diverse, remains very high. Results from empirical case studies that have looked at the occurrences of violent conflicts in countries affected by globalization are inconclusive as to whether there are increases or decreases in this area. Finally, consideration is given to food security issues, as is witnessed in the agricultural sector. Global market demands may only call for certain crops, and farmers hoping to profit from international trade at higher prices may change their crops over time to meet the demands.

Social and Political Globalization

What is interesting about globalization in reference to human security issues is that social and political globalization both contribute to an increasing awareness of these issues. The vast communication and social media networks that can be accessed via technology such as mobile phones enables the intermingling of ideas and facilitates the reporting of human security issues as they happen. Citizens affected by nepotistic and corrupt governments or subjected to human rights violations by their employers are able to communicate with the rest of the world or form coalitions of people suffering similar fates. Multinational companies seem to be developing an awareness of this and know full well that human rights violations can sway customers or lead to legal action, which can have a major impact on their reputation.

Globalization has undoubtedly contributed to the economic growth of many nations and has helped keep costs down for various goods in the developed world. However, it is a multifaceted issue that involves economic, political, technological, and sociocultural considerations. Furthermore, debate remains as to whether it benefits all stakeholders involved or if it contributes to and complicates social problems and human security issues for members of an emerging economy. More research is needed to better understand the relationships among globalization in the developing world and its direct and indirect effects on human security issues such as worker exploitation, food security, and internal conflict. By better understanding how cultures and societies react to globalization and abide by trade policies we may be better positioned to further develop policies and regulations that govern globalizing activity, thus reducing the negative impacts and creating positive outcomes for human security.

Despite the positive aspects of globalization, such as advances in knowledge and technology, the other side results in a highly uneven distribution of wealth, power, populations, and natural resources, and consequently causes pervasive inequality, massive poverty, a lack of access to universal health care and education, and ultimately the presence of contagious diseases. All of these issues continue to threaten the social and economic well-being of many developing or undeveloped nations. Caroline Thomas and Peter Wilkin (1999, 1) indicate that while human security entails "a condition of existence in which basic material needs are met and in which human dignity, including meaningful participation in the life of the community, can be met," because of a maldistribution of resources "[p]overty is the ultimate systematic threat facing humanity" and causes fundamental barriers to human well-being and development. Moreover, apart from poverty and other associated factors with globalization, one other significant meaning/definition that can be developed is *cultural globalization*. In fact, advances in technology, particularly in the areas of communication and transportation, have increased global cultural interactions. The contemporary information age and marketing of popular brands from industrialized nations to less-industrialized ones has caused important cultural and political implications as well. Cultural globalization is not a one-way trend: It also has negative aspects. In the presence of Western-dominated economic, political, and cultural trends, globalization has created some perceptions or fear of homogenization of diverse cultures, and more specifically the Westernization of national and subnational cultures.

Globalization, Religion, and Insecurity

One of the areas where globalization has had a major impact is on religion (and its resurgence in the post–Cold War world), ethnicity, and ultimately how people see their sense of identity in the world. Alongside ethnicity, religion in the post–Cold War period has become a much more salient feature within the developing world, and globalization to a large extent has caused many states to reassess their identity and the challenges to ethnic and religious distinctiveness in the late twentieth century. In this sense the problems of globalization have given pause for thought over how states are formed, how they are maintained, and how they fall apart. How states have used the tools afforded to them is crucial in the outcomes of political security, stability, and socioeconomic development, and all of these aspects have had a major effect on the lives of ordinary people and their sense of human security. It also shows to a large extent that the state has failed to manage religion in many ways, particularly in Pakistan, for instance, and other states that have disintegrative tendencies and weak state apparatus. It's important because the levels of violence associated with religion and religious ideology have risen dramatically in recent years. Since 9/11, Pakistan has seen tens of thousands of deaths associated with religious violence, and in recent years the death toll has risen dramatically. And if these states do not already endure (or have endured) large amounts of religious and ethnic strife, they certainly have the potential to do so.

Globalization as discussed has also had a major impact on the ability to connect at breakneck speed from any part of the world and communicate the level of human insecurity taking place in depth.

The Case of Syria's Chemical Weapons

The case of Syria is important here, which has been suffering a civil war for several years (since 2011). On 21 August 2013, Syrian government forces shelled a suburb of Damascus, the largest city in Syria. Within hours of the assault, videos, images, and television footage began to surface showing what appeared to be victims of a chemical weapons attack. International governments scrambled to ascertain the veracity of the claims, and traditional media outlets quizzed experts on the potential chemical weapons used. This attack reportedly killed 1,429 people, including 426 children. By 23 August, a mere two days after the attacks, Britain and France accused the Syrian government of the incursion and began to call for military strikes against Syria. Within a month of the attacks, on 21 September, Syria applied to join the international convention banning chemical weapons, agreed to hand over all chemical weapons, and agreed to turn over all data concerning its weapons arsenal to the Organisation for the Prohibition of Chemical Weapons.

While the use of chemical weapons would likely have been discovered in time, it is unlikely that such a swift resolution could have been achieved without the effects of the attack being placed online for the world to see. Instead of a newspaper report with a total number of killed and wounded, websites such as Reddit and YouTube allowed the world to see the human cost of chemical war merely hours after it occurred. This is part of the impact that the globalization of media and instant reporting can have on human security issues. Of course politics prevails, especially since the United States and Western allies were unwilling to intervene in what would be regarded as a humanitarian crisis. In the end the real victims of these actions are the innocent civilians typically caught up in someone else's war.

The Arab Spring

Much of the Arab Spring was also extensively promoted and communicated through the use of social media, and globalization ensured that these social movements attempting transformation did not go unnoticed. These uprisings occurred in authoritarian, often dictatorial countries that had appeared immune to democratic political and social change. Suddenly things began to turn, and human security agendas were exposed through the use of social media.

Social media use brought the conflicts themselves out of the hands of generals and government officials and into the hands of every person capable of viewing a webpage or accessing social media. In human security terms, these movements and the reactions they caused were truly bottom-up revolutions, even if they have failed to live up to the massive expectations of the participants and onlookers alike. While the movements certainly had unified goals, such as the overthrow of corrupt or brutal regimes, social media granted a voice to anyone with an Internet connection and a picture or video to upload. Facebook and Twitter among other mechanisms gave voices to individual protesters, and rather than simply being part of "a group of protesters," these individuals were heard and gave a face to the uprisings.

Pakistan: A Case Study in Human Insecurity

In terms of examples, Pakistan is often cited as a case study in terms of human insecurity. It's seen as a weak or failing state with little control over its own institutions and a grave inability to provide public goods and services for its population. The reasons are fairly evident:

- Pakistan is a major front on the War on Terror(ism)—and yet also an epicenter, a point underscored by Osama bin Laden having been based there in his last few years and Pakistan's borderlands being home to or safe haven for extremists. These are ungoverned spaces.
- Pakistan is one of the world's most dangerous states, mainly because its estimated nuclear weapons capacity has been tallied at between 70 and 120 usable nuclear devices and it sees its major enemy as its neighbor, India, which also possesses large numbers of nuclear weapons.
- Pakistan's borderlands, in terms of state formation and state (in)cohesion, largely constitute ungoverned spaces, beyond the realm of state control, subject to regional religious and tribal forms of governance, and also the site of international military operations.
- Affecting international relations and internal stability, Pakistan's military and broader government has been fiercely criticized by the United States (which generally but cautiously sees Pakistan as an ally) for their failure to rein in extremist insurgency within Pakistan's formal borders and the terrorist activities based there but operating beyond its borders.
- Pakistan itself recognizes the importance of state cohesion and the strategic importance of addressing Islamic insurgency. Former Interior Minister Rehman Malik (notably the "interior" not "foreign" ministry) recently stated, "We are not just fighting for Pakistan, we are fighting for the whole world. If this country is destabilized,

the whole region is destabilized" (Tisdall 2011). And indeed, Islamic insurgency has targeted Pakistani military with varying international and domestic rationales.

According to the 2013 Fragile States Index on failed states, Pakistan ranks thirteenth, which is exceptionally high for a "Western" ally. Failed states are categorized by a variety of factors, including demographic pressures, factionalized elites, weak human rights, few public services, a state that has become delegitimized in the eyes of many of its population, high levels of group grievance, and uneven development. In Pakistan these are the most important factors. The splintering of Pakistan into different regions with different ethnic and tribal affiliations has contributed to incoherence in national identity as different groups cling to their local identities and ethnic affiliations.

Another framework centers on globalization, particularly the dislocating and unsettling impact of globalization on individuals and how this impacts the state. Many identities appear in a state of fluctuation as norms and traditions offered by a protective community appear to sustain a global onslaught. Anthony Giddens (1991, 243) describes this through a lens of "ontological security and existential anxiety." In the case of the former, individuals require or need a sense of continuity and order in their lives—a sense of safety. When this safety and security is undermined (e.g., by the rapid pace of globalization), they experience the latter "anxiety" and, in Giddens's perspective, such anxiety favors a resurgence of religion that can provide some security for people. The fact that economic insecurity has forced people around the world into growing poverty and marginalization has increased the strength of nonstate actors like religious groups because people have lost trust and faith in the state and state institutions to deliver and increase human insecurity.

CONCLUSION

Human security has become part of the global lexicon in security and development terms in the post–Cold War period. It is something that all governments, regional institutions, and international governmental and nongovernmental institutions have to deal with as they work in an ever-connected world. Corporations are increasingly concerned with the impact of social responsibility and being held accountable for environmental and social damage in their operations in the developing world. Working to improve human rights and human security has now become firmly, if reluctantly, entrenched on their agendas.

This book is based on two fundamental premises:

- We argue that human security encompasses more than just "freedom from fear." It includes looking at the larger, holistic picture of the collective environment that individuals find themselves in. It is intimately linked to the idea of "freedom from want." Individuals and groups who experience grave economic and food security situations are more likely to live in fear than prosperous and healthy communities and individuals. In other words, it is contextual.

- In expanding the definition of human security to include human development, we agree with the UN report that cited seven linked types of human security, including political, food, personal, economic, environmental, health, and community forms of security, which are connected and interlinked to one another.

At the beginning of May 2003 a summary report from the Commission on Human Security, led by Amartya Sen, was presented to the UN secretary-general. The report acknowledged the role of globalization in the cases where states were unable to provide security to their citizens; it focused on the development of individuals and communities and their protection and empowerment in the light of globalization. The commission provided a set of 10 recommendations, which are discussed throughout this text:

1. Protecting people from violent conflict
2. Protecting people from the proliferation of arms
3. Supporting the security of people on the move
4. Establishing human security transition funds for post-conflict situations
5. Encouraging fair trade and markets to benefit the extreme poor
6. Working to provide minimum living standards everywhere
7. According higher priority to ensuring universal access to basic health care
8. Developing an efficient and equitable system for patent rights
9. Empowering all people with universal basic education
10. Clarifying the need for a global human identity while respecting the freedom of individuals to have diverse identities and affiliations (Ministry of Foreign Affairs of Japan 2014; ICB Japan 2015).

Human security and the need to attain it is not just a passing fad. In the post–Cold War period we have not seen any increase in the collective human security of individuals or nation-states. Freedom from fear and freedom from want are enormous aspirations for the human race, and we still have a long way to go. Thinking of how we can and why we should attain these goals will rely on how well we can put human security ideas into practice and how we can implement the values that these ideas represent on a global scale.

KEY TERMS

Asian Values; Civil Wars; Crimes against Humanity; Development; Empathy; Empowerment; Freedom from Fear; Freedom from Want; Globalization; Good

Governance; Human Security; Interdisciplinary; International Criminal Court (ICC); Intrastate Conflict; Liberal Imperialism; Millennium Development Project; National Security; Nonstate Actors; Ottawa Treaty; Realism; Types of Security: Economic, Political, Environmental, Community, Health, Food, Personal; UNDP *Development Report 1994*; Universal Declaration of Human Rights

FURTHER READING

Alkire, Sabina. 2003. "A Conceptual Framework for Human Security." Working Paper 2, Center for Research on Inequality, Human Security and Ethnicity (CRISE), University of Oxford.

Kaldor, Mary. 2007. *Human Security*. Cambridge: Polity Press.

Okubo, Shiro, and Louise Shelley, eds. 2011. *Human Security, Transnational Crime and Human Trafficking: Asian and Western Perspectives*. New York: Routledge.

Paris, Roland. 2001. "Human Security: Paradigm Shift or Hot Air?" *International Security* 26 (2): 87–102. http://dx.doi.org/10.1162/016228801753191141.

Reveron, Derek S., and Kathleen A. Mahoney-Norris. 2011. *Human Security in a Borderless World*. Boulder, CO: Westview Press.

Tadjbakhsh, Shahrbanou, and Anuradha M. Chenoy. 2007. *Human Security: Concepts and Implications (Routledge Advances in International Relations and Global Politics)*. New York: Routledge.

WEBSITES

Beyond Intractability: www.beyondintractability.org

Centre for the Study of Globalisation and Regionalisation: www2.warwick.ac.uk/fac/soc/pais/research/researchcentres/csgr

Eldis: www.eldis.org

Human Security Report Project: www.hsrgroup.org

Institute for Environment and Human Security: http://ehs.unu.edu

International Criminal Court: www.icc-cpi.int

United Nations Development Programme: www.undp.org

United Nations Trust Fund for Human Security: www.un.org/humansecurity

Yale Centre for the Study of Globalization: www.ycsg.yale.edu

Chapter 2

CONFLICT IN THE POST–COLD WAR ERA

Peace is not the absence of conflict but the presence of creative alternatives for responding to conflict—alternatives to passive or aggressive responses, alternatives to violence.

Dorothy Thompson (Women's International League for Peace and Freedom 2014)

INTRODUCTION

The post–Cold War era has led to new ways of thinking about conflict. We contend that conflict (and the study of conflict) has changed and been transformed from a traditional international relations security and realist approach that emphasizes conflict *between* states (**interstate conflict**). While this is still important, the significant conflicts in the period since the end of the Cold War have been *intrastate* rather than *interstate*. The examples of Afghanistan, Somalia, Iraq, Syria, Myanmar, Sudan, and the Congo, among others, are good indicators of this trend. More often than not these conflicts have involved a substantial ethnic and identity component, and often these conflicts, as in the case of Syria, have had major cross-border implications, spilling over into other states' territories and threatening their internal stability. Meanwhile the creation of an Islamic state by ISIS (albeit a self-proclaimed one) is seen as changing the rules of the global game in the twenty-first century. The security threats in the post–Cold War and post-9/11 period have also significantly changed as we are dealing with the rise of different global actors (essentially nonstate groups) who rely on complex networks and new and different technologies and methods to promote and exacerbate conflict. Indeed some of these groups are defined as much by the term *network* as by anything else. The theater of war was redefined after 11 September 2001 with the attacks on the World Trade Center in New York City. Suicide bombing, while not a new form of warfare, became a topic of special attention following this attack. The theater and meaning of terrorism has also been transformed with the rise of Islamic jihadism. Special attention will be given to the challenges surrounding ethnic violence and religious violence, as well as conflict over scarce resources and the environment later in this text.

A case can be made that the world of the twenty-first century is not about peace and harmony, but about conflict and violence. Indeed, the news media—whether print, broadcast, or the global Internet—seem to emphasize innumerable conflicts, with many of them affecting the lives of ordinary people that live far away from the area of the conflict. In the era of globalization, we appear to know far more about what is happening in our world than was the case in the immediate post-1945 period. Whether we pay enough attention to that fact is a good question, as many people seem immune to the continuing levels of human insecurity. In fact, many in the West view these conflicts as having little relevance to their daily lives and appear to have conflict and poverty fatigue. However, the post–Cold War era seems to have generated new and different forms of conflict, which we need to pay attention to, and questions need to be asked about how we can reinvigorate these debates. We will explore some of these questions within this chapter.

PEACE IN OUR TIMES?

It would be hard to argue that the twentieth century itself was a peaceful time. Eric Hobsbawm (1996), a Marxist historian, argued that nearly 187 million people "were killed or allowed to die" in conflicts between 1914 and 1918 in what he termed an "age of extremes." It was certainly the bloodiest century on historical record. Interstate wars on the whole accounted for most of these casualties. Roughly 15 million people were killed in World War I, and another 50 million died in World War II. The Korean and Iran–Iraq Wars cumulated in the death of nearly 4 million.

And yet intrastate conflict had also yielded high totals during this period, even before the end of the Cold War. Twenty million people died under Stalin's policies in the former Soviet Union; tens of millions died under the Communist regime in China (often through mass starvation and famine); 6 million died in the Holocaust; and a million more perished under the Khmer Rouge regime in Cambodia. The **genocide** in East Timor killed hundreds of thousands of people in what some regard as one of the worst genocides in proportionate terms in post–World War II history. Since 1998, at least 5 million people have died in the Congo.

The twentieth century was a century of violence, with the state being the main agent in the exercise of violence against ordinary civilians. Revolutions, anti-colonial insurrections, guerrilla warfare, terrorism, and ethnic and religious internecine violence emerged as significant contenders to state power over the last 100 years. In armed conflicts since the end of World War II, the fact that 90 percent of the casualties have been civilians is telling. Early on in the twentieth century, even before details of mass genocide had been provided, one author could argue that "the curse of privilege to be the most devastating or most bloody war century belongs to the Twentieth; in one quarter century it imposed upon the population a 'blood tribute' far greater than that imposed by any of the whole centuries combined" (Sorokin 1962, 342). These experiences have by and large produced deep and abiding scars on ordinary people. The wounds in the latter half of the twentieth century and beginning of the twenty-first centuries have started to be addressed in various forms. The institutionalization of memory in the form of commemorative sites of conflict (war memorials, heritage tourism, cultural heritage, government and institutional public policies of war memory, as well as private commemoration through travel and pilgrimage to key sites of conflict) has been important. The formation of truth commissions and inquiries into the past by the state, particularly during times of transition to democratic governance, and also war crimes tribunals and international criminal courts, which are determined to ensure that past injustices do not go unpunished, has been crucial in helping societies move on. And we have seen official state apologies to victims of past abuse in efforts to heal wounds and divisions. Much of the impetus for these efforts lies in the increasing push for democratization in authoritarian states since the end of the Cold War and the fact that the process and intensity of globalization has made past and present conflicts ever more salient. The global and social media have been able to locate victims of conflict in real time, allowing for instant history and evaluation of events.

We can also argue that in the post–Cold War period the meaning of the state has been undergoing a period of redefinition away from the traditional statist-realist perspective as the predominance of the superpowers has been challenged by intra-state and external-state actors. For instance, human security, human rights issues, refugees, ethnicity, gender issues, and the environment, among others, have emerged as crucial global themes in international politics at the close of the twentieth century. Democratization and globalization have become key elements for many social scientists in explaining these global changes. The collapse of the Soviet Union and authoritarian regimes in Eastern Europe, Latin America, and elsewhere has carried the process of democratization further. Democracy has also emerged as the legitimate form of government in Southern Europe (Spain and Portugal only became democracies in the mid-1970s) and in parts of East Asia. The development of the

Arab Spring in 2011, in a region known to be reluctant to accept democratic overtures, is also beginning to produce political and social change. It will be far more difficult now to reverse these trends. Political change has forced these issues out into the open in a way that is difficult to ignore. With the movement toward democratization, the quest for human security and peace will become more pronounced as people's aspirations seek to be met.

The Post–Cold War Blues?

With the end of the Cold War many people had hoped that an era of peace and tranquility might develop. Francis Fukuyama (2006) declared the **"End of History"** had arrived with the ascendance of liberal democracy and market capitalism. The major power blocs no longer threatened mutual and global annihilation, international governmental organizations were strengthened, and free trade was supposed to bring nations together in mutual self-interest. The United States emerged unchallenged as the sole superpower to dominate political and economic life.

Benjamin Barber (1996) posited two different worlds existing side by side in the New World Order. On the one hand, there was a scenario where much of humanity was caught up in a form of re-tribalization. War, conflict, and strife were the predominant images of this descent into identity and ethnic politics. There was the phenomenon of Lebanonization, reflecting that particular society's descent into disintegration and factionalism. There would be a struggle against any form of homogeneity, unity, or interdependence that would undermine globalization and the development of global norms. Barber called this struggle **jihad**. The second force was a result of the rush to homogeneity through globalization where everything across cultures begins to look and feel the same. Just as McDonald's in one country is roughly similar to McDonald's in a vastly different country, so the forces of homogeneity spurred on by globalization would bring everyone in line while endorsing similar material wants (this process has been called **McDonaldization**).

The answer to this paradox is still unclear. On the one hand we get lost in the supermarket of consumerism and lose much of our identity or assume a new one, while on the other we still have essentialist and identity impulses that cause us to define ourselves as the "other"; Scotland's recent referendum, where 45 percent of the population voted for independence, is a good example of this. Barber's theory posits that we are simultaneously falling apart and coming together. Neither of these alternatives seem to offer much hope; they are both undemocratic in nature and certainly do not seem to be under any institutional control. At roughly the same time, the conservative political scientist Samuel Huntington (1996) developed a text that claimed we were going to witness the **clash of civilizations** in the not too distant future, and that

Western civilization was under threat from different civilizational groups, like Islam. Huntington was criticized quite strongly for his views.

The Nexus of Conflict

This chapter has a limited amount of space to deal with the myriad conflicts in the world today, but some important considerations in understanding conflict in the contemporary world should be noted:

- Conflicts develop and change over time—a sense of history and context is important.
- Any conflict is a complex phenomenon involving psychological, sociological, economic, ecological, and political variables, among others.
- There is more than one side to any conflict. Being aware of multiple points of view and different perspectives is critical to analyzing and understanding conflict.
- Some conflicts take on intractable features. They become more complex and deadly and resist any resolution until the other side gives in, or the conflict is never fully resolved.
- While compromise and accommodation through negotiation is a conflict resolution strategy, the key actors in any conflict may refuse this approach, making it more difficult to compromise.
- The last resort—attempting to end a conflict by force and violence—may cause more conflict and bloodshed.
- And finally, thanks to the social media, globalization has enabled even the most remote and smallest conflict to become known on a global scale.

Tracking Conflict, Building Peace

The tracking of armed conflicts since the early 1980s through the Uppsala database shows that the number of interstate wars worldwide peaked in the 1980s and remained consistently high during the early 1990s. Since then, the number of wars has steadily declined before rising in 1999 to 40 wars in 36 countries. In 2013 there were 28 active armed conflicts in 25 countries, which was an increase from 26 armed conflicts in 23 countries in 2012. Africa continued to host the greatest number of armed conflicts (12) and the Americas the fewest (1) (Uppsala University 2015). Project Ploughshares (2015) reports that armed conflict is not a consequence of failure in the international system as much as it is due to the failures of national governments and societies to meet the basic human needs of their citizens.

In these terms, it doesn't get more basic than this: Without peace there can be no lasting development. It is no coincidence that almost half of the countries in the bottom third of the **Human Development Index** have experienced serious conflict in the past decade, and impoverished countries with low incomes are 15 times more likely to face civil war (UNDP 2002).

How do we, as global citizens and a collective community with empathetic values, respond to this? How can we promote peace? When Boutros Boutros-Ghali, former secretary-general of the UN, popularized the term **peacebuilding**, he referred to it as the post-conflict phase of communal violence. More recently, it has come to refer to all activities, whether before, during, or after conflict, that deal directly with conflict and peace issues. Peacebuilding is about intensifying efforts to establish lasting peace and to resolve conflicts peacefully. It refers to **conflict prevention, conflict resolution**, and post-conflict reconciliation activities. The focus here is on the political and socioeconomic context of conflict rather than on the military or security aspects, and external support for peacebuilding should be seen as an adjunct to local efforts and not a substitute for them. Central to this definition is the role and promotion of good governance. Many underdeveloped states lack fundamental aspects of good governance and human security, and thus their citizens and populations feel insecure and lack the basic necessities of life and well-being that promote good governance and human security, resulting in a cycle of insecurity. There is an astonishing lack of physical security in these countries, and citizens cannot feel secure when conflict continues to plague their lives. The year 2005 ended with 32 active conflicts in 27 countries. Africa and Asia hosted most wars, accounting for four out of five (84 percent) of the world conflicts (more than five out of every six armed conflicts raged in Africa or Asia during 2005, with more than one-quarter of African and almost one-fifth of Asian states affected by one or more wars). Throughout the 1990s, there were 57 conflicts in 45 locations.

These conflicts have produced another aspect of human insecurity: the displacement of people through conflict or conflict-related problems. One of the most telling aspects of human insecurity has been the rise of the refugee and migrant problem. When looking at refugees in particular, one sees that in 1978 the United Nations High Commission for Refugees (UNHCR) was involved in helping approximately 4 million people. In 2006, the number of "people of concern" to the UNHCR was over 20 million, or 1 out of every 375 persons on Earth. The vast majority of refugees are women and children. When the UNHCR opened for business on January 1, 1951, it had a staff of only 34 people, based mainly in Geneva, with a budget of US$300,000. In more than five decades, the refugee agency has grown into a global operation with 252 offices in 116 countries, a staff of more than 6,000 people, and a budget of US$1.2 billion.

An Alternative View

We have argued over the last few pages that conflict remains high on a global basis. Steven Pinker (2011), however, uses data based on battle deaths, not civilian deaths, to conclude that human violence is declining. As an evolutionary psychologist who stands by the idea that history is progress, he attributes the present more "peaceful" human behavior to the brain's neuroplasticity, which means that the human brain has learned over time that alternative behavioral strategies to violence work better. In other words, humans are being guided by our "better angels." Pinker sees the mass killings of the twentieth century as an aberration to the general trend of world pacification and peace progress. The post-1946 increase in civil wars and challenges by insurgent groups are seen as being stoked by the two superpowers, the USSR and the United States.

Pinker, however, is criticized for ignoring the anti-liberal views of Enlightenment thinkers, who favored violence as an instrument of social transformation; for considering mass killings in developing countries as evidence of their "backwardness"; and for his lack of concern for those paying the price for America's peace. Pinker does have a point, though, that overall violence has decreased in terms of warfare and bloodletting. Regardless, human insecurity still looms large when millions of people's economic, political, and social aspirations go largely unfulfilled.

CONFLICT AND ITS VARIANTS

We should be aware that the post–Cold War era is an arena where the global system is being transformed and where the forces of globalization change and affect the nature of conflict(s), sometimes in minor and sometimes in major ways. Such conflicts grow in complexity as the international community is drawn into the conflict—conflicts that may seem to be in a very remote part of the world, but are connected to us through the phenomenon of globalization.

Conflict itself is a phenomenon that evokes strong personal and national emotions. Importantly, conflicts are less state-to-state affairs now. We have separatist insurrections and rebellions where intense violence takes place over who will govern the state and how it will be governed. Moreover, new kinds of war need to be examined. Within the context of globalization, large numbers of governmental and nongovernmental organizations have emerged that promote a side in a conflict, try to resolve the conflict, or can be on the receiving end of the conflict. Either way, conflict has become a globalized problem that affects all actors in the international arena.

The origins and generators of conflict may not have changed much in the post–Cold War era—poverty, ideology, inequality, the environment, and economics are all important facets. However, globalization has changed the intensity of conflict and the tactics used by parties that create conflict and the peacemakers who try to resolve and manage it. We also take an analytic perspective and understand that many conflicts degenerate into difficult and seemingly unsolvable problems. Their intractable nature makes peaceful resolution difficult.

The nature of the conflicts can be divided into the following central thematic principles:

- Conflict of separatism and identity
- Conflict over the environment and natural resources
- Terrorism and new deadly conflicts
- Economic and social conflicts

The argument is that these kinds of conflict are not the only types, but also the most important facets in the post–Cold War era, in the sense that they have come to define conflict and are inextricably linked to human security both at the individual and collective level. We strongly believe that human security is linked to political, social, and economic development and that these concepts work to complement each other. We also argue that human security and human rights are intimately linked and bound together. Human security is unthinkable and unrealizable without good human rights practices and vice versa.

New Wars and State Decline

There have been a number of common elements that have been described in contextualizing conflict following the end of the Cold War. One of the most important analyses comes from the work of Mary Kaldor (2013), who argued that we were witnessing a period of "new wars." This was an attempt to link failed states, internal state conflict, and the increasing inability of the state to control its territory and govern. The themes throughout her work discuss the factors involved, including the ethnic basis of conflict; the brutal effects of violence on civilian populations, including displacement and the fractionalization of countries; the use of detention, torture, and rape as weapons of warfare; and the increasing criminalization of the different groups involved. We can see several of these elements in the Syrian crisis that erupted after the Arab Spring.

Such conflicts are also characterized by how long they last and how they are transformed given the increasing weakness of the state to control affairs. Kaldor's argument undermines traditional international relations theory by pointing out that the state itself is no longer the main actor in the conflicts that have emerged after 1990. Internal and ethnic conflicts among others have weakened the ability of the state to command a monopoly over legitimate violence. Because of this we have other actors emerging: insurgents, guerrilla groups, terrorists, and criminals who have stepped into the political and social space that the state once occupied. The increasing privatization of war is another good example, with private security firms and organizations attempting to capitalize on conflict in the absence of the state (i.e., executive outcomes). The privatization of war has led to the increasing use of mercenaries, who are individuals or organizations paid by the state to act on its behalf in the conduct of military and other operations. They have been used by the United States, for instance, in Afghanistan since 2001 and Iraq since 2003. These are not new aspects of warfare in some sense because mercenaries have always been a part of the history of warfare. What differentiates them now is the degree to which democratic governments employ them in conflicts and allow them to take over traditional state activities. This leads to serious questions of accountability.

New forms of conflict also include environmental ones, such as the process of global warming and climate change, which results in land degradation and conflict over resources. Such crises are manifesting themselves on a global scale with claims and counterclaims for land and resource ownership. To some extent the new forms of post–Cold War conflict are still rooted in the same trend of thinking—to conquer and dominate other nations and emancipate those that feel oppressed and marginalized by their system of governance—but these conflicts are intensifying under the forces of globalization. The fact that we are seeing other nonstate actors rise to prominence in the post–Cold War period has also undermined the state in pursuing its basic and extraneous goals.

Failed States and Conflict

We can trace many human security problems to the failure of states to provide basic security needs for their citizens and communities. The term **failed state** has some historical roots, but again derives much of its meaning from the literature following the end of the Cold War. Failed states can typically be characterized by their problems more than by some overarching theory of international relations. Essentially we see that failed states experience a near or total collapse of their institutional framework and a descent into chaotic forms of law and order. Some of them, like Somalia (often seen as the world's number-one failed state), are seen as anarchic. They represent societies that have endured long periods of conflict and are unable to cope with it, and thus appear to be the equivalent of a nation-state that is exhibiting a mental and nervous breakdown.

Examples of Failed States

There is an index of failed states, which is compiled every year and is based on a variety of indicators. All of these indicators speak to human security criteria, although this is not necessarily the intention of the authors. In 2015 the top 10 failed states fulfilling these criteria (or not fulfilling them, as the case may be) were South Sudan, Somalia, Central African Republic, Sudan, Democratic Republic of Congo, Chad, Yemen, Syria, Afghanistan, and Guinea (Fund for Peace 2015).

The failed states version of events has of course been criticized. Some argue that too much attention has been paid to the developing world in their failure to live up to the expectations of developed countries. Some critics, like Noam Chomsky (2006), have argued that the United States is a failed state. He argues that a failed state is one that fails "to provide security for the population, to guarantee rights at home or abroad, or to maintain functioning (not merely formal) democratic institutions." Based on that definition, Chomsky views the United States as the world's biggest failed state, one that has consistently failed its citizens. Chomsky is known for being critical of the United States, but here he is making a valid point: It's difficult to generalize and stereotype states as failed based only on a few criteria and factors that are open to interpretation.

In the next section we look at how context is important. The failed states argument attempts to provide some sort of context, but ultimately ends up categorizing states on a number of criteria that may or may not be the most accurate way of assessing them. In fact, it's almost impossible to assess conflict without analyzing the context within which it occurs.

The Significance of Context

Context in any conflict is extremely important because it enables us to understand and comprehend what is at stake. In many cases, political, social, economic, and cultural contexts must be taken into consideration to understand the key variables that result in the conflict and what contextual obstacles surround resolving and preventing conflict. It is imperative that context is analyzed to begin to attempt to resolve conflict. Root causes must be addressed to prevent conflict from reoccurring in the long term. Heidi and Guy Burgess (2003) stress that deeply rooted differences in religion, culture, or worldview can be irreconcilable. Moreover, a history of colonialism, ethnocentric racism, sexism, and human rights abuses creates power imbalances throughout the social structure of a society. Struggles over land, water, employment opportunities, and wealth also lead to conflict, especially when there is scarcity or unequal distribution. The notion that some conflicts are "intractable" is of great importance here. When describing intractable conflicts, Burgess and Burgess mention three causes of conflict: irreconcilable moral differences, high stakes distributional issues, and domination or "pecking order" conflicts. They contend that "intractable conflicts can be particularly paradoxical, as they cause disputants to destroy themselves ... in an effort to destroy the other."

In this way, understanding the context allows us to fundamentally appreciate the factors pushing and pulling the conflict, causing it to act and react as it does.

Essentially, by understanding the context we are able to not only draw up a more holistic understanding of the conflict, but also to know where the roots lie and from what angle to tackle them.

Social context is largely intertwined with cultural context, and understanding the dynamic interplay between culture and conflict can illuminate previously missed "drivers" or influences of a conflict. Culture helps us make sense of the world; it shapes our worldview, our sense of belonging, and our feelings of safety. When these are challenged, we react. However, what is important is that individuals are conditioned and influenced by culture to respond to certain triggers that initiate conflicts and the factors that affect their escalation and de-escalation. This means that conflict and culture are both local, because each is deeply anchored in human experiences and actions, and global, because of the large-scale, system-level consequences. Understanding these dynamics is essential in trying to analyze a conflict.

WHAT IS NEW ABOUT POST–COLD WAR CONFLICT?

Conflicts have changed since the end of the Cold War, and it's important to study these changes. It is clear, for instance, that interstate conflicts have declined, but we have seen a new increase in intrastate conflict. Colin Gray (2005) argues that the nature of war has remained the same, but the actual reasons for conflict are changing. The argument is that "these [post–Cold War conflicts] are wars about identity, as well as historic wrongs, myths and legends, they are not about reason of the state" (10). As long as certain communities or ethnic groups feel marginalized by their governments, there will always be conflict within the boundaries of a country. For example, much of the fighting in the Congo is rooted in historical wrongs.

Failed states have also played a large part in the conflicts during the post–Cold War period. Not only have they been a cause of conflict, they also seem to be caught in a vicious circle that continually generates conflict. Failed states and ungoverned spaces, for instance, are attractive to terrorist groups and networks that can generally operate with impunity within their territory, simply because the state does not have the capacity nor the will to challenge such groups. Such prolonged intrastate conflicts were described by the former UN Secretary-General Boutros Boutros-Ghali as follows:

A feature of such conflicts is the collapse of state institutions, especially the police and judiciary, with resulting paralysis of governance, a breakdown of law and order, and general banditry and chaos. Not only are the functions of government suspended, but its assets are destroyed or looted and experienced officials are killed or flee the country. This is rarely the case in inter-state wars. (quoted in Thürer 1999)

One of the characteristics of failed states is that they are often riddled with ethnic factions and problems of identity. States that face these kinds of problems are in severe trouble because they have to struggle to keep a sense of unity in the face of disintegrative forces. Often they face these severe problems while in the midst of conflict (such as Syria). In the next section we look at some of these intractable conflicts and why they are so difficult to deal with.

Ethnic and Identity Conflicts

Political movements reacting to oppressive government regimes or trying to achieve autonomy or independence have been a feature of the world throughout its history. In the post–Cold War era the number and intensity of these movements has increased—and so has the use of force and violence on both sides. Internal conflicts have become the most common form of armed conflict. Steven David (1997) notes that the number has not increased markedly since the end of the Cold War, nor has the intensity changed, but their relative importance has risen, their emergence in post-Soviet states has become important, and scholars of contemporary warfare have refocused on internal conflicts in an attempt to determine their causes and suggest remedies. What they are finding, however, is that the wide range of contexts and complexities make generalizations difficult and contradictory. The various internal war data sets David uses indicates a steady increase in the number of internal conflicts but no surge after the Cold War nor any increase in casualties or material devastation.

Furthermore, and abetting these internal conflicts, which are becoming increasingly globalized, the media and advances in technology have enabled organizations to promote their views on a worldwide basis. If we look at the way in which Islamic fundamentalist jihadist groups, for instance, have managed to propagate their views through social media and advanced technology, we can see how the media and globalization have interacted.

Yet the causes of ethnic conflict are never straightforward and tend to be oversimplified by the media. One method to develop a more meaningful understanding of such violence often used by scholars and analysts is a "mapping" approach to the origins of the violence. There are several approaches to conflict mapping, including the Harvard approach, human needs theory, and the conflict transformation approach (see the box below). While each of these perspectives offers unique and valuable insights into mapping violent conflict, they all call for a deeper understanding of the violence at hand. Some of the key questions to make sense of any conflict include the following:

- Why is the conflict happening? What is it over?
- Who are the key actors—individuals and organizations—involved?

- What primary and secondary demands are being made? How are they made?
- Have the issues changed from the original dispute?
- What strategies and actions have the actors/participants used in the conflict?
- How has the conflict changed over time?
- What resolution efforts have taken place? Have any been successful? Why or why not?
- What are your personal feelings about the conflict? How does this influence your analysis?

By asking these questions, the researcher is able to develop a deeper understanding of a conflict's origins. Conflict mapping not only brings new insight into the structural challenges driving violent struggle, it is also a case study method that ensures analysts develop a more meaningful understanding of often complex and confusing information.

Three Approaches to Mapping Conflict

1. The Harvard approach emphasizes the difference between positions (what people say they want) and interests (why people want what they say they want). It argues that conflicts can be resolved when actors focus on interests instead of positions and when they develop jointly accepted criteria to deal with these differences.
2. Human needs theory argues that conflicts are caused by basic "universal" human needs that are not satisfied. The needs should be analyzed, communicated, and satisfied for the conflict to be resolved.
3. The conflict transformation approach sees conflicts as destructive or constructive interactions, depending on how conflicts are dealt with or "transformed." Conflicts are viewed as an interaction of energies. Emphasis is given to the different perceptions and the social and cultural context in which reality is constructed. Constructive conflict transformation seeks to empower actors and support recognition between them.

Source: Mason and Rychard 2005.

Conflicts over Separatism and Identity

The Congo is a place where conflict has taken root and appears to be very difficult to shake off; it seems to be an intractable conflict where people have invested so much in the actual conflict that there seems to be no end in sight. It's rooted in many complex issues, including resources, ethnic violence, and identity, among others (see the box below for a brief history of the conflict). In this case we will look at the context of the conflict in terms of human security.

Some people might argue that by its very definition the conflict in the eastern part of the Democratic Republic of Congo (DRC) is intractable. The stakes involved in the conflict are extremely high, and many lives have been lost with even more at risk. The levels of human destruction confirm Mary Kaldor's "new wars" argument in that we have seen horrific casualties in the Congo during this new period following the Cold War. There are disputes within the DRC involving citizenship and land tenure, violent ethnic divisions, and, importantly, the coveted rich minerals that lay buried in the soil of the North and South Kivu provinces. The point is that the conflict in the Congo is not just about any one thing; conflicts rarely are. They operate on multiple levels, and each level usually is dependent on the other.

Since the end of the Second Congo War (1998–2003), renewed fighting between Hutu militias and government forces have displaced thousands of civilians in the region, creating massive human insecurity, chaos, and hardship on scales never seen. Even now, rebels like M23 (March 23 Movement) continue to operate in the region, with allegations of killings, forced recruitment, and illegal detention of civilians.

The Roots of Human Insecurity in the Congo

Early Congo

In order to understand human insecurity and the present conflict in this region, it is important to contextualize the situation by briefly assessing the fractious history of the country. Discovered by the Portuguese in 1482, the "Kingdom of Kongo" became a major source of slaves for European traders. Hired by King Leopold II in 1879, Henry Morton Stanley established trading posts along the Congo River, resulting in the 1884 Berlin Conference on Africa and appointing Leopold as sovereign of the "Congo Free State." This was the only time one Western monarch controlled an entire country as his personal fiefdom. Leopold proceeded to expand his own economic interests, monopolizing ivory and rubber production while enslaving the native populations in a brutal, bloody period lasting until 1908, when, under international pressure, the Belgian government annexed the country, renaming it the "Belgian Congo."

Independence

Despite new rule, the Congo remained mired in poverty and inhumane conditions. After a struggle following the end of World War II, the DRC achieved independence in 1960. But hasty Belgian decolonization resulted in a fragile state with almost no real central government and a burgeoning ethnic and regional conflict problem.

The Conflict in the DRC

The war in the DRC has resulted in an estimated 5.5 million deaths since it first began in 1998 and has been called Africa's First World War. Importantly, the conflict has become the most deadly war in terms of civilian deaths since World War II, with approximately 45,000 people dying per month from hunger, preventable disease, and other factors as a result of the ongoing violence. The conflict has been fueled by ethnic tensions, the collapse of a formal economy, and extreme levels of poverty. The main driver of the conflict, however, has been competition for the vast natural resources (such as coltan, tin, gold, copper, and diamonds) found in the North and South Kivu provinces. After decades of misrule, the Congolese region of Eastern DRC has become a chaotic whirlpool of armed rebel groups intent on inflicting political violence, which is aggravated by the presence of foreign-backed groups, each with their own economic and political agenda motivated by greed and grievance.

Conclusion

A peaceful resolution to this conflict is a long way off. Without goodwill and good intentions on the part of the government, without resolution of issues about land tenure, including recognition of citizenship that respects all ethnic origins, without objective international mediation, and, finally, without social reconstruction, the prospects for peace in the region are empty and desolate to a large extent.

Gender-Based Violence

Gender-based violence against women has increasingly taken on new dimensions in the post–Cold War period. It has intensified and accelerated, and now women in the developing and even developed world have become subject to all sorts of heinous crimes that are detrimental to their personal and physical security. There is much literature on this subject, and analysts are increasingly expressing this view in terms of security. While the literature on the problem is increasing exponentially, unfortunately solutions are not. We have included some of the key texts in the Further Reading section at the end of the chapter.

Due to the fact that women have not been conceived of as the main actors in war, they have often been left out of the more conventional forms of analyses. They are seen as less likely to be involved in the forms of traditional combat compared with their male counterparts. Typical stereotypes paint women as passive and more receptive to peacebuilding activities rather than violence and aggression. This is sustained through a conservative ideology and set of attitudes that has been part of the history of gender relations.

It's important to note that recently casualties involving women in conflict and war has sharply risen. There are roughly 10 times as many civilian casualties of war today as there were at the beginning of the twentieth century. Women and children as civilians (and in many cases forced or conscripted children into war) have become gravely endangered as a result of these conflicts, not only because of the levels of violence aimed at them but also because the results of the violence have engendered massive economic and social insecurity in their countries and across borders.

Rape as a Weapon of War

Women have become frontline victims in wars and are now targeted for rape in many conflict scenarios. Rape has become a widely used weapon of war as a means to achieving certain military and political ends. It's even more difficult to solve this problem because most of these crimes go unreported and unacknowledged. These figures are astonishing, but they are only half the story. The DRC (Congo) is one of the worst offenders of this type of crime. In the five years following 1998, an estimated 40,000 women were raped. And soldiers openly bragged about their crimes, such as one 22-year-old perpetrator in Kivu who announced "Twenty-five of us gathered together and said we should rape 10 women each, and we did it," he said. "I've raped 53 women. And children of five or six years old" (P. Jones 2013).

Kaldor's new wars thesis provides an exceptional framework for understanding the asymmetric violence that occurs when women and girls are raped for the purpose of perpetuating violent conflict. Rape is a severe violation of someone's person, a crime against their physical and mental being. It is also an expression of one group's power over another, a form of domination and a way of expressing control. Communities and families are destroyed. The United Nations Development Fund for Women (UNIFEM) has argued that rape "has become a means of achieving military ends. Rape under orders is not merely an aggressive manifestation of sexuality, but a sexual manifestation of aggression" (Alberdi 2008).

During the 1998 Yugoslavia War Crimes Tribunals, rape and sexual enslavement were officially declared to be crimes against humanity, thus identifying "rape as a weapon of war." Further, it was defined as more than simply a by-product of armed conflict, but as a tactical tool employed by armies and militia to inflict trauma on enemies. The Congo is party to the Rome Statute of the International Criminal Court, which specifies that "acts of rape, sexual slavery, enforced prostitution, forced pregnancy, enforced sterilization, or any other form of sexual violence of comparable gravity can constitute war crimes or crimes against humanity" (International Committee of the Red Cross 2015). While the conflict in the DRC has escalated the use of rape to levels never before seen (in fact, the conflict is definable by the use of rape), the perpetrators of these acts remain largely unpunished. The reasons that individual soldiers rape are convoluted and complex, but as a broad military strategy the use of rape is highly effective: It stigmatizes women and families, undermines communities, terrorizes and instills fear in the general population, demoralizes enemy combatants when perpetrated against their families, and is a much cheaper weapon than bullets.

Gender and Caste Violence in India

Rape is common all over the world, but gender violence doesn't end there. Even in the world's largest democracy violence against women has become a norm rather than an exception. India has recently drawn some controversy because rape and violence against women has taken on new proportions. In recent years there have been many controversial protests against this kind of violence. While dowry deaths were the crime that haunted India during the 1980s, rape—especially gang rape in rural or urban India—has become the crime that defines the country in this decade. India has a long history of overlooking or dismissing the deliberate sexual violence inflicted on women in religious riots, and an equally long history of ignoring the torture, lynching, and murder of men, women, and children from less-privileged castes across the country.

One of the most horrifying aspects of the caste and rape crimes is how normal they are, fitting the general pattern of crimes committed within the normal structure. The need to end the collective denial is urgent if the country is to acknowledge just how widespread the epidemic of violence is and how savage the caste and gender wars have become. Those on the receiving end of the killings and rapes are so often the poorest, the most marginalized, the most profoundly silenced. At the start of 2013, there were mass protests in every city in India following a horrific gang rape and protests in other countries have followed suit, so there is a tide of collective action willing to address this issue even if governments seem to be incapable. Jason Burke (2013), a reporter for *The Guardian*, has described some of this:

> It had long been known that Delhi had a problem with sexual violence. . . .
> According to India's National Crime Records Bureau, registered rape cases in
> India had increased by almost 900 per cent over the past 40 years, to 24,206
> incidents in 2011, while murder cases had gone up by only 250 per cent over
> 60 years, and incidences of riot had actually dropped. But Delhi, with its population of 15 million, registered 572 cases of rape, compared with 239 in Mumbai,
> India's commercial capital, with its bigger population, in 2011. There were just 47
> reported in Kolkata.

But no one knows quite what proportion of attacks these figures represent. Some activists say that 1 in 10 rapes is reported; others say it is probably more like 1 in 100. One poll in 2011 found that nearly one in four Indian men admitted to having committed some act of sexual violence; two-thirds of the sample came from the capital, Delhi.

But rape is not the only problem. Economists Siwan Anderson and Debraj Ray (2010) estimate that in India, more than 2 million women go missing in a given year. They found that roughly 12 percent of the missing women disappear at birth, 25 percent die in childhood, 18 percent disappear during their reproductive ages, and 45 percent go missing at older ages. They found that women died more from "injuries" than from giving birth—injuries, they say, "appear to be an indicator of violence against women."

Clearly, many Indian women face threats at every stage of their lives—violence, inadequate health care, inequality, neglect, bad diet, and a lack of attention to personal health and well-being. Analysts say deep-rooted changes in social attitudes are needed to make India's women more accepted and secure. There is a deeply entrenched patriarchy and widespread misogyny in vast swathes of the country, especially in the north. And the state has been found wanting in its protection and development of human security measures designed to protect vulnerable populations.

Environmental Conflict

Conflict over the environment has gone through various stages and taken on several different layers. There is little doubt that the boom we see in parts of Asia and the rest of the world has resulted in seriously harmful effects to the environment. The paradigm of modernization demanded these countries follow a Western-like trajectory, with economic development leading to political and social development. The result for countries like China has been an environmental disaster as it seeks to increase its economic power and consumer development on a scale the world has never really seen before. An entire industry of development studies emerged after World War II that tried to explain economic, social, and political growth.

Indeed, it was the failure of "development" policies to bring about growth in less-industrialized countries that were accounted for by the invention of "modernization" as a new way of looking at things. From the perspective of neoliberal thinking and globalization, "modernization" has enhanced living conditions in local communities. The Green Revolution has dramatically increased yields through the introduction of hybrids, especially in corn, rice, and other cereals, and mechanization has lessened the burden of physical work done by farmers. However, these accomplishments can have a different meaning if they are analyzed from the perspective of those communities. The substitution of "traditional" farm methods (i.e., those that are congruous with local conditions) for modern farming methods required the introduction of fertilizers, pesticides, and tilling systems to support increasing yields of cash crops for the export market. These new technologies generated, in many cases, an imbalance between expanded production and local conditions that resulted in a great deal of environmental destruction.

By the 1970s the impact of modernization practices on the environment began to become noticeable all over the world. However, while less-industrialized countries continued to be burdened by internal social, economic, and political problems and an increasing external debt, industrialized countries were confronted with increasing scientific evidence of environmental damage. Increased public awareness about the seriousness of the environmental problems faced by most industrialized countries resulted in societal concerns focusing mainly on the physical expression of environmental problems and in ways to control them and the damage caused.

Today, emerging voices have found expression in environmental movements, and feminist theory and local struggles have significantly challenged the dominance of the modernization paradigm. New social movements are becoming more visible and articulating new approaches to development and social organization. The environment is an area where social struggle, conflict, and new claims are and will continue to be made.

From the standpoint of social policy, the green movement can be divided into two main groups, depending on the role they attribute to the state. One brings together social organizations (NGOs) that take a locally based approach to development and consider that the state should play only a secondary role (i.e., green anarchists). The other accepts that the state has an important strategic role to play in guaranteeing a fair and democratic treatment of the needs and interests of the different sectors of society (Barry and Doherty 2001).

The 1972 Club of Rome's report, *The Limits to Growth*, marked the beginning of a global preoccupation with the potential consequences that pursuing development policies grounded in the idea of unrestricted economic growth could have on the natural environment (Meadows et al. 1972). In 1980, the North/South Brandt Commission Report also anticipated a "rising demand in the South for the goods and services provided in the North." Furthermore, although the development of the Asian "Tiger" economies was not yet fully underway, and the so-called "newly industrialising countries" were still taking faltering steps toward development (Page and Redclift 2002, 2), the potential increase in the demand for basic resources reinforced the perspective described in *Limits to Growth* as the foundation for development policies. A few years later, in 1987, before the dismantling of the Soviet Union, the Brundtland Commission report, *Our Common Future*, introduced into the general vocabulary the concept of "sustainable development," which represented a change in policy decision making, signaling an attempt to integrate development and the environment (Brundtland 1987).

Until the late 1980s, development and environmental policies were basically a matter of national interest. However, the detection by British scientists working in Antarctica of the ozone hole created international pressure that culminated in the Montreal Protocol on reductions in chlorofluorocarbon (CFC) gas emissions, signed in September 1987. After the Montreal Protocol, a series of multilateral agreements were signed regarding the exploitation of the so-called "global commons" (wildlife, the atmosphere, and marine environments). More recently, a "second generation of multilateral environmental agreements have tended to bridge sectors, and to be based more in 'systems'; they are more holistic in design. This second generation really commenced with the Earth Summit held in Rio de Janeiro in 1992" (Page and Redclift 2002, 3).

Edward Page and Michael Redclift (2002) indicate the need to distinguish between *environmental security* and *ecological security*. Environmental security refers to the material effects of environmental changes on the living conditions of human populations, while ecological security deals with the impact of human activities on the natural environment. "It is suggested that we need to look hard at the legitimacy of our actions, and avoid confusing human rights in civil society [environmental security] with our obligations to environmental sustainability [ecological security or the rights of nature]" (71).

Page and Redclift also suggest that threats to human and state security from environmental conflicts can be related to two main issues: one associated with conflicts over the ownership and control of vital resources (water, land, oil, forests, and fish) and the other related to serious environmental degradation that can undermine the security of the state. They also assert that three basic elements have contributed to the shift in emphasis away from restricting threats to security to military conflicts: (1) the breakdown of the Soviet Union, (2) the expanded interconnection of economic relations that can lead to global financial crisis, and (3) the "increasing evidence . . . that certain environmental changes could well endanger the existence of whole communities, as well as exacerbating already existing social evils such as poverty, mortality, morbidity, overpopulation and so on" (Page and Redclift 2002, 28).

Conflicts over the Environment and Resources

Environmental conflicts are one of the most important conflicts facing the developing and developed world today as competition over natural resources increases exponentially. These kinds of conflict take on various forms and have different and multiple impacts in different contexts. Conflicts over climate change have come to the fore in recent years because climate change seems to pose such a threat to human security and life. This and everything associated with it have the ability to create and maintain conflict, which of course affects vulnerable people to a large extent.

As reported by the BBC, American scientists have argued that shifts in climate are strongly linked to much of the increase in violence around the world. These scientists contend that small changes in temperature or rainfall are associated with a rise in all types of violent crimes perpetrated by individuals, as well as group conflicts and ultimately war. It seems no one is safe from climate change. Predicting the future based on this information, the world is likely to become more prone, not less, to violence. They report a "substantial" correlation between climate and conflict.

This is illustrated through a recent increase in domestic violence in India during times of drought as well as an increase in assaults, rapes, and murders when heat waves occur in the United States. In addition, the report views rising temperatures as related to conflicts, among them ethnic violence in Europe and civil wars in Africa. The researchers estimate that a rise in the overall temperature of 2°C (3.6°F) will lead to increases in personal crimes by about 15 percent and group conflicts in some regions by more than 50 percent.

However, other researchers have questioned these findings. Dr. Halvard Buhaug from the Peace Research Institute Oslo in Norway concluded that conflicts are linked to other factors, such as high infant mortality, proximity to international borders, and high local population density. Although scholars debate the link between climate change and conflict, there is a case to be made that changes in the natural environment can fuel human competition for resources that may lead to an increase in human insecurity.

Even dissenters like Buhaug (2015) have noted that armed conflict may increase a community's vulnerability to climate change while "ill-advised climate adaptation plans have the potential to trigger resentment and conflict." One thing is for certain: the question of whether climate change threatens human security is unlikely to disappear any time soon.

Source: Adapted from Morelle 2013.

When we see these conflicts and how there might be post-conflict reconstruction and peacebuilding, we need to know the effect a conflict has had on the environment and what stress effects this has had on the people living within that environment.

However, it is true that the world's natural environment and natural resources have increasingly become a conflict arena as governments seek new sources of energy to maintain the lifestyles their populations have become accustomed to. These conflicts may not involve violence in the initial stages, but the consequences in the longer term point to conflict opportunities, particularly over access to resources and the benefits to be gained from them. One of the proposed solutions is to control world greenhouse gas emissions. However, there is controversy over whether this is a human-made problem or just a natural warming process. In the United States, opposition to global warming has become a conservative political cause that is well funded by the oil and automobile industry.

A second theme focuses on Earth's scarce resources and their use. Two examples—water and oil—have generated intense and bloody conflicts between communities and states. Oil poses special problems because it is found in abundance in some countries but is scarce or nonexistent in others, and since its discovery it has become the center of major disputes in many places around the world. Oil usage closely correlates with economic development—India and China are rapidly developing economically and also using increasing amounts of oil for its "energy needs." Some credit oil as the real justification for the Iraq wars—it was all about energy, not weapons of mass destruction (which were never found). China is becoming a vast user of oil as it develops and has openly played politics to protect its energy security—as China's record in the Sudan illustrates clearly.

Climate Change and Threats to Human Security

People are taking action because climate change has serious impacts, both locally and globally. For example, "in 2007, scientists from the International Panel on Climate Change (IPCC) predicted that warming oceans and melting glaciers due to global warming and climate change could cause sea levels to rise 7–23 inches by the year 2100. Worldwide, densely populated coastal communities and infrastructure that supports them would be affected (such as city buildings and homes, roads, ports and wastewater treatment plants). Some would be flooded or more vulnerable to storm damage. In flat terrain, the shoreline could move many miles inland" (Washington State Department of Ecology 2012). Other effects are also serious. In some places, floods or drought could become more frequent and more severe. Even seemingly less dramatic local changes in temperature, precipitation, and soil moisture could severely impact many things that are important to human, animal, and plant life.

Jon Barnett and Neil Adger (2007) argue that climate change has a significant impact on human security via a reduction in resources and a weakened ability of the state to deliver protection from climate disaster, thereby increasing the likelihood of conflict:

> The vulnerability (potential for loss) of people to climate change depends on the extent to which they are dependent on natural resources and ecosystem services, the extent to which the resources and services they rely on are sensitive to climate change, and their capacity to adapt to changes in these resources and services. In other words, the more people are dependent on climate sensitive forms of natural capital, and the less they rely on economic or social forms of capital, the more at risk they are from climate change.

They also rightly point out that human security implications from climate change vary given the globally diverse dependency on natural resources throughout communities. Different regions will experience different human security threats from climate change.

China, the largest energy consumer and producer in the world, needs to secure resources and is competing with other large consumers, such as the United States. For example, there has been a developing geopolitical conflict between the United States and China over Chinese oil and gas interests. China's most popular newspaper issued a cautionary statement in October 2011 stating that nations involved in territorial disputes in the waters should "mentally prepare for the sounds of cannons" (Reuters 2011).

In 2010, US, Australian, and British governments argued that they should not be targeted for increased measures to address greenhouse gas emissions unless China and India were also subject to this targeting based on the combination of these two countries' large populations, strong economic growth, and high use of energy and materials. In terms of international relations, this is an important issue. Penalizing developing countries for the historical problems caused by developed countries is particularly unfair, especially if the poor countries' emissions are for basic needs and development while rich countries' emissions are more about luxury consumption and lifestyles. This is an issue that will not be resolved easily, particularly as countries in Asia and elsewhere catch up with developed countries.

One writer, Idean Salehyan (2008), argues that climate change cannot be used yet to predict increasing conflicts. He explains the rationale given by supporters of climate change as a factor for increased civil conflicts: resource scarcity, competition over the means to sustain livelihoods, rising sea levels, natural disasters, disrupted economies, reduced availability of natural resources, and many more that lead to mass migration. Further, competition between the haves and the have-nots will increase global and intrastate inequalities, further contributing to conflict. Salehyan argues, however, that those linking climate change with increased violent conflicts fail to consider human agency, technological innovations, and the role of political institutions in managing conflict.

There is a fair amount of research regarding whether resource scarcity causes more conflict, but at times it does not always appear accurate. Some have suggested that it is the *combination* of factors that lead to conflict and resource scarcity that is more important. Alex Evans (2010), for instance, suggests that poor people and fragile states will be at the greatest risk, and weak governance is a contributing factor to the problems associated with resource scarcity. While it's difficult to show a direct link between climate change and violent conflict, there are multiple factors that contribute to the realization of conflict, and the effects of climate change play an integral part in solution development. However, to say that climate change or resource scarcity is solely responsible for violent conflict is in part misleading and misses recognizing the complexity of the various potential threats to human security.

Terrorism and New Deadly Human Security Threats

New methods of waging conflict and "war" have been developed throughout history— whether based on technology (e.g., gunpowder, aircraft, missiles) or new tactics and methods (e.g., suicide bombing, counterinsurgency). However, the 9/11 attack changed the study and practice of war significantly.

What has been called **terrorism** has emerged as a strategy favored and used in conflicts to achieve objectives—which may only be to kill people. The term may be overused now, as the **"War on Terror"** seems to have become political rhetoric rather than an operational set of policies. Terrorism involves violent attacks on targets that include people who may have nothing to do with the conflict or the perpetrators—these attacks are not on police, army, or government targets. The attacks may be carried out by groups and individuals acting independently of any state organization's funding or approval, although some rogue states may fund, train, and allow such operations to be launched from their own territory if the targets are within a perceived enemy's country.

Terrorist methods vary, from hijacking aircraft to bombing planes, trains, buses, village markets, or banks to assassinating government officials. The technology of weaponry now enables explosives to be small, easy to hide, difficult to detect, and detonated by remote control. A new pattern emerging is the extensive use of "suicide" bombers— those who kill others but also kill themselves.

Private wars between combatants—none of which are government linked—have existed in the past. The "mafia" type of violence between competing gangs has been a feature of real life and has been glorified in fiction and film. Gang violence of this type seems to have become quite open in Mexico, as rival gangs involved in the drug smuggling business openly attack each other with automatic weapons. The large gang of Dawood Ibrahim based in India, Pakistan, and the United Arab Emirates has operated for years and is implicated in bombings in Mumbai, murders, as well as normal gang activities of smuggling, gambling, and extortion.

The dilemma of a global war on terror and its relationship to human rights is a crucial issue that has helped define terrorism, human security, and human rights in the early twenty-first century. This has constituted the "paradigm" for most of US foreign policy during this period, and by extenuation for many other states as well, either in reaction to (for the most part) or in making their own initiatives. A central argument is that states have used the war to legitimize their own regimes and stifle opposition, particularly in nondemocratic states where there is a history of repression, thus denying human security to their populations.

Human Rights

One of the most important developments in human security and international relations in the post–Cold War period is the central focus on human rights on a global scale. This is of immense importance not only for the victims of rights abuses, but also for scholars and activists who try to shape agendas in the international arena. There have been many debates regarding the balance between (human) security and human rights. The attempt in this text will be to emphasize these debates and provide the background about how they emerged and how they may be resolved (or not) in the contemporary era. We will also indicate the differences between the pre-9/11 international human rights regime (which was witnessing some improvements) and the post-9/11 regime, which appears to be in the process of being dismantled as security concerns have taken precedence over human rights abuses (domestically and internationally).

Essentially this is a new security environment that emerged after the Cold War but was not fully realized until after 9/11. One of the problems the modern state faces is how to balance national security while simultaneously allowing for recognized civil liberties. In April 2005, the UN created the post of special investigator to investigate counterterrorism measures that violate basic human rights.

How the Context Has Changed in Dealing with Human Rights/Human Security

One of the crucial paradoxes in the global War on Terror is that the US government argues that human rights are a critical part of its foreign policy. The protection of fundamental human rights was a foundation stone in the establishment of the United States over 200 years ago. Since then, a central goal of US foreign policy has been the promotion of respect for human rights as embodied in the **Universal Declaration of Human Rights**. The United States understands that the existence of human rights helps secure peace, deter aggression, promote the rule of law, combat crime and corruption, strengthen democracies, and prevent humanitarian crises.

The threat to the United States from terror has increased. In the decade after 1985, there were only two terrorist incidents on US soil with foreign involvement: the bombing of the World Trade Center in February 1993 and the occupation of the Iranian mission in 1992 by five opponents of the Iranian government. Between 1990–5, there were 32 recorded domestic incidents of terror. The threat levels have been viewed as asymmetrical—that is, a condition of war where adversaries are likely to attempt to circumvent or undermine an opponent while exploiting weaknesses using methods that differ significantly from the usual mode of operation.

Despite these kinds of arguments, one could point out that policy and rhetoric do not match reality. In practice, we see scenarios of a realist, security, state-centered–driven view of rights, which sees rights as expendable in times of national crisis and emergency (i.e., the War on Terror), on the one hand versus a universalistic, idealistic, nonstate–centered view of human rights and human security as being non-negotiable on the other hand. Our argument will be that the former has triumphed over the latter as the *modus operandi* for the "new" world order following 9/11. We are living in a world in which rights have become tempered by the need to balance the rights and civil liberties of the individual with a need for the security of the state and the people who live in it. Already this "state of emergency" has had significant implications, not just in the United States but around the world, in curtailing individual rights. Take the case of the young Brazilian electrician shot dead in the Stockwell tube station in London on 22 July 2005 after being suspected of being a potential bomber. It might be argued that Jean Charles de Menezes's individual right to life was not respected because the perceived collective security of the larger public was placed as a higher priority. In this sense the rights of the individual appear to have been deemed lesser in nature to the rights of a larger group. Ironically this view resembles an early Asian authoritarian values argument about rights, which argues that the rights of the community should take precedence over those of the individual. Jean Charles de Menezes was a victim of police incompetence, albeit in difficult conditions. However, the conditions that led to the fatality were created by the state's pursuit of a war on terror, and therefore in some ways constitute an abridgement of the individual right to security. A set of fears have emerged with this war that have created the conditions that allow for such tragedies to occur. In short, the War on Terror has circumvented aspects of the rule of law, a keystone of Western liberal democracies. Human security ultimately is denigrated in both the individual and the collective senses.

Patterns

We might see several patterns emerging as a result of this. The first is that human rights concerns are currently and look set to continue to be outweighed by security concerns. This can be argued despite the defeat of some of the British government's security legislation in Parliament. It is not just terror attacks themselves, such as those that took place on 11 September 2001 in the United States or 7 July 2005 in London, that have created a climate of fear and mistrust—the War on Terror itself has helped create this climate. This climate of fear and insecurity is present even among the most liberal and erstwhile tolerant members of the community. People who were once liberal in their attitudes toward asylum seekers and refugees, for instance, have become increasingly conservative toward such groups. A climate of Islamaphobia has also developed, with increased attacks on Muslims and people associated with the Muslim faith. The human security and human rights of people have declined as a result.

Humanitarian interventionism came to be based to some extent on the notion that human rights abuses were taking place and that it was acceptable to intervene to protect these rights. This led to a closing of the divide in the Cold War between the advocates of second-generation rights (social and economic rights; the communist countries) and the supporters of political and civil rights (advanced liberal democracies in general). It also allowed for some integration between previously opposing camps.

The Intersection of Human Rights and National Security

At the heart of the War on Terror and its relationship with human rights is the balancing act that liberal nation-states must conduct between the security of its citizenry and the protection of basic rights and freedoms. The intersection of national security and human rights principally involves the issue of friction between individual security and state or regime security. At the most fundamental level, there is no contradiction between state interests and individual interests if it is accepted that the state originated in individuals organizing to protect themselves from the perils of **anarchy** and persisted because it proved cost effective compared to the alternatives. To some extent states are designed (in liberal thought) to protect the security of individuals, but they must also secure themselves *against* those individuals who might be a threat to the state, including dissidents, terrorists, separatists, and agents of enemy governments. There is no doubt that security is also a human right. Article 3 of the Universal Declaration of Human Rights points out that "everyone has the right to life, liberty and security of person" (United Nations 1948). These are rights that terrorists seek to abolish when they kill, maim, or injure in their actions. How we balance that right with the larger goals of security is an even more difficult dilemma for the modern nation-state.

CONCLUSION

This chapter has argued that we are facing new challenges when it comes to conflict in the post–Cold War era. With the end of the Cold War many people had hoped that an era of peace and tranquility might develop. The major power blocs no longer threaten global annihilation, international governmental organizations have been strengthened, and free trade has been endorsed to bring nations together through shared economic self-interest. Human rights prospects appeared to be improving on a global basis, and the United States emerged unchallenged as the sole superpower to dominate political and economic life. However, internal power struggles persisted in many countries and ethnic and separatist movements flourished, promoting violence to achieve their objectives that in turn led to the increased conflicts and civil wars within states.

The conflict in Syria and the countries affected by the Arab Spring also reflect the internal nature of conflicts despite the fact that many of these conflicts have spilled over into neighboring countries. To a large extent, the whole international system has undergone change, and conflict has been restructured. After 9/11 the entire scope and theater of war was redefined by the United States and its Western allies. Moreover, the end of the Cold War and the continuous expansion of the new neoliberal economic system have resulted in increased prosperity for much of the industrialized world and the power elites in less-developed countries, while the large majority of the world's population has benefited only marginally if at all. Conditions of poverty, environmental degradation, and alienation from Western modernity have brought about religious, ethnic, and political violence, which has resulted in civil wars, terrorist acts, and in some cases "failed states."

One thing that we should be aware of is that it is impossible to understand conflict without understanding the context and environment within which that conflict has developed. Several trends emerged after the Cold War world and have continued; we conclude this chapter by summarizing them here:

- The shape, nature, and intensity of conflict have changed in the post–Cold War period. This has changed our perspective on the relations between states and forced us to rethink our traditional views.
- Security as a concept and reality has changed. International relations theorists have been forced to consider other forms of security, in particular the new and emerging concept of human security.
- From a historical point of view, contrary to conventional wisdom, we have seen that interstate war is *not* the main source of violence or physical insecurity, and this holds true for contemporary periods.
- While armed violence is declining there has been a shift in the post–Cold War period to new forms of war and intrastate ethnic warfare. This latter form of conflict often appears highly brutal and intense (i.e., the 1994 Rwandan genocide of Tutsis by Hutus).

KEY TERMS

Anarchy; Clash of Civilizations; Conflict; Conflict Prevention; Conflict Resolution; Democratization; Failed State; End of History; Gender-Based Violence; Genocide; Human Development Index; Identity; Interstate Conflict; Intractable Conflict;

Intrastate Conflict; Jihad; McDonaldization; Peacebuilding; Post–Cold War; Terrorism; Universal Declaration on Human Rights; War on Terror

FURTHER READING

Barnes, Joe, and Amy Myers Jaffe. 2006. "The Persian Gulf and the Geopolitics of Oil." *Survival* 48 (1): 143–62. http://dx.doi.org/10.1080/00396330600594348.

Battaglini, A., and J. Scheffran. 2011. "Climate and Conflicts: The Security Risks of Global Warming." *Regional Environmental Change* 11 (1): 27–39.

Fjelde, Hanne. 2009. "Buying Peace? Oil Wealth, Corruption and Civil War, 1985–99." *Journal of Peace Research* 46 (2): 199–218. http://dx.doi.org/10.1177/0022343308100715.

Johnstone, Sarah, and Jeffrey Mazo. 2011. "Global Warming and the Arab Spring." *Survival* 53 (2): 11–17. http://dx.doi.org/10.1080/00396338.2011.571006.

Kaplan, Robert. 1994. "The Coming Anarchy." *Atlantic Monthly*. http://www. theatlantic.com/magazine/archive/1994/02/the-coming-anarchy/304670/.

Kaplan, Robert. 2002. *The Coming Anarchy: Shattering the Dreams of the Post Cold War*. New York: Knopf Doubleday Publishing.

Le Billon, Philippe. 2001. "The Political Ecology of War: Natural Resources and Armed Conflicts." *Political Geography* 20 (5): 561–84. http://dx.doi.org/10.1016/S0962-6298(01)00015-4.

Shah, Anup. 2012. "Climate Change and Global Warming." *Global Issues*. http://www. globalissues.org/issue/178/climate-change-and-global-warming.

WEBSITES

Conflict Information Consortium: http://conflict.colorado.edu

Equality Now: www.equalitynow.org

GBV Prevention Network: http://preventgbvafrica.org

International Committee of the Red Cross: www.icrc.org/en

International Peace Institute: www.ipinst.org

International Relations and Security Network: www.isn.ethz.ch

UN Women Watch: www.un.org/womenwatch

Uppsala Conflict Data Program: http://pcr.uu.se/research/UCDP

Chapter 3

HUMAN RIGHTS AND THE RULE OF LAW: FOUNDATIONS FOR HUMAN SECURITY

It was never the people who complained of the universality of human rights,
nor did the people consider human rights as a Western or Northern imposition.
It was often their leaders who did so.
Kofi Annan, former UN secretary-general (quoted in Alves 2000, 498)

INTRODUCTION

In December 2013, the world mourned the passing of a great human rights defender, former South African President Nelson Mandela. Once described as the "grandfather of the world," his memorial service was attended by royalty and heads of state from at least 84 countries. Politicians came from far and wide to bear witness to the passing of a great leader who urged peace and reconciliation over violence and revenge.

Mandela spent 27 years in prison for his opposition to his country's brutal and racist **apartheid** system. Apartheid in South Africa, which started in the 1940s and would last for nearly 50 years, was structured so that the white minority population controlled the black majority through political and social segregation. Mandela not only inspired national resistance, he embodied the international human rights community's contempt for South African oppression. But what makes Mandela's story so important is that he was not always supported by his contemporaries; rather, he was often classified as a dangerous revolutionary and ideologue.

In a little over a decade, the South African government would charge him with "statutory communism," "high treason," and sabotage. In 1964, he was sentenced to life imprisonment on the infamous Robben Island. Meanwhile, many Western governments, including the United States and the United Kingdom, continued to support the apartheid regime in the name of its anti-communist stance. The former British Prime Minister Margaret Thatcher labeled Mandela's political party, the African National Congress (ANC), "a typical terrorist organisation" for its affiliation with the South African Communist Party. Only in 2008 did the United States officially remove Mandela from its terrorist watch list, nearly two decades after he was freed from prison and 15 years since he had been democratically elected as the president of South Africa.

The story of Mandela is a source of inspiration for human rights defenders. It involves a grassroots resistance movement against an oppressive regime, the power of a philosophical idea like rights, the triumph of justice through reconciliation, and all within a context of nonviolent healing. For apartheid to end, Mandela and his supporters had to break laws, challenge all levels of government, and prepare for an aggressive state response that would likely involve imprisonment, **torture**, or even death. Officials in apartheid South Africa operated with impunity, while human rights defenders faced great risk. South Africans had to reclaim their rights from a state that had hijacked them, a struggle that symbolizes the modern human rights movement.

This chapter sets out to explain the relation between the international human rights movement and human security in developing states. We are concerned with the ways in which rights are respected and why they are often violated in the world's poorest regions. Here, we do not explore rights through a top-down statist approach—that is, a study of **human rights** as entitlements that are protected by international law and normative philosophy. Rather, we approach the topic through a bottom-up approach that looks at **dysfunctional institutions** that are the product of corruption, weak **rule of law**, and an overall lack of political will. By *political will* we refer to governments that have no intention of or interest in improving human rights within their territories while purposely violating fundamental legal principles such as impartiality, neutrality, and an independent judicial system. These dysfunctional systems undermine human security by failing to protect and promote human rights while jeopardizing vital public interests, since the courts are unable to protect the rights of citizens. To begin, we start with a review of the human rights movement while discussing the ideas behind the concept itself.

MAINSTREAMING INTERNATIONAL HUMAN RIGHTS LAW

The international human rights movement is one of the most important struggles to emerge out of the twentieth century. While claims over rights have been advanced throughout history, they were often declared by one group over another to exert power. For example, Jack Donnelly has shown that many societies rejected basic rights to entrench social hierarchy and empire. For example, traditional Hinduism entrenched a hierarchy of social relations based on duties and obligations within the **caste** structure. Those finding themselves at the lowest end of caste have the least amount of rights compared to those that belong to a higher class. One group in particular, known as the Dalits or "untouchables," were completely left out of the system, thereby establishing deep discrimination and intolerance within the system that still impacts over 200 million people today. In the world's oldest continuous civilization, Chinese emperors believed the "Mandate of Heaven" gave them a right to govern those within the civilized borders of the Middle Kingdom, while those outside were deemed barbarians. The Confucian code of ethics argued that rights must be earned and could therefore be taken away by the state. In the Muslim world, there is debate on whether principles of universal human rights can be found within the Islamic holy works. While themes of rights and dignity are presented, ancient Islamic doctrine is more concerned with the dynamics of state duties and the responsibility of citizens (Donnelly 2013). Indeed, as history has shown, rights claims have proven to be highly political and have been more concerned with preserving status quo power structures than protecting an individual's rights.

Europe was no exception. The monarchs took special interest in declaring themselves defenders of the faith and holders of divine rights. Such celestial privileges demanded citizens obey their king, who governed under the authority of God. Yet the Western concept of natural rights would emerge as a powerful tool to challenge absolutism through appeals to reason. Europe's Renaissance and Enlightenment saw philosophers such as Thomas Hobbes, John Locke, and Jean-Jacques Rousseau claim that humans had certain inalienable rights drawn from natural law, such as the right to life. Still, Europe's Renaissance was marred by violent colonial expansionism and mercantilist economic models that saw resources extracted from around the world though slavery and servitude. Europeans often viewed those outside their culture as savages needing to be occupied and trained on how to be civilized. The slave trade, the destruction of Indigenous societies in the Americas, along with the direct occupation in territories throughout Asia are just a few examples of colonialism at work. Europe's transformation from mercantilism to an emerging capitalist system was violently imposed on societies the world over. **Social Darwinism**, a worldview that promoted the supremacy of powerful individuals and races over others that were perceived as inferior, was well established in elite European circles. The stage was set for one of the most violent periods in human history: the early twentieth century.

The horror of the World Wars, the Holocaust, and the spread of violent ideology drove European governments to turn abstract notions of rights into functioning legal code. As Jack Donnelly (2013, 78) has noted, it was "by necessity rather than superior virtue they [the West] got a jump on the rest of the world in developing the response of human rights." Such extreme levels of European violence led to the adoption of the Universal Declaration of Human Rights (UDHR) on 10 December 1948. As the declaration's preamble notes, "Whereas disregard and contempt for human rights have resulted in barbarous acts which have outraged the conscience of mankind, and the advent of a world in which human beings shall enjoy freedom of speech and belief and freedom from fear and want has been proclaimed as the highest aspiration of the common people" (United Nations 1948). Not only does the UDHR signify a major turning point in the human rights movement's long political struggle, it also sought to establish freedom from fear and want while laying down a foundation for the legal conventions that would follow. Today, every government in the world has signed and ratified at least one human rights convention, while 80 percent of states have ratified four or more treaties.

It is for this reason that we argue the modern human rights movement as seen today is a recent phenomenon. While there have been important human rights events throughout history, such as the signing of the Magna Carta, the American and French Revolutions, the Treaty of Westphalia, and the abolishment of slavery, to name just a few, the codification of human rights law marks a milestone in human innovation. Legal principles and guidelines of international human rights law provide a basic set of criteria that work to strengthen human security. There are currently 18 human rights treaties that deal with a range of themes, including gender, Indigenous rights, as well as rights of the child. These treaties have been drafted to protect the most vulnerable and marginalized groups in any society. When these laws are rejected, undermined, or ignored by governments, human security is lost.

UNDERSTANDING HUMAN RIGHTS

If your community was given a choice between having access to free primary schooling or clean drinking water, which would you chose? This question is not hypothetical for many in the developing world who experience pervasive levels of poverty. What many in advanced industrialized countries consider to be essential services of life continue to be out of reach for billions of people. But can access to education be considered less of a fundamental right than drinking water? For modern rights advocates the answer is no—the state has an equal responsibility to provide both. There is no hierarchy when it comes to basic human rights as outlined in the UDHR, pointing to the central claim that all rights are equal, inalienable, and indivisible. When governments do not consider all rights as equal, thereby denying protection to vulnerable or marginalized groups, a deep sense of insecurity and fear seeps into populations as human security is denied.

Basic human rights have also been referred to as **first-generation rights**, or negative rights. These are the rights that are generally protected so long as the state refrains from committing a violation against the individual. For example, the state must not arbitrarily arrest you, bulldoze your house, or torture you while in custody. These rights are set out in the UDHR and should be considered a *minimum* baseline for human rights. Within a first-generational rights paradigm, there is no expectation that government ought to provide goods or services for the community, such as social welfare assistance. Rather, the emphasis is on limiting political power that can easily be abused by those in positions of authority. They have also been referred to as *civil-political rights* since they outline the protection of political liberties and empowerment. This is the spirit of human rights: a check on state authority. Human security calls for assurances that citizens are able to live and work within a community without fear of government.

Second-generation rights, or positive rights, are the rights that you gain by the state doing something for you. These are the rights that you probably argue most about with your family and friends. Should the state provide social assistance for those who are unemployed? Should new parents be entitled to one year maternity or paternity leave? Should the state be providing free medicine for patients with chronic illnesses? These socioeconomic rights are disputed throughout the world because they directly question the role of the state in providing basic security for individuals. They are referred to as second generation because these claims require governments to move beyond the minimum threshold set out in first-generation rights defined in the UDHR. These types of rights are fiercely contested since they involve a diverse range of stakeholders who demand entitlements that require state resources involving the redirection of tax revenue to fund services such as education, social housing, or health care. Support for second-generation rights is often ideologically divisive and can differ greatly between communities and states.

Finally, there is an emerging field of scholarship that focuses on **third-generation rights**. These rights are associated with collective claims and culture. The rights to clean air or water are collective claims centered on the environment. The African Charter on Human and Peoples' Rights is an example of an international agreement calling on participants to respect collective rights as well as those of the individual. Adopted in 1981, the charter is unlike Western equivalents in that it calls for regional unity and cooperation. The charter states, "parties to the present Charter shall individually and collectively exercise the right to free disposal of their wealth and natural resources with a view to strengthening African unity and solidarity" (African Commission on Human and Peoples' Rights 1986, article 21, section 4). Similarly, calls from many Indigenous communities throughout the world also argue for minority group claims. In 2007, the adoption of UN Declaration on the Rights of Indigenous Peoples (UNDRIP) was a major victory for advocates of collective and cultural rights. Yet as Karen Engle (2011) has argued, it remains to be seen if the UNDRIP has the ability to entrench the notion of "collective rights" outside the sphere of historical bias that the international human rights community holds toward the special status of the individual.

As you can see, third-generation rights are more difficult to define as they can be broadly interpreted. There are even critics within the human rights movement, who see these types of rights as problematic since they take away from the claim that rights are individual-centric. Despite the controversy over third-generation rights, it is impossible to dismiss the importance and influence of group claims, which are now regularly advocated by UN agencies and human security specialists. Table 3.1 summarizes the three generations of rights and some examples of each.

This discussion of generational rights might sound philosophical and abstract. But this is for good reason, if we remember that human rights started as ideas that have since come to be understood as real and of substance. If a professor asked you to go out into the "real world," find human rights, and bring them back to the classroom, what would you bring? This question points to the wider difficulty of reconciling individual perceptions of how we ought to identify and advocate for the protection of rights. For example, is capital punishment a human rights violation? The UDHR clearly declares that every individual has a right to life, but can an individual lose this right, especially if he or she has committed a heinous crime against the innocent? Would providing the leader of a genocidal military unit with the right to live deny justice to the families of victims who experienced **ethnic cleansing**? As we discuss throughout this book, individual perceptions, notions of justice, and the belief in **cultural relativism** make answering this question complex. In fact, the idea of rights as an ethical and moral appeal backed by international treaty is controversial.

On the one hand, rights claims are normative in nature, since they assert universalism. Generally associated with the liberal philosophical tradition, advocates of **universalism**, such as John Locke and Immanuel Kant, claim that humanity strives to find

Table 3.1   Three Generations of Rights

First Generation (Civil-Political Rights)	Second Generation (Socioeconomic Rights)	Third Generation (Collective Rights)
Right to life	Right to health care	Right to clean air
Right to shelter	Right to housing	Right to culture
Right to work	Living wage	Collective rights
Right to food	Social insurance	Sustainability
Freedom of religion	Right to education	Social development
Free speech	Some civil liberties	Democracy
No torture and fair trials	Maternity leave	Right to the Internet

truths that can be observed throughout the world. For universal human rights advocates, there can be no justification for violating an individual's rights on any grounds. For consistency, this rule must also apply to war criminals, terrorists, serial killers, and pedophiles.

To the contrary, those who subscribe to the concept of **cultural relativism** believe that not all rights should apply to all societies. Culture matters for relativists, and those who advocate universal notions of rights are taking on a **neocolonialist** worldview by demanding others adopt similar rules and regulations as those in the West. This perspective allows for pluralistic notions of how rights are managed within the state, where the government becomes the adjudicator of human rights. From this perspective, individuals may be denied the right to life under extreme circumstances where a serious crime has been committed. Other rights may also be denied under the pretext that societies are different and governments have a right to enact laws that are contrary to the UDHR. Cultural relativism has a long history of being used by nondemocratic regimes to suppress political opponents and weaken gender-based rights movements.

The Asian Values Thesis: Social Harmony as Human Security?

Is it possible to have human rights in authoritarian political environments? The answer is not as simple as you might think and brings about some arguments that governments can create secure and safe environments by placing collective security above the rights of the individual. One of the more powerful arguments in support of collective security over that of individual human security centers on the Asian values thesis.

In the early 1990s, a small faction of political elites based in Singapore, including former President Lee Kuan Yew and diplomat-turned-academic Kishore Mahbubani, presented universalists with a powerful human rights critique in what became known as the Asian values thesis. Proponents argued that Western governments who promoted human rights did so to gain political leverage over societies that lacked the ability to develop and enforce human rights laws. The concept argued that Western notions of rights did not fit with Asian values, which called for social harmony over individual rights.

They suggested Asians preferred family, the community, and the collective over individualist notions of rights, and governments in Asia needed to take on a paternal role over society. Asian values advocates placed economic development above all other rights. The argument was simple: How can you think about rights when society is so poor that it can't feed itself? The concept was embraced by some governments, such as China, Indonesia, and Malaysia, but was rejected by others, such as India, the Philippines, and Japan. The concept was also criticized for promoting authoritarian governance policies, since it argued that a government's rights should always trump that of the individual.

Still, the argument that communitarian-based rights claims focusing on culture could bring security for the group not only offers an alternative approach to human security but also challenges the need to place the individual at the center of the rights debate. While the concept has now been largely discarded by academics and governments alike, the theory did manage to cause much controversy throughout the human rights world.

From our perspective, *human rights can be understood as a basic set of universal guarantees that all individuals possess from birth*. We borrow from Jack Donnelly (2013), who sees rights as something that one has simply because he or she is human. They are inalienable and separate us from other organisms, such as animals and plants, while capturing the literal meaning behind the UDHR. Human rights offer the individual a framework for thinking about the arbitrary use of force by the state. We must point out that only governments can commit a human rights violation according to the law. While other actors commit abuses, they are not human rights violations since this domain is exclusively reserved for the state. We therefore see the human rights movement as an effort to *empower* and *protect* individual human security.

Our intention here is not to develop another argument on the theoretical underpinnings of human rights; rather, we hope to show the link between human rights and human security. The next section argues that governments who cannot guarantee the basic human rights of their citizens are manufacturing environments of insecurity. What's more, and as we discuss throughout this book, denying basic services can lead to structural violence that does not require physical acts by the state. Not providing individuals with access to clean drinking water, safe housing, or nutritional food undermines the very foundation of society. The freedom to live in dignity does not exist where rights are denied.

MAKING THE CONNECTION BETWEEN HUMAN RIGHTS AND HUMAN SECURITY

In 1961, British lawyer Peter Benenson (1961) published a groundbreaking letter in the London *Observer* entitled "The Forgotten Prisoners." The article, which also marked the early beginning of Amnesty International, stressed that human rights violations did not just occur in communist countries. Benenson accused Western governments of violating the UDHR by arresting citizens for believing in ideologies that ran counter to that of the governing regime. Many of these prisoners were held in detention without trial and often tortured to extract confessions that would give the state just cause to hold them. The world would later refer to these individuals as prisoners of conscience since they were detained on account of their belief system. The notion that anyone could be imprisoned for thinking pointed to a troubling fact: Even democratic governments could be purveyors of human insecurity. While Benenson's letter galvanized the human rights world, it serves as a stark reminder of the gap between international legal commitments by states and the enforcement of such declarations at the national level.

The inability of states to honor their international legal obligations is one factor that drives human insecurity in the Global South. The disregard for human rights by states risks undermining the legitimacy of international law altogether. Rights advocates will continue to draft cutting-edge laws and regulations, but what good are these documents if they are not implemented by governments? Convincing governments to surrender legal sovereignty can prove difficult, especially when there could be negative implications for the regime. Still, governments do endorse human rights laws despite the political risk, but why? There are at least three reasons why international human rights laws are often advocated by governments yet not enforced.

First, *governments may sign international human rights treaties to build their reputation*. For example, there are 155 countries that have signed and ratified the Convention against Torture and Other Cruel, Inhuman or Degrading Treatment or Punishment (CAT). Parties to the CAT have legal obligations to eliminate torture in their societies, yet many of these countries use torture as a method of policing to extract confessions. While signatories accept the CAT as legally binding, many endorse the treaty knowing it will not be enforced at the domestic level. Few governments would admit that torture is used as a policing mechanism in their country, but by signing such treaties political leaders can bolster their standing by laying claim that they are committed toward implementation. Governments want to be perceived as responsible actors within the community of nations. Political leaders also care about what others think and may calculate the risks associated with not endorsing international norms. Indeed, signing human rights agreements can increase an illiberal regime's political capital.

Second, *governments may sign treaties knowing they are unable to enforce the laws because they simply have no capital*. Implementing international norms is expensive, but no country wants to be perceived as weak and incapable of enforcing its own legal obligations. A lack of institutional capacity requires states to prioritize scarce resources. For example, Bangladesh is one of the world's poorest countries. Although there has been steady growth over the past decade, 43 million people in that country still live on less than US$2/day, while one-quarter of the population lacks food security (see the box below for more information). For Bangladesh, which has been referred to by Paul Collier (2008) as a **bottom-billion** state, using resources to end hunger will take priority over other areas such as training police to end torture. Collier's term "bottom billion" is used to describe the number of poor who fall within the world's lower echelon of economic vulnerability.

Governance and Food Insecurity in Bangladesh

There can be no human security when governments are unable to provide their citizens with basic access to food. Achieving food security demands that an individual has continuous access to and availability of nutritious provisions. While global poverty numbers are on the decline, hundreds of millions of people living in both the Global North and South struggle to access food. One country experiencing high levels of food insecurity is Bangladesh.

This South Asian state is one of the poorest, most densely populated and disaster-prone countries in the world. In 2010, over 30 percent of the population (48 million people) lived below the poverty line, while high levels of inequality contribute to the country's food insecurity. The damage caused by floods, droughts, and hurricanes contributes to the country's poverty cycle by undermining efforts to reduce poverty and raise the health standards of children. Vulnerability of low-income households is high, because natural disasters often destroy food sources and drive families to withdraw their children from school.

Bangladesh ranks 146th on the 2013 Human Development Index (HDI) and 68th out of 79 countries on the Global Hunger Index. The World Food Programme (WFP) estimates that 37 million people are food insecure, resulting in low dietary options with little foreseen change across all income groups. Roughly 41 percent of children below the age of five in Bangladesh experience high rates of chronic undernutrition, while an estimated 7 million of these children never reach their full physical and mental potential. Endemic poverty and undernutrition is causing irreparable damage to future generations of Bangladeshi youth who have little access to education and thus no way of escaping the poverty trap.

International aid organizations like the WFP work in Bangladesh to help reduce poverty. The group has operated in the country for 40 years. The WFP Bangladesh Nutrition Strategy focuses its aid priority on a child's first 1,000 days of life. The WFP also works with local authorities in supporting over 2.7 million children through a National School Feeding Programme, which provides vitamins and mineral biscuits to school-aged youth.

The WFP also offers educational programs on health and hygiene, emergency preparedness programs during times of natural disasters, as well as providing small one-off cash grants to women in communities deemed as ultra-poor. In 2012, the WFP distributed nearly US$6 million in humanitarian aid to help build the capacity of Bangladesh's food programs.

The case of Bangladesh raises the issue of government capacity. Are poor countries that are unable to feed their populations committing a human rights violation? There is no easy answer to this question. On the one hand, Bangladesh is a young and proud nation that has struggled since its independence to raise its development levels, given its colonial past. Yet at the same time, the government is accused of endemic corruption while political violence is common.

The debate surrounding the right to food in Bangladesh should not be considered outside the context of poverty and development. As the country continues to develop, higher good governance expectations will likely follow. Until then, it is unlikely that the politicians in Dhaka can resist international aid as it works to feed its population (World Food Programme 2014).

Third, *governments may sign treaties with the intent to develop and implement future laws.* For example, authorities in China face serious challenges when it comes to implementing human rights laws at the domestic level; however, the government continuously engages the international community on rights issues through multilateral organizations and under the auspices of legal development. The words *human rights* have now been incorporated into the preamble of China's constitution, while the government has signed and ratified 25 major international human rights conventions. For China, signing international treaties signals a commitment that the government hopes to further develop the legal capacity of the state.

There are two controversies that run through each of the above points. First, how do bottom-billion countries promote human rights when there is no funding or **political will** to implement rights protection locally? Again, *political will* refers to the motivation behind the decisions made by governments and state officials. If there is little incentive for authorities to act and enforce human rights, the motivation is low and will result in weak implementation. Second, how do citizens achieve security when the state fails to deliver on its rights duties? Individuals may be forced to establish their own security regimes by relying on family, friends, and community networks. When the state cannot fulfill its rights obligations, the community may establish itself as the only legitimate source of human security. Both these questions point to the inherent link between human rights and human security.

The remainder of this chapter tries to address these questions by first shifting the focus to governance. We then highlight the relationship between weak governance and dysfunctional state institutions. Finally, we discuss the relationship between human rights and nonstate actors in the Global South.

GOVERNING HUMAN RIGHTS AND SECURITY

When the state prioritizes certain rights over others there can be little human security. Asian values had set out to justify economic development over political freedoms. Political rights such as free speech were seen as subordinate to economic security, a role that should be reserved for the state. The question is what should individuals expect from government when human rights are at stake? Here, we draw on theories of international relations that offer valuable insight into the behavior of governments on the international stage.

Realism argues that the individual should expect nothing more than what the state offers. The world is anarchic and can only be pacified by the security guaranteed by the state. Rights are thus the domain of states. When governments use the language of human rights, they are doing so purposely in an effort to leverage their own self-interest. The concept of rights is therefore easily manipulated since it is states that give them any sense of inherent legitimacy. Statist approaches to rights not only allow for a legalist defense of a government's decision to reject or promote certain rights, it also leaves room for cultural relativism. For political philosophers such as Edmond Burke, David Hume, as well as realist scholars like Hans Morgenthau, rights are derived from human convention that has been developed by states. In this sense, realists see human rights as a mechanism to further state interests.

On the other hand, **liberalism** places individual autonomy at the center of the political world. The state has a responsibility to ensure both negative and positive **liberty**. Negative liberty refers to the absence of external threats against the individual. Rights advocates such as John Locke, John Stuart Mill, and Robert Nozick argued that as long as the state refrains from committing a violent act against the individual, negative liberty can be achieved. Other scholars, such as Jean-Jacques Rousseau, Karl Marx, and John Rawls, believed governments must ensure positive liberty. Here, the state must set the conditions so that individuals can achieve their full potential. This might require the state providing basic education or access to health care. Positive liberty requires the state to act and govern in a way that ensures services to the citizenry. For liberals, human rights realization requires governments to ensure elements of both negative and positive types of liberty.

A final international relations approach to consider in terms of human rights is **constructivism**. Unlike those advocating the realist or liberal worldview, constructivists see human rights as ideational interests that have emerged over time as normative concepts. The mainstreaming of human rights is able to occur since institutions, governments, and individuals have all established them as legitimate claims that must be protected by law. These shared values thus emerge as an ideational norm that is to be governed by transnational agencies. As Tim Dunne and Marianne Hanson (2009) note, constructivists see human rights as a result of "interstate order" that "has been transformed by the emergence of universal values." From this perspective, governments will follow and respect human rights since they risk diplomatic backlash for deviating away from international norms. Therefore, international institutions matter in governing human rights norms.

From a human security perspective, the discussion above is important because it offers three contentious perspectives on the role of government. Yet what should we think about theory when presented with real-life struggles such as childhood illiteracy, extreme poverty, or gender discrimination? Nobel Laureate Amartya Sen's (2005) **capabilities approach** offers one of the most powerful arguments for good governance. For Sen, security cannot be achieved until governments take a holistic approach to human rights. He asks how an individual who is not poor yet has no right to vote can be considered free? Sen sees development of the individual as central to achieving development of the state. Human rights and liberty are at the core of human security.

What Sen's argument highlights is the importance of strengthening the social contract between the individual and the state. **Social contract theory** has been written on extensively since the times of Plato. The basic idea studies the relationship between an individual and government. For example, you pay taxes and promise to not take up arms against your government. In exchange, the government paves roads, provides basic services, and protects you from violence by offering police services. If either side breaks the contract, then the other may engage in an act of protest. If you don't pay your taxes the state may arrest you and place serious restrictions on your liberty. But if the state can't guarantee your security, you may decide to reject the government as a legitimate sovereign and demand a new ruler. Here we draw on social contract theory to contextualize rights within the human security paradigm.

The social contract emerges prior to the creation of states since it is an agreement between individuals in what John Rawls (2009) calls the *original position*, or what others have referred to as the **state of nature**. The state of nature is a hypothetical thought experiment that seeks to explain how humans interacted prior to the creation of societies. The theory argues that people enter social contracts with one another to survive. In the state of nature, fear and the human desire to rationalize drives us to make agreements with each other to ensure we are not met with impending doom and insecurity. The social contract is therefore an agreement between individuals that outlines our human rights. Once we have entered into social contracts, we form governments and states. Governments are, therefore, the mechanism for ensuring the protection of pre-established rights that have been defined in the state of nature.

Social contract theory is valuable for framing human rights as inalienable and indivisible entitlements. States that deny basic human rights are not serving their sole purpose in *protecting* and *empowering* individuals. There is no human security so long as the state fails to respect human rights. There is also no security when the state is unable to protect the individual rights of victims. For instance, **honor killings** in Pakistan are illegal, yet many perpetrators carry out such acts with impunity. The state's failure to protect and deliver justice robs these women of their basic human rights.

Human Insecurity in Pakistan: The Case of Honor Killings

Violence against women is a widespread type of human rights violation that occurs throughout the world. South Asia is no exception, with many communities experiencing endemic levels of assault on women who defy patriarchal traditions that are culturally and judicially entrenched in the community. Honor killings are one form of violence that has been reported in Afghanistan, Pakistan, India, Nepal, and many other parts of the region. Such murders violate a range of fundamental human rights laws, such as the right to life, due process, and the presumption of innocence.

Honor killings have a long history and signify a traditional form of justice that has nothing to do with the rule of law. Women are perceived to be the possession of men and may be killed in the name of a family's honor or in retribution for tainting the household's reputation. For example, in Pakistan the practice is associated with a traditional system of *jirga* or *panchayat* rule where tribal councils have not acted to prevent such killings and have at times encouraged them. These systems empower local tribal councils to pass judgments that run parallel to the country's legal institutions. Honor killings target not only women, but also men and young girls who have brought "dishonor" to the family. The Asian Human Rights Commission (AHRC 2015) writes:

> In cases where a woman is believed to have "dishonoured" her family with immoral conduct (having a male friend, marrying a man of her choice or seeking divorce), all those responsible should be killed or otherwise punished. Inevitably, the undefined concept of "honour" and of what undermines it leads to almost every act of female disobedience amounting to "dishonouring" the family. In fact, it is merely the rumour of a woman's inappropriate behaviour that damages the "honour" of her family and hence the truth of such an allegation does not need to be established.

Honor killings are not only abominable acts of male aggression, but also clear signals of state failure and dysfunctional rule of law. When governments are unable to hold those accountable for such violence, communities live in fear. In 2013, the AHRC estimated that honor killings were carried out against 350 women and 270 men in Pakistan alone.

Source: Adapted from Asian Human Rights Commission 2015.

We now turn our attention to state institutions that provide security, or in our case contribute to insecurity and the dysfunctionality of justice.

HUMAN INSECURITY AND DYSFUNCTIONAL INSTITUTIONS

Dysfunctional institutions are one of the most common causes of human rights violations in the developing world. By *dysfunctional* we mean state institutions that do not work to their full capacity on account of corruption, poverty, as well as political interference. Institutions that cannot deliver basic human services are contributing to an environment of state-directed insecurity. By *institution* we mean government agencies and fundamental guiding principles that guide the state in its day-to-day operations. We focus on the concept of constitutionalism, the importance of judiciaries, the impact of police and military, as well as state surveillance. These institutions are the guardians of human rights. When they are dysfunctional, societies live in fear, human development suffers, and people live in a state of insecurity.

Corruption is one of the primary drivers behind dysfunctional institutions and has cost the developing world over US$6 trillion during the past decade (Dawson 2012). Not only does corruption undermine the capacity of bureaucracies and other agencies because it diverts valuable tax money away from the system, it also undermines investor trust while marginalizing those who cannot afford to pay bribes. Indeed, bribery is one of the more prevalent types of corruption found in the developing world. Citizens often have to pay "tips" or leave "tea money" to receive basic services such as attending a public hospital or securing a meeting with a state official. In bottom-billion countries, it has been reported that children have to pay their public primary school teachers to remain in class. Other types of corruption involve patronage and nepotism, which stifles competition as elites are able to award government contracts to friends and family. This enables rent-seeking and ensures resources stay within the hands of a small elite group with little trickle-down effect throughout the economy.

Types of Political Corruption

Rent-seeking: The act of manipulating a political system to enhance personal wealth by receiving economic gains on account of state policy decisions.

Bribery: An illicit payment or gift that is used to achieve a personal gain by influencing a decision maker in either the private or public sector.

Nepotism: When political elites show favoritism to family members and close friends by awarding lucrative government contacts through unfair bidding processes.

Patronage: The awarding of government positions and contracts based on political loyalty rather than merit.

A second explanation for dysfunctional state institutions centers on economic hardship and poverty. Institutions that are underfunded cannot perform, while the prospects of corruption within institutions rises since civil servants are more likely to accept bribes. In advanced economies, bureaucrats are offered high salaries in part to reduce the likelihood that they will be corrupted. In developing countries, many depend on bribes as part of their salary. For example, the average civil servant in Cambodia earns less than US$86/month (Morton 2014). Professional development and resources also have an impact, leaving the government with few options other than offering less services. As discussed later in Chapter 7, poverty has raised questions of how development should be managed, especially within government institutions. The **aid versus trade debate** has sparked wide-ranging opinions about the utility and sustainability of foreigners funding state institutions in the developing world.

A final factor impacting the efficacy of institutions is political interference. When politicians pressure the bureaucracy and judicial apparatus to rule in the government's favor the public interest is compromised. Abuse of political power can result in unfair market practices that are the result of corrupt behavior like nepotism. The private sector will lose faith in the judicial process and may cite political instability to justify divestment. Human rights are also at risk since police and judges act according to political directives rather than the rule of law. If courts ignore constitutional supremacy on account of the directives of political elites, democracy does not function and legal systems become dysfunctional.

Constitutions are the first of four areas we highlight that are especially vulnerable to dysfunctional institutions. Human security is undermined when a country's constitution cannot protect individuals within a society because of political manipulation. For example, Russia's 2013 law that targets the lesbian, gay, bisexual, and transgendered community by calling for a ban on "gay propaganda" to minors is a troubling example of a legal system not upholding universal rights. Although the Russian constitution guarantees equality and freedom of expression, the laws were passed by ideologues seeking to uphold the rights of children and the traditional family. Russia's State Duma passed the law in a unanimous 436–0 vote. Those found in violation of the law face heavy fines, a significant prison term, and possibly even deportation for foreigners (Elder 2013). The Russian example shows how constitutional protections can be disregarded when political entrepreneurs and ideological appeal has more authority than the legal system. Laws in any country that deny minority rights that are protected by state law and the UDHR not only weaken constitutionalism, they also signal a more nuanced authoritarian assault on **civil society**.

Ineffective policing is another example of dysfunctional institutionalism that leads to human rights violations. Police officers are agents of the state who we are most likely to see on a daily basis. But if we ask how you perceive police authority, what would your response be? How do you feel when you see a police officer? Do you trust him or her? What feelings do you have when you are in a car and a police officer is following you? Are you concerned that you will be pulled over, dragged out of the car, and tortured? This is the reality for most people living in illiberal regimes. Police officers are *the* primary violator of human rights in the community. They are agents of the state entrusted to keep stability at all costs. But what happens when police lack training, have no oversight, or are dependent on bribes to pay for their own equipment? The result is generally a manipulation of the law. Police become dependent on bribes, while torture serves as an effective mechanism to achieve a confession and solve a case. Dysfunctional policing breeds feelings of insecurity and fear within the community.

A third state institution often responsible for human rights violations is the military. In many countries the military is responsible for carrying out some of the governments most heinous crimes. Although state-armed forces can be seen as a source of pride and security, they can also instill fear in populations. Examples of extreme human rights violations involving the military have been widely reported the world over, such as the Srebrenica genocide where the Bosnian Serb army slaughtered nearly 8,000 Muslim men and young boys who had sought refuge in a UN-sanctioned safe zone. Other crimes committed by military units can involve covert extrajudicial killings, as seen in the Philippines. Human rights groups, as well as former UN special rapporteur on extrajudicial, summary, or arbitrary executions Philip Ashton, have cited rogue military units as responsible for conducting hundreds of assassinations against human rights activists, journalists, and political opposition figures. These murders are typically carried out by armed men dressed in black who pull up beside their victims on motorbikes, causing significant fear within the activist community.

Extrajudicial Killings and Kenya's War on Terror

Police that operate outside the rule of law are agents of human insecurity. There should be no difference if a search warrant is being carried out on a shoplifter to that of an alleged gang leader. Society and judicial systems must hold state security forces accountable and these systems must be transparent. A community that cannot trust its police officers lives in fear. The fight against terrorism has been one battle that has seen state security forces in many countries perform illegal acts. Kenya is no exception, as seen in the case of Kassim Omollo.

On 17 June 2013, a Kenyan anti-terror police squad stormed the home of Omollo, a suspected terrorist, killing him in a shootout after the suspect allegedly failed to surrender to police commands. Yet reports filed with the Justice Initiative and Muslims for Human Rights claim the death was little more than an extrajudicial killing. Omollo's family has alleged that the police entered the home between 3:00 and 4:00 AM, where the victim was with his wife, Fatima Muhammed, and their four children.

According to the family, six soldiers in masks told the couple that they had been sent to kill them, but if they paid the intruders a bribe they would spare their lives. Kassim and Fatima gave the men 67,000 Kenyan shillings (US$800) and jewelry that was in the house. The men then threatened to rape Fatima while Kassim would be forced to watch. When he protested, the armed men once again said they would kill him. After the soldiers pulled his young son and three daughters aside, they shot Kassim once in the chest and three times in the head.

The police then took Fatima to another room, showed her weapons and bullets that allegedly belonged to her husband, then took her fingerprints and forged a witness statement on her behalf acknowledging that the weapons were found in the residence. Fatima was subsequently charged and sent to Shimo La Tewa Prison until she was eventually released on bail.

The story of Kassim and Fatima is all too common in many countries where the rule of law is weak and institutions like the police depend on heavy-handed tactics such as extrajudicial killing, torture, and forced confessions to achieve results. These challenges are often structural and originate from institutional corruption, a lack of due process, limited resources, and dysfunctional investigative procedures.

While Kenya has seen a serious increase in terrorist threats over the years, the country's anti-terror police operate outside the scope of the law and with relative impunity. The police unit has carried out dozens of extrajudicial killings against alleged radical Islamic militants, all of which contribute to an erosion of the judicial system. Security forces that do not adhere to the law risk undermining human rights and serve as a serious threat to human security.

Source: Open Society Justice Initiative and MUHARI 2013.

A final characteristic of the state that has the potential to undermine constitutional rights worth mentioning is surveillance. Both advanced democracies and authoritarian states rely on surveillance as a means to achieve state security while potentially jeopardizing individual rights. Achieving state security at the expense of individual liberties is controversial. The divisiveness of Americans toward former US intelligence analyst Edward Snowden and his role in exposing mass surveillance techniques used by the National Security Agency is a case in point. While many have branded him a traitor, others have referred to him as a patriot (Shiffman and Trotta 2013). Either way, state surveillance is not to be taken lightly and is used as a method of control over civil society in all countries throughout the world.

The 2014 **coup d'état** in Thailand saw the government demanding that nearly 400 prominent political opposition figures, academics, and activists report to military instillations throughout the country (Fenn 2014). The purpose was to keep tabs on those who might be considered agitators of the military regime. Coups are always illegal, even when bloodless, since an unaccountable branch of the state seizes power from the government. Coups involve a suspension of constitutional rights and a disruption in market activity, require an expansion of the state surveillance apparatus, and bring about a general sense of human insecurity.

How should individuals respond to state-sanctioned violence through human rights abuses? We consider three bottom-up approaches to achieving rights protection when top-down protection fails, including social movements, nongovernmental organizations, and the private sector. These groups represent nonstate actors, and each has a unique ability to confront human insecurity in the Global South. Unlike governments, nonstate actors are not restricted to think in terms of an anarchic system that requires them to hold on to power. This group can act independently and provide resources when the state is unwilling. They work in communities at the grassroots level, building trust with individuals who cannot depend on the state. Stephen Hopgood (2013) has gone as far as saying that activist civil society groups will represent the future of the rights movement as nation-states become more inclined to adopt relativist approaches to rights. He writes:

> There is a deep divergence between the concept of human rights shared by elites, largely until now located in the west (what we might call Human Rights), and what those rights mean for the vast majority of the world's population (what we might call human rights). Human Rights are a New York-Geneva-London-centered ideology focused on international law, criminal justice, and institutions of global governance. Human Rights are a product of the 1%.
>
> The rest of the world, the 99%, sees human rights activism as one among many mechanisms to bring about meaningful social change. By their nature, lower-case human rights are malleable, adaptable, pragmatic and diverse—they are bottom-up democratic norms, rather than top-down authoritative rules.

Hopgood's argument is striking and helps us frame human rights within the context of nonstate actors. We therefore first turn our attention to the importance of social movements in the context of bottom-up narratives of rights justice.

Social Movements

Social movements are the coming together of like-minded individuals for the purpose of forwarding a social cause. They are often not well organized, are spontaneous in nature, and are generally understood as informal networks between activists. They have broad goals but seek to influence policymakers to bring about social change. Protest and civil disobedience are tools used by activists to raise awareness of their cause. The purpose is to mobilize civil society into action and respond to state aggression through strength in numbers.

In 2000 the city of Cochabamba, Bolivia, saw a powerful social movement unfold where tens of thousands of residents took part in general strikes demanding an end to the government's attempt to privatize water (The Democracy Center 2000). Under the advice of the World Bank and the International Monetary Fund, the Bolivian government had granted rights of Cochabamba's water to an American corporation. The San Francisco–based firm, Bechtel, had also been assured that they had exclusive rights over rain water, streams, and local wells.

South America's poorest country saw the price of water skyrocket, resulting in a popular uprising against the government's privatization laws. The government invoked martial law and sent in the military to quell the protests. The government pulled back and informed Bechtel their investment could not be protected, forcing the company to shut down operations. Cochabamba's "water wars" significantly damaged investor confidence and resulted in a lawsuit against the Bolivian government. It would take another five years before Bechtel would settle the dispute for two symbolic boliviano coins (about 30 cents US).

Water wars in Bolivia demonstrate how a grassroots social movement can carry enough pressure to influence political change at the top. It also captured the imagination of activists in the Global North, which saw anti-neoliberal protests rise around the world. At one point activists in the United States occupied the lobby of Bechtel's headquarters, while San Francisco's city council denounced the firm's legal action against Bolivia through an official resolution.

Nongovernmental Organizations

A second nonstate actor that plays an important role in the Global South is **nongovernmental organizations (NGOs)**. NGOs have the ability to bypass government and connect with those impacted by rights violations directly. As will be discussed in Chapter 5, NGOs are able to run publicity campaigns to raise awareness of rights violations while monitoring the activities of oppressive governments through on-the-ground research. Meanwhile, international NGOs are able to be critical of governments through the safety of foreign offices, often resulting in governments being forced to officially respond.

The Asian Legal Resource Centre (ALRC) is a Hong Kong–based NGO that holds consultative status with the United Nations Economic and Social Council (ECOSOC). The ALRC spends most of its time dealing with breakdowns in the rule of law throughout the Asia region. The group's primary focus is torture and its impact on communities. The ALRC, along with its sister organization the AHRC, rely on an "urgent appeals" system to communicate rights violations with other activists around the world. The system depends on informants, networks, and technology to ensure accurate information is received. The box below outlines how a typical appeals process works.

Dynamics of an Urgent Appeals Process

1. An individual is illegally detained and brought to a detention center. Members of the community may suspect that the individual is being tortured.
2. Local activists investigate, ask police questions, and try to resolve the situation.
3. If no resolution occurs, activists will text message or call the AHRC associate in the country, who then calls the police station to try to resolve the situation.
4. If no resolution occurs, the associate gathers all the information and sends it to the main AHRC/ALRC offices in Hong Kong.
5. Campaigners in Hong Kong then call the police station to find out more information, demanding assurances of the individual's well-being and the nature of the detention.
6. If no resolution occurs, the AHRC will draft a statement in the form of an "urgent appeal" to be disseminated throughout its networks.
7. The AHRC asks its network of activists to send letters of "appeal" directly to government officials in the country along with international human rights observers. The direct contact details of the police station are also provided.

The appeals process can take less than 24 hours from the time of illegal detention to the direct intervention by activist networks. Not only does it demonstrate how NGOs handle human rights on the ground, it shows how organized civil society groups can have a direct impact on a rights case, bypassing the state.

The Private Sector

A final nonstate actor we want to explore is the private sector. Why should the private sector care about human rights? This question is not easy to answer, since most companies are more concerned with maximizing profit and improving shareholder value. There is, however, a long history of connecting human rights abuses with corporate behavior. As a result, attitudes within companies are changing, with businesses laying out strategies "to do no harm" while operating ethically within their spheres of responsibility and influence. Moreover, the private sector is finding it easier to make the connection between sustainable growth and stable legal systems: It is difficult to make money in dysfunctional economies that are riddled with corruption, political instability, and weak rule of law. Industry has started to step forward through various initiatives, such as the United Nations Global Compact and the Global Reporting Initiative. As will be discussed more in Chapter 8, the business community can play an important role in the Global South.

Business and Human Rights

There are numerous examples of businesses violating human rights around the world. This box presents only a small sample of some of these abuses.

Historical Abuses: Companies have profited from slavery and the slave trade; by providing goods and services to Nazi Germany that enabled war crimes and crimes against humanity; from forced labor in Asia during World War II; and by selling products to the apartheid government in South Africa and military governments in Latin America that were used in perpetrating abuses.

Killings: Blackwater (now Academi), a private American military company, was sued over shootings in Baghdad in 2007 that left 17 civilians dead.

Environmental Health: A US-owned company operated an outdated lead smelter in La Oroya, Peru, where 99 percent of children in the area were found to have unacceptably high levels of lead in their blood.

Rape and Sexual Abuse: Multinational beer companies hire "beer promotion women" in Cambodia to promote their products in bars. But many companies allegedly do not do enough to protect the women (who are often teenagers) from rape and abuse.

Torture: Security companies hired by international diamond firms in Cuango, Angola, were reportedly responsible for beatings, attacks with machetes, sexual abuse, torture, and killings. The victims were artisanal miners.

Child Labor: Uzbekistan forces children to work in cotton fields without pay, then sells the cotton in international markets where it is bought and used by major companies.

Freedom of Expression: Yahoo! China handed over private user data about dissidents to the Chinese government, which then imprisoned the dissidents.

Indigenous Peoples and Displacement: In India, a mining company is accused of displacing a tribal group from its traditional lands without obtaining consent or providing adequate compensation.

Complicity: Burmese soldiers providing security for a pipeline that was developed by major oil companies forced villagers to work on the pipeline and shot and tortured protesters.

Discrimination: Walmart has been accused in a lawsuit of systematically discriminating against over 90,000 of its female employees in the United States. Some employers in France have insisted that employment agencies refer only white workers to them, according to prosecutors.

Labor Rights: Foreign companies operating in Colombia have been sued for allegedly paying paramilitaries who intimidated and killed union leaders.

Access to Water: In India, beverage companies have allegedly depleted groundwater supplies in rural villages.

Workplace Safety: Hundreds die every year in Chinese coal mines.

Source: The Business and Human Rights Resource Centre 2015a.

What should be clear is that the private sector faces human rights situations on a daily basis. There is a key distinction between rights abuses by industry and rights abuses by government, because a business can only be held complicit in rights violations. Legally, international human rights are reserved for states. Prosecutors cannot bring a CEO or a multinational corporation before the international court of justice. However, when corporations work with governments who commit violations, they risk being accused of complicity and may be brought before national judicial systems.

In 2004, for instance, an Australian/Canadian company called Anvil Mining was accused of helping the government of the Democratic Republic of the Congo reclaim a mining concession that had been taken over by a small-scale rebellion. The "Kilwa incident" saw Anvil use its planes to fly military personnel into the region, where they proceeded to systematically kill over 100 people. Human rights activists sued and brought the case to the Supreme Court of Canada, but the case was later thrown out on jurisdictional grounds. While the case against Anvil did not succeed, it raised serious questions about how far a company could go before it would be considered as contributing to rights violations (McBeth 2014).

In 2011, another Canadian mining company was implicated in human rights violations in Papua New Guinea. Barrick Gold Corporation, the world's largest mining company, was accused of hiring security guards who terrorized the local community. Barrick's 450-member private security forces were accused of murder and at least six gang rapes on women they had detained for illegally mining at the company's Porgera mine site. Barrick was subject to an entire Human Rights Watch report, whose findings were later presented before a parliamentary committee in Ottawa (Human Rights Watch 2011). However, unlike the Anvil case, Barrick has acknowledged the need to investigate and work with authorities to ensure the security of the community. Indeed, when the state is unable to protect individuals from rights violations, companies can work toward improving human rights within their sphere of influence and responsibility by following international best practice standards (more in Chapter 8).

CONCLUSION

There is a deep connection between human security and the protection of human rights. When rights are violated by state actors such as police and security officials, societies live in fear and struggle to protect the social contract that guarantees a basic level of rights that are inalienable, inseparable, and universal. This chapter has set out to connect some of the more pressing issues of human rights and human security, including the rule of law, good governance, and the role of the private sector.

We have argued that the power of the state has the ability to protect rights but also to take them away. While terrorism and new wars give states new agendas to enhance surveillance powers and provide the pretext to justify heavy-handed security measures, there has never been a more important time for bottom-up approaches to rights protection. The importance of civil society in organizing, documenting, and pressuring governments to provide rights is critical. Economic development and the right to a secure environment are inherently linked. When governments fail or refuse to recognize this connection, human insecurity is the only outcome.

Finally, human rights should not be confused with human security. While each concept does relate to one another, they are not mutually exclusive. States with strong human rights records enjoy higher levels of human security than those that do not. Dysfunctional institutions, which undermine the rule of law, contribute to a state of human insecurity because governments are unable or unwilling to deliver services and offer protection. Human rights are therefore an essential requisite for communities that experience high levels of human security.

KEY TERMS

Aid versus Trade Debate; Apartheid; Bottom Billion; Bribery; Capabilities Approach; Caste; Civil Society; Constructivism; Corruption; Coup d'état; Cultural Relativism; Dysfunctional Institutions; Ethnic Cleansing; First, Second, and Third-Generation Rights; Honor Killing; Human Rights; Liberalism; Liberty; Neocolonialism; Nepotism; Nongovernmental Organizations; Nonstate Actors; Patronage; Political Will; Prisoners of Conscience; Realism; Rent-Seeking; Rule of Law; Social Contract Theory; Social Darwinism; State of Nature; Torture; Universalism

FURTHER READING

Christie, Kenneth, and Denny Roy. 2001. *The Politics of Human Rights in Asia*. London: Pluto Press.

Donnelly, Jack. 2013. *Universal Human Rights in Theory and Practice*. 3rd ed. Ithaca: Cornell University Press.

Dunne, T., and N.J. Wheeler, eds. 1999. *Human Rights in Global Politics*. Cambridge: Cambridge University Press. http://dx.doi.org/10.1017/CBO9781139171298.

Hopgood, Stephen. 2013. *Keepers of the Flame: Understanding Amnesty International*. Ithaca: Cornell University Press.

Ignatieff, Michael. 2001. *Human Rights as Politics and Idolatry*. Princeton, NJ: Princeton University Press.

Nozick, R. 1974. *Anarchy, State, and Utopia.* New York: Basic Books.

Rawls, John. 2009. *A Theory of Justice.* Cambridge, MA: Harvard University Press.

Rose-Ackerman, S. 1978. *Corruption: A Study in Political Economy.* New York: Academic Press.

Ruggie, John. 2007. "Business and Human Rights: The Evolving International Agenda." Corporate Social Responsibility Initiative, Working Paper No. 31. http://www.hks. harvard.edu/m-rcbg/CSRI/publications/workingpaper_38_ruggie.pdf

Sen, Amartya. 2005. "Human Rights and Capabilities." *Journal of Human Development* 6 (2): 151–66. http://dx.doi.org/10.1080/14649880500120491.

Thompson, M. R. 2001. "Whatever Happened to 'Asian Values'?" *Journal of Democracy* 12 (4): 154–65. http://dx.doi.org/10.1353/jod.2001.0083.

WEBSITES

Amnesty International: www.amnesty.org

Asian Human Rights Commission: www.humanrights.asia

Business and Human Rights Resource Centre: http://business-humanrights.org

Global Rights: www.globalrights.org

Human Rights Foundation: https://humanrightsfoundation.org

Human Rights Watch: www.hrw.org

International Commission of Jurists: www.icj.org

Journalists for Human Rights: www.jhr.ca

World Organization Against Torture: www.omct.org

Worldwide Movement for Human Rights: www.fidh.org

PART TWO

Chapter 4

GLOBAL GOVERNANCE, SECURITY, AND CONFLICT

The pursuit of peace and progress cannot end in a few years in either victory or defeat. The pursuit of peace and progress, with its trials and its errors, its successes and its setbacks, can never be relaxed and never be abandoned.
Dag Hammarskjöld, former secretary-general of
the United Nations (2014)

INTRODUCTION

There are more refugees in the world today than at any other time in the modern era. By the end of 2015, nearly 60 million people had been displaced on account of war and natural disaster (United Nations News Centre 2016). How should governments and international agencies address such tragedy? Should we entrust governments, international organizations (IOs), or communities to develop strategies for dealing with transnational crises? This chapter takes a macro-level approach to analyzing such pressing challenges, which are often brought on by violent conflict, and how human security is affected by them. We discuss how global governance mechanisms, such as the United Nations, the World Bank, and the International Labour Organization, struggle to strengthen individual and collective human security in the developing world and the challenges they face. We discuss several of the challenges that a "top-down" approach to development may bring, while arguing that such interventions can lead to protracted humanitarian crises. We also introduce arguments for denying aid, especially to so-called "rogue" regimes, even during times of natural disaster and complex emergencies, while considering the impact of multilateral efforts in managing conflict using peacekeeping, peacemaking, and peacebuilding strategies. We are therefore concerned with how multilateral organizations impact bottom-billion societies and individuals living in conflict zones.

Globalization and the pressures of **collective action** by states also play a role in how multilateral governance is designed. The collective action problem occurs when states support multilateral governance policies out of fear of diplomatic sanctions, for the purpose of enhancing ones political standing, or to avoid economic repercussions. This approach suggests that states may become **"free riders"** on controversial governance and not voice opposition to the policy. For example, the government of Canada withdrew from the Kyoto Protocol, citing the agreement as weak without China and the United States. Canada was able to justify its position by free riding the policy positions of the world's two largest carbon dioxide emitters (China and the United States). From a human security perspective, this is problematic since governments will support multilateral policy that appeases elite political interests.

If we recall Hopgood's criticism of global human rights mechanisms and context from Chapter 3, he points to a serious disconnect between global institutions and civil society. Political elites representing states are well represented in these organizations, while those who are impacted by their policies are far from present. As Kostovicova and Glasius (2011) have suggested, bottom-up approaches to governance are concerned with noninstitutionalized policy outcomes. We agree and have outlined the impact of civil society on governance and development in Chapter 5. This chapter, however, is concerned with the *structural reality of sovereignty* and its impact on global governance and human security.

Richard Falk (2014) has written extensively on this challenge and identifies *horizontal* and *vertical* themes that shape sovereignty. By horizontal, he is referring to diplomatic and trade relations between sovereign states, exclusive membership to state-driven multilateral institutions, as well as general governance obligations that require the management of transnational economic and social flows. By vertical, Falk is concerned with the structural inequality between states, which sees powerful governments draft geopolitical policy around their own self-interests, such as economic trade regulations, humanitarian interventions, and when to use force against a noncompliant state. From this perspective, multilateralism is a state-centric project with little room for bottom-up perspectives on how to govern. Here, Falk turns the debate around and asks if global governance can be reimagined within a framework of human security. Falk's solution is to rethink the system and push toward developing humane global governance. Falk differentiates between global governance and human global governance as follows:

> The current system of global governance is shaped by the primacy accorded to the security of states, and especially of capital with regard to trade and investment.

Humane global governance is, in contrast, dedicated to the security of people and to development paradigms that are people-oriented, giving priority to food, water, health, and employment security rather than fulfilling the expectations of billionaire venture capitalists and hedge fund managers. (3)

For Falk, the management of the **global commons** must evolve beyond the realm of nation-states, especially if we are to seriously consider human security. We will return to this concept later in the chapter, but first it is important to understand what we mean by "governance" and how such a system became fundamentally state-centric.

GOVERNANCE AND HUMAN SECURITY

Thomas Weiss and Rorden Wilkinson (2013, 5) define global governance as "the totality of the ways, formal and informal, in which the world is governed." It involves a multilateral (as opposed to bilateral) process of designing law and policy that is implemented and enforced by international organizations. Still, there is no "world government," and many IOs are little more than transnational bureaucracies that are managed by a board of directors who happen to be nation-states. IOs are therefore managed by self-interested entities known as *governments*. It is worth remembering that we are talking about *governance institutions* and not discussing *world government*. Not only would calls for a world government be highly complex and unrealistic, there are extreme power imbalances within existing intergovernmental structures, with some countries wielding much more authority than others. The concept of world government brings about all kinds of ethical questions we do not want to get into here. Instead, we are concerned with the challenge that IOs face in creating human security because they are governed by states.

What, then, is the capacity of such organizations to rein in human security, such as development assistance, advocating human rights, and protecting victims of state-sanctioned violence? The answer is debatable at best. While some groups such as the United Nations have placed human rights at the center of its organizational mission, the concept has historically been absent from other IOs, such as the World Trade Organization and the World Bank. While themes of human security have started to make inroads with **intergovernmental organizations (IGOs)** as these groups try and grapple with the many new threats facing communities in the post–Cold War era, weak political will and collective inaction can derail the work of those dedicated to improving the security of people in need. When these organizations fail to deliver security, it is the states that occupy the organization's board that fail, not the IGO itself. These are political bodies that are used to serving the interests of nations. There is, however, a standing international civil service that manages these organizations.

This professional class is well educated, highly skilled, and devoted to the governance ideal. But there is nonetheless a gap between the professional civil service and the political bodies that direct the organizations.

There are other types of global governance regimes that are managed by nonstate actors that cover human security themes, such as the *Global Reporting Initiative*, which provides a tool for businesses to measure and minimize their social and environmental impact on communities; the *Equator Principles*, which offer guidelines to financial institutions to help identify questionable clients whose business may run counter to the principles of the United Nations; as well as the now defunct *Business Leaders Initiative on Human Rights*, which was a six-year collaborative effort by industry to find practical ways to implement the Universal Declaration of Human Rights in daily business operations.

International NGOs are also playing a leading role in governance by developing networks with activists and civil society groups around the world. One example is the *World Social Forum*, which began as a shadow conference of the World Economic Forum to protest the organization's commitment to neoliberalism and global economic deregulation. Since global governance can have different meanings, a precise definition is difficult to outline and is often disputed within academic circles. We can, however, outline a general sense of themes that are expected of IGOs and international NGOs alike when it comes to governing.

For some authors, like Gerald Caiden (2009), there are several expectations that can ensure the integrity of global governance regimes. First, these groups must operate in a cost-effective and efficient manner when managing the *scarcity* of resources. Mismanagement of resources will call the organization's credibility into question and raises the specter of corruption. Second, these groups must be consistent in applying *universal* principles of management while moving away from particularism. Inconsistency in governance risks undermining the impact and efficacy of resource management. Standards and equality must be employed to reduce corruption and rent-seeking activities. Third, a strong sense of *professionalism* must carry these organizations, especially when faced with adversity and hardship. International civil servants should be rewarded based on merit, not patronage, thereby ensuring best practice standards. A final two conditions outlined by Caiden worth mentioning are perhaps the most important themes associated with governance: transparency and accountability.

Transparency and accountability reduce mistrust on account of the wide democratic deficit that exists between the public and elite governance institutions. The **democratic deficit** is a critique of governance institutions where the voting public has little influence over the undemocratically elected civil servants designing and implementing policy. The public has no direct say in how these organizations are managed, nor are many of these groups upfront with how they reach decisions. Meetings are often held behind closed doors and work via an "invite only" process. **Epistemic communities** are left to design, approve, and reject policy that IOs adopt. Peter Haas defines epistemic communities as follows:

> A network of professionals with recognized expertise and competence in a particular domain and an authoritative claim to policy-relevant knowledge within that domain or issue-area. Although an epistemic community may consist of professionals from a variety of disciplines and backgrounds, they have (1) a shared set of normative and principled beliefs, which provide a value-based rationale for the social action of community members; (2) shared causal beliefs, which are derived from their analysis of practices leading or contributing to a central set of problems in their domain and which then serve as the basis for elucidating the multiple linkages between possible policy actions and desired outcomes; (3) shared notions of validity—that is, intersubjective, internally defined criteria for weighing and validating knowledge in the domain of their expertise; and (4) a common policy enterprise—that is, a set of common practices associated with a set of problems to which their professional competence is directed, presumably out of the conviction that human welfare will be enhanced as a consequence. (Haas 1992, 3)

Epistemic communities contribute to the democratic deficit of global institutions because these unelected experts are consistently approached to help draft policy. Whichever elected officials have been appointed by the public, they will be screening policy options designed and manipulated by epistemic communities. These groups are very much a function of the policymaking process at all levels of government. Yet when organizations are transparent, public mistrust may be reduced since the community has more information about how decisions are reached by policy experts. When there is no accountability, those holding positions of influence are able to make decisions with impunity that could negatively impact the organizations meant to serve the public interest and enhance human security. Such blanketed power causes mistrust in governance bodies at both the international and domestic level. As will be discussed in the next chapter, citizen groups and NGOs are responding in unique ways to many of these challenges.

Yet there are other facets of global governance that pose setbacks. The rise of **regionalism** along with the internationalization of conflict brings new questions concerning the role of border security and the ability of weak states to solve their own governance issues. As Paul Collier (2008) has pointed out, bad neighbors can have detrimental effects on the growth of an economy. On the one hand, regionalism provides a unique opportunity for diversity in governance if we consider pluralism an important component of elite structures. The African Union (AU), the European Union (EU), and the Association of Southeast Asian Nations (ASEAN) are all examples of regional governance bodies that advocate on behalf of their member states. Even when members have conflicts with one another, these IGOs may insist on a regionally driven solution. For example, the AU has frequently called for "African Solutions to African Problems." While not endorsed by all, a regional approach to conflict management and crisis has its benefits.

Darfur: An Experiment in African Peacekeeping

Peacekeeping has always been a controversial proposition, considering it involves sending foreign soldiers into sovereign states to manage everything from complex peace processes to humanitarian emergencies. Many of the peacekeepers know nothing about the country they have been deployed to beyond a short crash course provided by their government or locally engaged UN officials. How, then, are peacekeepers to carry out their duties when they know very little about the people they are meant to be protecting?

One method being tested by the United Nations and the African Union is a type of hybrid peacekeeping in the Darfur region of Sudan. The mission involves both regional and international forces who make up a 26,000-strong force that is jointly commanded by UN and AU authorities. The African Union/United Nations Hybrid operation in Darfur (UNAMID) is the first shared command of a peacekeeping mission. It was developed after the Sudanese government refused to allow a traditional peacekeeping mission the right to operate within the country. By approving the hybrid mission, the government hoped the initiative would maintain an "African character." The UN Department for Peacekeeping Operations along with the AU Peace and Security Directorate was tasked with providing logistical support for the mission.

Since the mission's inception in 2007, it has been plagued with a lack of funding, personnel, and political will from donor countries. Critics have suggested that UNAMID lacks the functional capacity to carry out its mission and struggles to protect civilians and support humanitarian relief. As one observer noted, the mission is providing more "lessons learned" rather than demonstrating a "best practice" approach to peacekeeping. Still, time will tell if hybrid missions are here to stay. At the very least, they offer an innovative attempt at collaborative peacekeeping and help champion the call for a regional response to regional problems.

Source: African Renewal Online 2010.

The theme of this chapter centers on the dynamics between human security and global governance. We argue that public participation in governance bodies can improve multilateral responses to conflict. While regionalism brings new challenges, it also brings opportunity for stakeholders looking for new approaches to intervention. As discussed in Chapter 6, military intervention under the banner of humanitarianism is controversial since it directly challenges the concept of sovereignty. We now turn to the issue of sovereignty within the context of global governance and conflict.

TWO CONCEPTS OF SOVEREIGNTY AND THE STATE

At the center of the controversy that is often associated with global governance is the issue of **sovereignty**. More precisely, what rights do states have within the international arena, especially with competing sovereigns? Moreover, do states have a responsibility to respect the rights of its own citizens? These questions have long concerned legal scholars, including the seventeenth-century Dutch jurist Hugo Grotius, who wrote extensively on these issues. For Grotius, the solution was international law as a mechanism to keep absolute power of competing sovereigns in check. As Winston Nagan and Aitza Haddad (2011, 433–34) write, "One of the most important contributions that Grotius made to the understanding of sovereignty in a climate of multiple sovereigns was his introduction of the idea that legal thought and legal reasoning, which implicated rationality, could be deployed in a way that brought reason to the conduct of sovereigns among themselves." In other words, the rules of sovereignty must be bound to international law. While Grotius clearly advanced the arguments for an emerging international order, he did not believe that states should be responsible for providing all requests made by its subjects, nor did he think subjects had a right to revolt against a sovereign:

> At this point first of all the opinion of those must be rejected who hold that everywhere and without exception sovereignty resides in the people, so that it is permissible for the people to restrain and punish kings whenever they make a bad use of their power . . . We refute it by means of the following arguments. To every man it is permitted to enslave himself to any one he pleases for private ownership, as is evident both from the Hebraic and from the Roman Law. Why, then, would it not be as lawful for a People who are at their own disposal to deliver up themselves to some one person, or to several persons, and transfer the right of governing them upon him or them, retaining no vestige of that right for themselves? (Stanford Encyclopedia of Philosophy 2011)

For Grotius, rights where perceived as commodities that could be traded and therefore surrendered to the sovereign in exchange for peace and protection. While the argument played a key role in advancing seventeenth-century liberalism, it has also been criticized for advocating illiberal principles that support authoritarian rule

(Stanford Encyclopedia of Philosophy 2011). The writings of Grotius should be understood as masterful works that try to deal with the conflict between the rights and responsibilities of the sovereign. Indeed, the issue of sovereignty is a debate that continues to this day.

Advocates for governance regimes and human security practitioners alike have questioned the right to state sovereignty, especially when governments are not protecting their citizens. Calls from within the international community, including the United Nations Secretariat, have emphasized a need for reframing the concept of sovereignty. Statist claims are becoming harder to justify in an increasingly interconnected world, especially when governments are unable to protect their citizens. In today's world, everything from violent conflict to food security is being questioned. Globalization has placed new pressures on governments who advocate for a more traditional type of sovereignty that rejects the influence of civil society groups. Indeed, globalization is changing the way sovereignty is perceived. Francis Deng, a former UN special adviser on the prevention of genocide, has pointed to the widening sovereignty gap that exists between a state's responsibility to govern effectively and its right to self-determination:

> I realise that this is an internal matter that falls under state sovereignty; I'm respectful of your sovereignty. But I do not see sovereignty negatively, as a barricade against the outside world. I see it as a very positive concept of state responsibility for its people. And if it needs support, to call on the international community. The subtext, in the right spirit of solidarity with the government, would be: But in this day and age of concern with human rights and humanitarian issues, the world will get involved in one way or another. So the best way for you to protect your sovereignty is not only to protect your own people and take care of them, but to be seen to be doing so, and to call on the international community if necessary. That's how you gain internal legitimacy; that's also how you gain external legitimacy and a respected place in the international community. (Deng 2011)

For Deng, the concept of sovereignty should thus be considered tantamount to a responsibility to protect a state's own civilians.

A new conceptualization of sovereignty began emerging at the end of the Cold War, but it was not mainstreamed until the Kosovo intervention that forced UN Secretary-General Kofi Annan to find some way of salvaging the legitimacy of the UN system. Given the West's determination to intervene regardless of the Security Council's decision, Annan had to take on the role of norm entrepreneur (someone interested in changing social norms) and reconceptualized the case for intervention in terms of human rights protection. In what became known as the *Ditchley Formula*, Annan published an article in *The Economist* magazine calling for two concepts of sovereignty: He argued that sovereignty was not only a right, but also a responsibility. Annan successfully saved the Security Council by highlighting an evolving international system where military intervention should be based on benchmarks that should be applied fairly and consistent, should involve extensive feedback from national policymakers, and should ultimately require the endorsement of the Security Council. This was a significant departure from the traditional view of **Westphalian sovereignty**.

Since the Peace of Westphalia, the world has organized itself around the concept of independent nation-states who hold a right to self-determination. Many of the Westphalian tenets have been entrenched within the international system through international law and the United Nations Charter. For example, in 1933 the Montevideo Convention on the Rights and Duties of States was signed at the International Conference of the American States by 19 governments. The treaty set out to provide a legalistic meaning of statehood by identifying four requisite features, including a permanent population, a defined territory, a recognized government, and a capacity to perform diplomatic relations with other governments. The Montevideo treaty was later incorporated into the workings of the League of Nations and remains the legal benchmark for what it means to be a state under international law. Of course, many scholars have pointed out that sovereignty and the legitimacy of statehood is more complex and requires the legitimacy of the individuals the state claims to represent.

Westphalian concepts of the world system have proved to be both positive and destructive for the world's most vulnerable communities. On the one hand, arguments centered on sovereignty and the right to self-determination have helped frame anti-imperialist movements throughout the world while empowering communities to reject foreign occupiers. On the other hand, such an approach is easily abused by regimes looking to consolidate their domestic power through violence and impunity. As a result, challenges to a Westphalian-based state system have emerged, often referred to as **post-Westphalian sovereignty**, all of which place greater responsibilities on states.

Three of the more powerful challenges to state sovereignty include international law, the global human rights movement, and the forces of globalization. International law demands that states surrender some level of sovereignty to participate in a multilateral legal initiative, many of which are designed to protect civilians from state power. For example, the United Nations Convention against Torture (CAT) demands that signatories of the treaty reject the use of torture as a mechanism for police investigation. With torture considered a legitimate method of interrogation in many countries, signatories of the CAT are prohibited from deporting anyone to a country that practices torture if there is a risk the claimant will receive such treatment on arrival.

A second challenge to state sovereignty is the international human rights movement. As discussed in Chapter 3, human rights emerged as an abstract concept that has found its way into international law. The CAT demonstrates how a movement can spread globally while gaining legitimacy through legal codification. Governments now face greater scrutiny when committing the gravest of human rights violations, including arbitrary arrests, summary executions, or enforced displacement. Even regimes that violate such rights often go to great lengths to explain their actions to the international community. International NGOs have emerged as major stakeholders in the transnational human rights movement in their efforts to hold states accountable for their actions.

A final challenge to sovereignty is the rise of globalization, which forces communities to think about global governance and humanitarian emergencies around the world. New actors, such as NGOs, multinational corporations, and transnational migrant networks, actively shape the global economy. Globalization has also increased the movement of labor, pollution, and disease. Many of these issues impact the autonomy and security of nation-states, forcing sovereign authorities to seek out collaborative solutions they would otherwise not entertain. For example, the **Montreal Protocol** brought governments together during the Cold War era in an effort to halt the depletion of the ozone layer and ban the use of chlorofluorocarbons (CFCs). In this case, governments were willing to surrender their right to produce and use a certain chemical in the face of an environmental crisis. Environmental crises brought on by the rapid industrialization of the planet have forced states to cooperate in new ways. Today, all countries in the world have signed and ratified the protocol, although not all have committed to each of the protocol's amendments. Indeed, the concept of sovereignty in the global era is changing.

Even with multilateral success stories like the Montreal Protocol, there is much debate within the international community on sovereignty. While advocates for global governance and cosmopolitanism have proved successful in challenging the traditional understanding of state boundaries, new nonstate actors have emerged that are committed to improving the lives of those in need. For example, there were hundreds of organizations and over 210,000 humanitarian relief workers involved in delivering aid to victims of the 2004 Indian Ocean tsunami, a disaster that killed over 350,000 people (Barnett 2011, 3).

What is certain is that there are many contradictions associated with concepts of global governance and sovereignty. While organizations do their best to remain impartial, they are dependent on governments. This becomes especially challenging when faced with prospects of interstate and intrastate conflict. Who decides when sovereignty should be violated? Moreover, who has the right to operate within conflict zones? This brings significant ethical challenges as global governance planners and governments find new ways to manage conflict. As Michael Barnett (2011) points out, the good intentions of Western humanitarians do not save lives. In order for human security to be achieved, stability often needs to be established through top-down governance. There is no freedom from fear during wartime.

MANAGING MULTILATERAL PEACE OPERATIONS

In November 2008, rebel fighters from the National Congress for the Defence of the People (CNDP) in the Eastern Congolese town of Kiwanja summarily executed 150 civilians. The victims were accused of being members of a local Mai Mai militia, who had allegedly been involved in an earlier attack on the CNDP. The rebel response was quick and brutal, with survivors describing total helplessness as fighters went door to door executing any young man or boy they came across. Human Rights Watch also reported cases of systematic rape and enforced disappearances of children. Despite the horrific violence, what makes the Kiwanja massacre especially troubling is that it occurred less than a mile away from an active United Nations peacekeeping mission.

The United Nations peacekeeping mission in Congo (MONUC) had 120 active "blue helmets" in Kiwanja. Thousands of civilians had fled the siege to the gates of the UN compound seeking refuge from their attackers. Still, the UN peacekeepers were unable to offer support in protecting civilians. The unit was significantly understaffed, had no local translator, suffered from a lack of intelligence information, and were unable to distinguish between civilians and combatants. The commander of the Indian peacekeepers based in Kiwanja, Lieutenant-Colonel H. S. Brar, suggested that his unit had been up against an "informational vacuum" filled with rumors and speculation (McGreal 2008). The tragedy in Kiwanja not only reveals a common criticism toward the effectiveness of contemporary peacekeeping, it also highlights many of the structural challenges faced by peacekeepers. This section highlights key concepts of peacekeeping while reviewing the operational complications of protecting civilians in armed conflict.

The UN defines **peacekeeping** as "the deployment of international military and civilian personnel to a conflict area with the consent of the parties to the conflict in order to: stop or contain hostilities or supervise the carrying out of a peace agreement" (Parliament of Canada 2000, note 4). As of June 2015, there were 16 active peacekeeping operations throughout the world that operate within a guiding framework based on consent of the parties involved, strict impartiality, and the use of minimal force unless in an act of self-defense. Peacekeeping was conceived of and introduced in 1956 by UN Secretary-General Dag Hammarskjöld and the Canadian Minister of Foreign Affairs Lester B. Pearson. Prompted by the Suez Crisis, Hammarskjöld and Pearson envisioned using soldiers for peace rather than conflict. The idea was well received by the General Assembly in part because it sought to reduce Cold War pressure from the UN Security Council, since permanent five (P5) members would not be able to contribute their own soldiers. It also provided an innovative approach to dealing with a major political crisis that clarified the role of the UN in the Middle Eastern region and had the support of two highly influential diplomats. Thus was modern peacekeeping born, an idea that would later be awarded the Nobel Peace Prize.

As we have discussed in Chapter 1, it is important to recognize that since the end of the Cold War the international community's understanding of conflict has changed. A shift from the more traditional interstate threats toward intrastate warfare has raised new questions on how military missions should respond to crises. Our definition of security has also changed, with a greater emphasis on human rights and resources allocation. Achieving human security requires a good education, a clean environment, access to health care, and even democratic rights. Nobel Laureate Amartya Sen's groundbreaking work has focused on precisely this by suggesting that poverty must not only be associated with financial well-being, but should be reframed to be understood within a wider human security framework. The changing nature of conflict, along with an increase in global terrorism and new wars, is altering the peacekeeping landscape. The emerging human security implications of conflict and displaced populations in the post–Cold War world have forced the UN to reconsider how its peacekeeping operations are managed.

In 2000, one of the most ambitious initiatives was launched to identify the areas of peacekeeping that needed to be reformed. The Report of the Panel on United Nations Peace Operations was a high-level study chaired by veteran UN diplomat Lakhdar Brahimi. The **Brahimi Report** offered a blunt assessment of many of the short fallings facing peacekeeping. It called for more funding, greater political will, more robust military capabilities, and greater collaboration between the Security Council and member states that contribute military personnel. Moreover, the report made the following recommendations:

1. The need for robust doctrine and realistic mandates
2. New headquarters capacity for information management and strategic analysis
3. Improved mission guidance and leadership
4. Rapid deployment standards and "on-call" expertise
5. Enhanced headquarters capacity to plan and support peace operations
6. Establishment of Integrated Mission Task Forces for mission planning and support
7. Adapting peace operations to the information age (United Nations 2000)

Brahimi laid out arguments that many senior officials within the UN system had thought: that force could play a role in peacekeeping operations. Disasters such as

Rwanda, Mogadishu, and Srebrenica (see the box below for more on this massacre) had led many to question the purpose of peacekeeping if it could not help the civilians it was designed to protect. Peacekeeping was destined to receive a "triple transformation," which involved greater political support resulting in an increase in operations, more complex mandates, as well as missions that have been largely perceived as normative in nature. The end of the Cold War meant fewer deadlocks on the Security Council, while the rise of globalization placed new pressures on governments to respond to an increasingly interconnected world.

Since the Brahimi Report, several other documents dealing with UN reform have been published. These include *A More Secure World: Our Shared Responsibility*, Report of the High Level Panel on Threats, Challenges and Change (2004); the Prodi Report (2008); the New Horizons Process (2009); and the Civilian Capacity Initiative (2011), as well as the Report of the High Level Independent Panel on Peace Operations (2015). Topics covered in these reports include everything from a proposed UN standing army (or vanguard army), using peacekeepers for counterterrorism measures, recruitment procedures, conflict prevention, organizational accountability, chemical and biological weapons, transnational crime, as well as civilian partnerships. While each of these initiatives seeks to modernize the UN by proposing reform strategies, it is estimated that only 20 percent of the recommendations are ever implemented. In referring to the recent High Level Independent Panel on Peace Operations (HIPPO), Sebastian von Einsiedel and Rahul Chandran (2015) note, "Like all of its worthy predecessors, the HIPPO's recommendations will live and die on the political strategy around its implementation. Unfortunately, there is no evidence that the High Level Panel managed to establish a political consensus around key ideas of the report." Despite the difficulty in achieving UN reform, departments within the UN system, like the Department for Peacekeeping Operations, have served as critical tools for promoting peace and security.

A Failure for UN Peacekeeping: The Srebrenica Genocide

In the summer of 1995, roughly 8,000 Bosnian men and boys were systematically murdered at the hands of a Serbian military unit led by General Ratko Mladić. The atrocity took place near the end of the Bosnian War (1992–95) and occurred within a United Nations "safe area" that was under the protection of 400 Dutch peacekeepers.

A UN declared "safe area" is a jurisdiction that falls under the protection of the international community. In 1993, UN Security Council Resolution 819 designated Srebrenica a "safe area" that was to fall under the direct protection of the United Nations Protection Force (UNPROFOR). The zone was to be demilitarized, although the surrounding areas of Srebrenica remained heavily armed.

In early July 1995, the Serbian military captured Srebrenica after it pushed back Bosnian forces into the UN enclave. The ill-equipped Dutch peacekeepers responsible for protecting the safe area were forced to negotiate a peace settlement with the occupying Serbian army. Video footage would later emerge showing General Mladić and Dutch Lieutenant-Colonel Thom Karremans raising a toast to their deal while Dutch peacekeepers were filmed drinking and dancing with the Serb army.

The next day Serb forces began separating Bosnian men and boys from the rest of the townspeople. They placed them on trucks and removed them to a nearby camp, where they were executed and buried in mass graves. The Dutch peacekeepers, along with the wider UNPROFOR mission, were accused of failing to protect the Bosnian refugees within a UN-sanctioned safe area.

Following the tragedy, the UN Secretariat and the Security Council said that member states had never felt that the safe area was truly safe. It was reported that "There was neither the will to use decisive air power against Serb attacks on the safe areas, nor the means on the ground to repulse them."

The killings at Srebrenica were the worst violence experienced in Europe since the end of World War II, and former Secretary-General Kofi Annan would later call it one of the darkest pages in UN history (United Nations General Assembly 1999).

The Five Types of Peacekeeping Missions

Alex Bellamy, Paul Williams, and Stuart Griffin (2010) group peacekeeping into five distinct types of missions. First, traditional peacekeeping, which is generally considered the most established type of operation, is committed to the "holy trinity" of impartiality, consent, and the minimal use of force. Traditional peacekeeping missions can range from small multinational observer missions of unarmed civilian personnel to larger military operations designed to place international forces between conflicting sides with the hope of eventually securing a peace agreement. In 1948, the first observer mission, classified as the United Nations Truce Supervision Organization (UNTSO), was dispatched to the Middle East to observe a cease-fire agreement following the first Arab–Israeli war. Based in Jerusalem, UNTSO remains the UN's longest-running observer mission to date.

The second type of mission refers to those that "manage violent transitions." First, these types of missions are designed to oversee state transformations from violence to peace: They set the conditions for negotiations between conflicting sides while managing the mediation process. The principle of impartiality is critical here to ensure that each side perceives the negotiators as neutral yet strong enough to see through agreements from beginning to end. Second, managing transitions requires a clear time frame that ideally ends with combatants signing a lasting peace accord and moving toward free and fair elections. These types of missions are considered multidimensional and often involve complex mandates. For example, the United Nations Transitional Authority in Cambodia (UNTAC) had a clear time frame (1991–93) that saw a wide range of military and civilian forces push for quickly held democratic elections. The idea was to empower local communities to take ownership of a new government. The elections were seen as a milestone in Cambodia's history and an opportunity to move beyond the horrors the country had experienced throughout the previous decades including civil war, occupation, and genocide.

A third type of peacekeeping can be called *wider peacekeeping*, which is also referred to as second-generation peacekeeping. These operations provide similar support to transitional missions yet occur during continued violence and often involve intrastate conflicts. The mandate of peacekeepers is also more robust, along with greater responsibilities, such as disarming combatants and providing humanitarian aid. More importantly, the mandate of each mission can change, making the work more flexible than the traditional approaches to peacekeeping. An example of wider peacekeeping was seen during the breakup of Yugoslavia through the work of UNPROFOR. The UNPROFOR operation (1992–95) was tasked with monitoring the cease-fire agreement between Serbia and Croatia, providing military protection during the delivery of humanitarian provisions, establishing a no-fly zone, designating and defending UN "safe areas," setting up a criminal court, as well as gathering and storing arms from belligerent fighters. While peacekeeping operations appeared to crossing over the impartiality line, many problems remained, especially on the rules of engagement.

The fourth type of peacekeeping operation involves peace enforcement. The nature of these missions involves the Security Council's efforts to end hostilities, typically through the use of military coercion. For example, the Council can authorize deadly force when it seeks out the application of Chapter VII of the UN Charter (Action with Respect to Threats to the Peace, Breaches of the Peace, and Acts of Aggression). Chapter VII allows the Council to deploy "air, sea, or land forces as may be necessary to maintain or restore international peace and security." Peace enforcement is concerned with collective security and calls for peacekeepers to respond to conflict using strategic military action. Former UN Secretary-General Boutros Boutros-Ghali outlined his vision of elite "peace enforcement units" in his influential 1992 report *An Agenda for Peace*. For Ghali, the units would serve as an indispensable prerequisite for peacebuilding activities and provide a much-needed boost to the legitimacy of the UN. However, without any standing UN army or the political will of the Security Council such initiatives have struggled.

An example of peace enforcement was seen during the Persian Gulf War (1990–91). Following Iraq's invasion of Kuwait and after repeated demands for then-President Saddam Hussein to withdraw his forces from the country, the Council invoked Chapter VII and deployed a multinational force led by the United States. The Gulf War was the first real post–Cold War test for the Council, and it successfully demonstrated the benefits of a unified Security Council, although it also showed that the success of peace enforcement operations is very much at the mercy of the P5.

A final type of peacekeeping is peace support, which involves a multidimensional force consisting of military and civilian personnel. Similar to what was suggested in the Brahimi Report, the goal of peace support operations is to help war-torn societies transition toward lasting peace. The end goal is to establish a liberal democratic type of government model by applying peacebuilding strategies like developing state institutions. Armed peacekeepers are assigned to protect sub-agencies of the United Nations that hope to establish and build state institutions. For example, the Australian-led International Force for East Timor was tasked with providing security for the interim UN administration (see the box below). The UN was responsible for training local police, delivering humanitarian aid, and overseeing Timor's 1999 referendum, which was marred by extreme **political violence**. In this sense, peace support operations can be important mechanisms for assisting UN humanitarian missions worldwide.

The Road to Security in East Timor

Communities that achieve human security are often those that have overcome difficult historical struggles. These struggles can be violent and are experienced at the local level and require grassroots support if they are to gain traction. One country that has taken control of its future through years of affliction is East Timor.

On 20 May 2002, the small Southeast Asian country's struggle for independence came to a historic end. East Timor's past has been both turbulent and traumatic, following centuries of Portuguese colonial rule then 25 years of Indonesian occupation. When the Portuguese withdrew from the country in 1975, the Indonesian Navy invaded and declared the territory a province of Indonesia, meeting popular resistance with violent force. The UN estimates that between 100,000 and 200,000 people died as a consequence of the occupation, and another 250,000 were forced from their homes.

In 1999, after decades of international pressure and a protracted internal conflict against separatist guerillas known as the Falintil, Indonesia granted East Timor the right to an independence referendum. Despite attempts to intimidate voters by a pro-Indonesian militia backed by the Indonesian military, the electorate showed overwhelming support for independence, with 78.5 percent voting in favor.

The results of the referendum brought widespread violence as the pro-Indonesian militia attacked the capital, Dili, killing an estimated 1,400 people and forcing the displacement of another 200,000. Some estimates suggest that

75 percent of all privately owned buildings in the capital were destroyed. Order was restored only after a United Nations peacekeeping force was deployed to the country on the invitation of the Indonesia government.

The UN Transitional Administration in East Timor was sent to investigate and arrest those responsible for the ongoing human rights abuses that occurred following the vote. The UN formed a serious crimes unit (SCU) that was designed as a hybrid judicial mechanism that oversaw the prosecution of those responsible. However, the majority of those responsible remained at large, and charges were generally brought against low-ranking members of the Indonesian Armed Forces. As the Center for Justice and Accountability notes:

> Out of a total of 303 arrest warrants that were issued, over 75 percent of those indicted remain at large. The SCU convicted 84 individuals, but the majority were low-level defendants who had participated in local pro-Indonesia militias. Only a handful of low-ranking members of the Indonesian Armed Forces were convicted, while the military and political leadership responsible for crimes against humanity were left with impunity. The outstanding warrant for General Wiranto—the commander of Indonesian troops in East Timor in 1999, who was indicted for crimes against humanity—is illustrative of the SCU's shortcomings. The East Timorese attorney general refused to cooperate with the SCU in arresting Wiranto, and the fledgling East Timorese government declined to authorize Interpol to issue an international arrest warrant. (Center for Justice and Accountability 2014)

The UN mission would stay in East Timor until May 2005, rebuilding and providing support for the country's post-conflict reconstruction agenda. Yet when gang violence once again flared up in 2006, the UN would return to cite poverty and unemployment as mitigating factors in the violence. The United States stayed in East Timor until 2012, assisting the country through national reconciliation and helping it develop its economy.

Still one of Asia's poorest states, East Timor struggles to improve human security for the 1.2 million people who have lived through decades of violence and occupation. While the international community has played a significant role in managing the country's post-conflict transition, no amount of international governance can achieve what local East Timorese can provide for themselves. Sustaining peace and improving human security must be recognized as a local struggle that begins at the grassroots level.

There are significant challenges with each of these types of peacekeeping operations. Some of the more difficult involve determining a clear mandate for each mission. Training of peacekeepers, along with a lack of resources and funding, is also a serious problem. Ensuring the "holy trinity" of impartiality, consent, and the minimal use of force is upheld also proves challenging, with members of the Security Council struggling to reach consensus on how to handle conflict. Indeed, political will has proven to be one of the central criticisms of the Council itself. The peacekeepers in Kiwanja discussed at the beginning of this section experienced elements of each of these problems. The ad hoc nature of peacekeeping missions also raises questions about what constitutes a legitimate threat to international security. Why was the Security Council able to intervene in Libya in 2011 but has refused to launch a similar mission in Syria?

It is no secret that peacekeeping has critics, who often point to the seemingly dysfunctional Security Council, but it is important to recognize that such initiatives are overseen by two very distinct bodies. The first is the Security Council, which is the only body capable of authorizing peacekeeping missions. The Council is a political body that is governed by nation-states who each bring their own interests to the table. When the Council meets to discuss the option of deploying peacekeepers, members must consider the long-term implications for approving such a move in relation to their own personal interests. For example, the Council's decision to send an observer mission to Syria but not approve any type of wider intervention comes down to political interests. While the Western powers of the United Kingdom, France, and the United States have all pushed for stronger action against the regime of Syrian President Bashar al-Assad, China and Russia have repeatedly invoked their veto power to reject any type of further sanctions. In doing so, China and Russia are considering the long-term geostrategic implications of their own interests in the region. Notably, Russia risks losing its only Mediterranean naval base in Syria if anti-Assad supporters are given control of the country, while China may be more concerned with how supporting foreign intervention could lead to a slippery slope of Western domination in the Middle East. The veto function should be considered a political mechanism. Although criticized, it remains an important tool of the Council to ensure that the world's great powers stay at the bargaining table.

On the other hand, the Department for Peacekeeping Operations (DPKO) within the United Nations Secretariat, which runs the day-to-day support for peacekeeping missions, comprises over 40,000 international civil servants who operate under the principles of impartiality. If the UN were a country, it would be the second-largest deployer of armed forces in the world after the United States (von Einsiedel and Chandran 2015). The DPKO is a dedicated branch of the UN system that has acted consistently in its commitment to international peace and security. In the case of Syria, the UN Secretariat has frequently called for greater efforts to end the violence, with Secretary-General Ban Ki-moon calling the situation a global "calamity." In a September 2012 address to the General Assembly, the secretary-general stated "[the Syrian conflict] is a serious and growing threat to international peace and security which requires Security Council action . . . We must stop the violence and flows of arms to both sides and set in motion a Syrian-led transition as soon as possible" (Ban Ki-moon 2012).

What is important to understand is that although the Council may show inconsistencies when endorsing missions, the Secretariat has shown great leadership in mobilizing the international community around peacekeeping in an effort to open new diplomatic space. As Ramesh Thakur (2006, 2014) reminds us, the UN's good offices (which generally refers to the pressure the secretary-general can apply based on the prestige of his position and the world community he represents) have been tirelessly working at preventative diplomacy, peace operations, and peace negotiations. Article 99 of the UN Charter allows the secretary-general to bring forward all matters deemed a threat to international peace and stability. For Thakur, the UN offers innovative and strategic solutions for dealing with human insecurity. Bernard Ramcharan (2008) agrees and has convincingly shown the effectiveness of preventative diplomacy dating back to the Concert of Europe. Ramcharan, a former acting UN high commissioner for human rights, shows how preventative diplomacy is closely linked to the charter, while high-level mediation can work to minimize violent conflict. Indeed, the work of the secretary-general not only works to advocate peace, the Secretariat is also actively involved in the promotion of peacebuilding and human security initiatives such as democracy, climate change strategy, as well as economic development.

Still, peacekeeping must be thought of as a top-down political option of the UN Security Council. It is a mechanism for stabilizing violent conflict to create the right conditions for building security, especially along contested boarders and within weak states. Peacekeeping holds local, regional, and international dimensions, as was seen in both the Darfur and East Timor cases discussed above. There is debate around how each mission should be managed, as they all have unique mandates. Yet as Jeni Whalan (2013) rightly argues, peace operations work to influence the behavior of local actors. Achieving legitimacy through local "buy in" is thus critical if peace operations are to succeed. Third-party interveners need to ensure their operations are designed to meet the needs of communities, or peace agreements and mediated settlements will fail.

GOVERNANCE AND INTERVENTION

The purpose of intervening forces is to set the conditions for peacemaking. Craig Zelizer and Valerie Oliphant (2013, 7) define peacemaking as "[a]n approach focused on resolving a specific conflict . . . through negotiations and/or other means, such as dialogue." Oliver Ramsbotham, Hugh Miall, and Tom Woodhouse (2011) suggest that

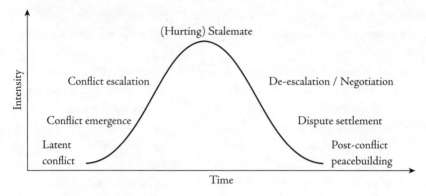

FIGURE 4.1 Mapping Violent Conflict

Source: Brahm 2003.

a negotiated settlement must be free of manipulation, yet parties should be persuaded to find a resolution. Talks generally involve a third-party intervener who is trusted by each side and works toward establishing trust at the international, national, and community level. Peacemaking seeks to establish a formal settlement between combatants. Unlike peacekeeping, which requires top-down governance strategies, peacemaking is often a bottom-up process and can involve nongovernmental organizations and other civil society members.

Peacemaking involves conflict resolution, which has significantly changed as a field of study and practice since the end of the Cold War. It is based on the premise that while conflict is a natural human condition, we struggle to find ways to resolve our disputes. Ramsbotham, Miall, and Woodhouse (2011) offer an exceptional study of the various approaches to conflict resolution, such as the **prisoner's dilemma**, coercion and enforcement, as well as noncoercive approaches such as mediation and good offices. They further differentiate and map the trajectory of violent conflict as it transitions from *latent* (hidden) to *overt* (open) conflict. See Figure 4.1 for a diagram of how violent conflicts can be mapped.

One type of peacemaking mechanism is mediation. **Mediation** is a voluntary process that involves a third party who serves as a messenger between each conflicting side to ensure they maintain control over the process and outcome. Facilitators can serve as mediators, but they are not problem solvers in that solutions must be reached by the parties. Top-down mediation through track-one diplomacy is considered high-level negotiation that involves governments. On the other hand, track-two diplomacy involves unofficial bottom-up dialogue led by civil society groups. From the statist perspective, track-one diplomacy is a stronger option to achieve a peace settlement.

Notice that peacebuilding relies heavily on nonstate actors to reach settlements. Bottom-up peacebuilding allows for the depoliticization of mediation while simultaneously building trust with actors from civil society who may be well established in the community. One group that has been extensively involved in mediating violent conflict are the Quakers, who embrace "restorative peacebuilding" that focuses on grassroots reconciliation and dialogue (see Princen 2001).

War, Ungovernance, and Gender-Based Violence

The long-term societal impact of armed conflict and poverty is destructive. War brings about all types of atrocities, one of which is gender-based violence (GBV). One study estimates that 48 women are raped each hour in the Democratic Republic of the Congo, with 12 percent of the country's women having been sexually assaulted (Adetunji 2001). Rape is endemic in the Congo, but it is also used as a weapon of war in the country's South Kivu province. As a weapon of war, rape traumatizes communities and instills fear in both men and women. The spread of sexually transmitted disease along with enforced pregnancies has led one UN peacekeeping commander to suggest it's becoming more dangerous to be a woman than an armed soldier during war.

Sexual violence is often carried out by both military and nonstate actors, such as warlords who often refer to themselves as freedom fighters. These groups do not follow the rules of war because they operate outside the Geneva Conventions. The UN Action Against Sexual Violence in Conflict (UN Action; 2015) has compiled the following statistics:

- Hundreds of thousands of women were raped during the 1994 genocide in Rwanda.
- An average of 40 women are raped every day in South Kivu in the context of the ongoing armed conflict in the Democratic Republic of the Congo.
- It is estimated that between 20,000 and 50,000 women were raped during the war in Bosnia and Herzegovina in the early 1990s.
- It is estimated that between 50,000 and 64,000 internally displaced women in Sierra Leone have experienced sexual violence at the hands of armed combatants.

Sexual violence in war is an ongoing crisis that is slowly gaining international attention. Yet the ability to govern or manage such violence in war is difficult, especially when dealing with armed nonstate actors who do not follow international law. Moreover, state-supported military units that are bound by laws are increasingly being called on by the international community to hold soldiers accountable for committing such violations. As Security Council Resolution 1820 (2008) has clearly laid out, "rape and other forms of sexual violence can constitute war crimes, crimes against humanity or a constitutive act with respect to genocide" (United Nations 2008). Indeed, governing gender-based violence and rape as a weapon of war will continue to gain ground within the international community.

International Tribunals and War Crimes

War crimes such as genocide, ethnic cleansing, and crimes against humanity are examples of extreme human rights violations or mass-atrocity crimes. These crimes are carried out against civilian populations on a grand scale where identifying perpetrators is increasingly difficult. When violence has reached such levels there are often calls for humanitarian military intervention, yet political will to launch such campaigns may be weak, especially when it involves violating the sovereignty of a state. The Responsibility to Protect (R2P) doctrine, which will be discussed in Chapter 6, specifically deals with the optics of such a challenge; however, here we focus on the judicial institutions that seek to prosecute those responsible for heinous crimes.

The International Criminal Tribunal for the Former Yugoslavia and the International Criminal Tribunal for Rwanda are two courts that sought to address the specific crimes carried out in each country. As Ernesto Verdeja (2013) notes, they were both established by the West in an attempt to bring justice to the communities impacted by genocide. While the courts are limited in their territorial reach and time frame, they are important steps in establishing legal precedent on how the international community responds to war crimes and mass atrocity. Verdeja further notes, "Both tribunals have made significant contributions to international law, including the definition of genocide, war crimes, crimes against humanity and violations of the 1949 Geneva Conventions, as well as furthered greater understanding of the concept of intentionality at the heart of genocide" (175).

While such tribunals offer hopes of justice to victims of war crimes, other tribunals have been criticized. For example, the Extraordinary Chambers in the Courts of Cambodia has been tasked with investigating and prosecuting those responsible for a genocide that took place in the late 1970s. Cambodia saw one-quarter of its population murdered by the genocidal Khmer Rouge regime under the leadership of Saloth Sar, better known as Pol Pot. When the UN established the court in 2006, Pol Pot had long been dead, along with other leaders responsible for the crimes. Still, the court did prosecute three senior officials involved in the atrocities, including Kaing Guek Eav (alias Duch), Nuon Chea, and Khieu Samphan. A fourth member being tried, who was well into his eighties, was deemed unfit to stand trial after he had been diagnosed with Alzheimer's disease. Indeed, could such a court that was established nearly three decades after the crimes serve a purpose? Despite the criticism over the courts costs and delays, advocates see the initiative as a key building block in Cambodia's healing.

There have also been hybrid tribunals, such as the Special Court for Sierra Leone, the War Crimes Chamber in the State Courts of Bosnia and Herzegovina, the Special Tribunal for Lebanon, as well as the Special Panels of the Dili District Court in East Timor, to name just a few. These courts are supported by the international community on account of each country's weak institutional capacity. Hybrid courts are controversial given the fact that outsiders often serve as lawyers, judges, and investigators. For example, the Cambodian tribunal discussed above is a hybrid court that had to find foreign judges since the vast majority of the country's legal population had been killed in the genocide.

A last judicial mechanism we wish to explore is the International Criminal Court (ICC). As briefly mentioned in Chapter 1, the ICC began operating in 2002 after the Rome Statute came into legal force. The treaty established the first permanent war crimes tribunal with a mandate to pursue perpetrators regardless of jurisdiction. Seen as a court of last resort, it was hailed as a breakthrough mechanism in the realm of international human rights and humanitarian law. However, the court has seen its fair share of criticism. First, the court has yet to carry out any successful prosecution that would be considered in line with its original mandate as highlighted in the Rome Statute. Part of this is due to the court's inability to arrest individuals that operate in jurisdictions that do not recognize it, such as Sudan, where the president has been indicted with war crimes since 2009. Second, the court has struggled to establish itself as an international institution of justice that has moved beyond the continent of Africa. There is a sense that the court is serving as a Eurocentric institution that is targeting the poorest countries in the world. Finally, the United States and Russia have not ratified the Rome Statute that gives the court legal recognition, while China and India have refused to acknowledge the ICC's jurisdiction. There is a view that without buy in from the great powers, the institution will struggle to gain international credibility. Still, the ICC should be considered a groundbreaking mechanism for addressing war criminals.

The final section of this chapter explores one approach for addressing such complicated and destructive violence: peacebuilding. We argue that such violence has resulted in the proliferation of peacebuilding activities at the UN. Peacebuilding operations can be identified as implementing cease-fire agreements, disarmament, and the facilitation of demobilizing combatants.

Since the end of the Cold War, the concept of **peacebuilding** has emerged as an ever-expanding approach to rebuilding failed states and ending violent conflict. Craig Zelizer (2013, 7) defines peacebuilding as an activity that focuses "on transforming relationships and structures in society to decrease the likelihood of future conflict." Peacebuilding can involve a range of activities, including conflict resolution, peacekeeping, diplomacy and dialogue, truth and reconciliation processes, as well as rebuilding state institutions. Zelizer identifies three types of contemporary peacebuilding components: (1) peacebuilding as a profession that involves individuals making a career out of conflict analysis; (2) peacebuilding as a sector involving transnational NGOs and activists looking to build peaceful dialogue and engage in humanitarian work; and (3) peacebuilding as a mechanism to develop post-conflict reconstruction programs involving a host of themes, such as gender equality and economic security. Each component touches on strategies to operationalize projects that seek to strengthen peace agreements, promote development, and improve human security.

Peacebuilding can thus be understood as both a pragmatic and conceptual approach for analyzing conflict to seek out remedies involving a diverse range of stakeholders. These stakeholders work to transform conflict in a variety of ways and involve a wide range of actors, from UN peacekeepers to humanitarian NGOs. For Zelizer, peacebuilding first involves identifying key stakeholders to ensure an appropriate intervention is designed and that all parties to the conflict are included in the dialogue. This also allows peacebuilders to assess power relationships within the group dynamic of combatant actors. Second, the context and background of the conflict must be established to understand historical grievances that might be driving the violence. Diverse interpretations of history often shape how conflict is understood by combatants. Peacebuilders must cut through the range of perceptions to establish a common context to ensure peace processes move forward. Third, peacebuilders should assess how conflicts escalate by identifying tipping points. Determining the moment when latent violence develops into overt conflict can help establish a framework for developing a cease-fire. It gives peacebuilders an opportunity to assess the level of violence and interaction between combatants prior to an escalation in violence. Finally, analysts should draw on theories and models of practice to determine the root source of the conflict, which may involve identity or socioeconomic issues. Conflict will continue so long as deeper understandings of the violence do not present themselves. However, it is important that analysts apply a range of theories in seeking out explanations, since conflicts are organic and relying on only one approach can result in a seriously flawed assessment (Zelizer 2013).

Peacebuilding therefore involves an interdisciplinary strategy for working in conflict zones that involves conflict assessment, strategic implementation, operationalization, and project monitoring. While NGOs and academics have actively been involved in exploring how peacebuilding can lead to conflict transformation by targeting drivers of conflict, so too have governments and international organizations. For example, a number of organizations offer toolkits for peacebuilders to use to develop conflict assessments, including Small Arms Survey, United States Agency for International Development, Search for Common Ground, CARE International, and many others. Each of these organizations has detailed guides on how to assess indicators that can be developed into peacebuilding assessments. Some groups draw on already existing frameworks developed through multilateral initiatives, such as the Geneva Declaration on Armed Violence and Development (2015). The declaration is now signed by over 100 states and offers resources for measuring violence built around three pillars:

1. Advocacy, dissemination, and coordination to raise global awareness about the negative impact of armed violence on development and the obstacles it creates to achieving of the Millennium Development Goals.
2. Measurability and monitoring to improve our understanding of the scope, scale, and distribution of armed violence and its negative impact on development.
3. Programming to develop and carry out commitments enshrined in the Geneva Declaration so as to make a measurable difference in the lives of individuals in affected countries and regions through concrete programs targeting risks and symptoms of armed violence.

While the Geneva Declaration is but one multilateral initiative to develop approaches to conflict transformation, multilateral initiatives involving UN agencies have been working on themes of peacebuilding and conflict for decades. In 2005, the World Summit approved the creation of the **United Nations Peacebuilding Commission (PBC)**. While the concept had been widely used within the UN system for years, the idea was not fully entrenched until the PBC was established. Set out to be an organization dedicated to sustaining peace and ensuring that post-conflict societies do not return to war, the PBC was designed as an intergovernmental body that is overseen by 31 rotating elected member states. Two other affiliated bodies of the PBC were also created at this time: the Peacebuilding Support Office (PBSO) and the Peacebuilding Fund (PBF). These institutions addressed a seemingly wide gap in the UN system that was failing to deliver security.

Commenting on the PBC's establishment, Rob Jenkins (2013) outlines five observations worth discussing. First, the vagueness surrounding the nature of peacebuilding in the 1990s played out during the formative years of the commission. This brought divergent views from bureaucratic and diplomatic actors who were all looking to advance the PBC in their own light. Second, the PBC became popular outlets for de facto political statements. Third, the UN's new peacebuilding approach did not eliminate the old guard, looking instead to keep the status quo within specific UN departments that claimed to run their own programs. Fourth, the commission was frequently used as a venue for states looking to push UN reform by promoting national agendas around peace and security. Finally, even with the early barriers facing the PBC, the institution emerged as a meaningful regime ready to work within the UN system.

The official PBC definition of peacebuilding can be understood as "a range of measures targeted to reduce the risk of relapsing into conflict by strengthening national capacity at all levels for conflict management, and to lay the foundations for sustainable peace and development" (United Nations Peacebuilding Commission 2015b). While seemingly vague, peacebuilding can refer to anything form multimillion dollar post-reconstruction development projects to small grassroots initiatives focusing on children's theater. The common theme between such initiatives is that they occur in post-conflict settings.

Support for the PBC has been widely received, especially during the time when the United States and its allies where struggling to rebuild institutions in Iraq and Afghanistan. The commission's mandate is jointly overseen by the UN Security

Council and the General Assembly. Early assignments of the PBC saw the commission look at development strategies in Sierra Leone and Burundi. In Sierra Leone, the PBC took on youth empowerment and employment, along with strategies for improving the capacity of democratic and legal institutions. In Burundi, the focus was on good governance, security, and the rule of law.

Roland Paris (2010) has argued that modern peacebuilding can trace its roots to the post–Cold War world. Liberal peacebuilding initiatives went operational throughout most of the post-conflict world, including Cambodia, El Salvador, Mozambique, Namibia, and Nicaragua. The early approaches to peacebuilding combined democratization with free market principles. For example, economic liberalization was incorporated into the United Nations Transitional Authority in Cambodia (UNTAC). The UNTAC mission was designed to take "control of key sectors of the country's administrative structures—foreign affairs, defense, security, *finance* and communications—in order to build a stable environment conducive to national elections [emphasis added]" (United Nations 2015). Paris points out that while such operations may have had good intentions, liberal peacebuilding has proved contentious. There have been several high-profile debacles, including one that saw belligerent fighters rearmed after they sought to contest the UN's democratization process.

Peacebuilding skeptics have been fierce or even "hyper-critical" toward the concept. Some of the more mainstream criticisms of peacebuilding center on the simple fact that most post-conflict societies are unable to sustain many initiatives that are introduced through peacebuilding strategies. For example, when trainers from advanced industrialized states teach police that torture is an illegal and outmoded method of interrogation, it fails to recognize that many post-conflict societies do not have the means to provide police with tools for advanced investigations or the resources to allow them enough time to carry out meaningful inquiries. Once the trainers leave, newly minted police often face pressure to achieve "confessions" to keep their jobs. Torture is a productive tool for agents of the state looking to promote their investigative skills. From this perspective, while peacebuilding in the area of anti-torture initiatives is important, the task cannot sustain itself without the development of other sectors, including the bureaucracy, the judiciary, and free press. Meanwhile, without a concerted effort to combat corruption many of these peacebuilding initiatives risk failing.

While peacebuilding has become a contested concept in the literature, it still holds significant support among United Nations member states and maintains a solid base within the humanitarian community. From a human security perspective, institutional capacity is an essential part of realizing one's human rights. Without a functioning police force, judicial system, or working bureaucracy, victims of post-conflict societies struggle to regain their security. Peacebuilding is, therefore, a fundamental part of improving human security.

Peacebuilding from Below: Guiding Principles for the Field

Below are the five key principles that are central to the programs run by International Alert, a peacebuilding organization.

1. **Active curiosity:** Successful programming involves the coming together of different people, organisations and ideas. Facilitating and managing this requires an openness and willingness to listen to and explore the ideas of others, while contributing new thinking of its own.

2. **Confidence with humility:** Alert is a peacebuilding organization with its own ideas and believes it can and has a mandate to change things. This confidence must be balanced with humility. If not, then arrogance will undermine the respect and trust that Alert needs to do its work. Part of this humility is living up to Alert's responsibility to question its own approach, and demonstrate how it has changed things for the better (i.e., how it has had an impact).

3. **Local ownership:** Alert believes that peace must be built by those that are members of the society affected by violent conflict. However, ensuring local ownership of interventions is not straightforward. In the conflict contexts where we operate, there exist complex relationships between different individuals and organisations. Indeed, an intervention can itself exacerbate differences and rivalries between groups if not handled with extreme care.

4. **Impartiality:** While we are explicit about our peacebuilding goals, we are impartial in that we do not take sides in our pursuit of these goals. We endeavor to be inclusive in our programming, seeking access to all relevant parties to the conflict. In our work we frequently come into contact with parties suspected of, and responsible for, grievous human rights abuses. Indeed, such contact may be a requirement of successful peacebuilding work. However, it in no way implies agreement with, or support for, the views or objectives of those parties. Our engagement is aimed at seeking specific peacebuilding outcomes and this involves us coming to decisions about what actions we can best take to achieve our peacebuilding goals.

5. **Cultural sensitivity:** In our posture and our work we endeavor to be sensitive to cultural differences. However, this does not undermine our fundamental belief that behaviors which do not respect human rights are plain wrong, and undermine peace. We therefore try to balance a respect for different values with a willingness to criticize and work to change some behaviors, even though they may be culturally acceptable.

Source: International Alert 2010. © International Alert.

CONCLUSION

This chapter has set out to discuss the connection between international governance institutions and human security. It has explored the connection between sovereignty, intervention, and security. While top-down approaches to addressing human security concerns can prove problematic, there is clearly a need for international leadership. Modern human security threats that push the limits of state sovereignty, such as terrorism, infectious disease, and civil war, all require a range of multilateral policy options by governments that are exposed to such risk. Indeed, no state in the world is immune from the potential spillover effects of these types of human insecurity.

Despite the many controversies associated with the UN's record and a perception that the agency struggles to enforce its own mandate, there is a desperate need for such an agency. Not only does the UN system offer a platform for nation-states to engage with one another through multilateral means, the organization also designs, implements, and delivers justice through criminal tribunals while offering valuable support for those engaged in post-conflict societies.

There is a clear need for such initiatives to be developed in full consultation with local constituents, who are the ones living through the conflict. Without consultation at the grassroots level, global governance strategies on human security will prove to be ineffective and unsustainable. We therefore argue that for human security to be achieved—especially in fragile states—insight from grassroots civil society organizations must reach the desks of top-down development planners. Only through continuous stakeholder dialogue involving a range of both local and international actors can peacebuilding achieve meaningful results.

KEY TERMS

Brahimi Report; Collective Action; Conflict Resolution; Democratic Deficit; Ditchley Formula; Epistemic Communities; Free Rider; Gender-Based Violence (GBV); Global Commons; Good Offices; Intergovernmental Organizations (IGOs); Mediation; Montreal Protocol; Peacebuilding; Peacekeeping; Peacemaking; Political Violence; Post-Westphalian Sovereignty; Prisoner's Dilemma; Regionalism; Sovereignty; United Nations Peacebuilding Commission; War Crimes; Westphalian Sovereignty

FURTHER READING

Barnett, Michael N. 2011. *Empire of Humanity: A History of Humanitarianism.* Ithaca, NY: Cornell University Press.

Bellamy, Alex J., Paul D. Williams, and Stuart Griffin. 2010. *Understanding Peacekeeping.* 2nd ed. Cambridge: Polity Press.

Deng, F.M., ed. 1996. *Sovereignty as Responsibility: Conflict Management in Africa.* Brookings Institution Press.

Falk, Richard. 2014. *(Re)imagining Humane Global Governance.* New York: Routledge.

Ramcharan, Bertrand G. 2008. *Preventive Diplomacy at the UN.* Bloomington: Indiana University Press.

Ramsbotham, Oliver, Hugh Miall, and Tom Woodhouse. 2011. *Contemporary Conflict Resolution.* Cambridge: Polity Press.

Thakur, Ramesh. 2006. *The United Nations, Peace and Security: From Collective Security to the Responsibility to Protect.* Cambridge: Cambridge University Press. http://dx.doi.org/10.1017/CBO9780511755996.

Weiss, Thomas G., and Rorden Wilkinson. 2013. *International Organization and Global Governance.* New York: Routledge.

Whalan, Jeni. 2013. *How Peace Operations Work: Power, Legitimacy, and Effectiveness.* Oxford: Oxford University Press. http://dx.doi.org/10.1093/acprof:oso/9780199672189.001.0001.

Zelizer, Craig. 2013. *Integrated Peacebuilding: Innovative Approaches to Transforming Conflict.* Boulder: Westview Press.

WEBSITES

Alliance for Peacebuilding: www.allianceforpeacebuilding.org

Centre for International Governance Innovation: www.cigionline.org

Council on Foreign Relations Global Governance Monitor: www.cfr.org/global-governance/global-governance-monitor/p18985#!/p18985

Peace Research Institute Oslo (PRIO): www.prio.org

Small Arms Survey: www.smallarmssurvey.org

United Nations Department of Peacekeeping Operations: www.un.org/en/peacekeeping/about/dpko

United Nations Peacebuilding Commission: www.un.org/en/peacebuilding

Chapter 5

HUMAN SECURITY AND
CIVIL SOCIETY

Silence has long been confused with neutrality, and has been presented as a necessary condition for humanitarian action. From its beginning, MSF [Doctors Without Borders] was created in opposition to this assumption . . . We are not sure that words can always save lives, but we know that silence can certainly kill.

Dr. James Orbinski, then-president of the MSF International Council, accepting the Nobel Peace Prize on behalf of MSF (Doctors Without Borders 2015)

INTRODUCTION

Civil society groups play one of the most important roles in the promotion and protection of human security. Media, nongovernment organizations (NGOs), and activists are vital in holding state actors accountable for violations of human rights, abuses of power, corruption, and other types of questionable state behavior. Yet these groups are often targets themselves by security agents looking to silence those in opposition to the state. And for good reason: Civil society groups such as Amnesty International, Greenpeace, and Global Witness all have a proven track record in campaigning against those who deny human security. These groups are on the ground, reporting and standing in solidarity with the most vulnerable and marginalized communities.

In this chapter, we explore the role of NGOs from a "bottom-up" approach to development and peacebuilding. We will show how these actors interact with other nonstate actors outside the realm of the state, such as terrorists and guerrilla groups.

We discuss the relationship between violence and insecurity, explaining how humanitarian activists work to enhance human security in the developing world.

One of the most divisive debates within the NGO community is intervention. At what point should foreign civil society groups concern themselves with the internal affairs of a sovereign country? Should aid workers interject only when war occurs, should they limit themselves to post-conflict reconstruction, or should they work to minimize poverty? NGOs are involved in all types of development activities that often seek to bypass state authority. When the state will not or cannot provide protection to its citizens, people-to-people aid can be an effective bottom-up approach to development.

Since the birth of the modern nation-state, governments have used the concept of sovereignty to justify their right to manage all matters that happen within their borders. Although the concept has served a purpose in protecting weaker states from the more powerful, the post–Cold War era demands that the right to sovereignty must also be accompanied by a responsibility to govern in such a way as to ensure the security of the population. Globalization and the growing interconnectedness between communities have led to new pressures on the UN Security Council to intervene when governments brutalize and oppress their citizens. But when calls for UN intervention fail and governments engage in asymmetric conflict, **global civil society** is increasingly playing a role in building security for those in need under the umbrella term of *humanitarianism*. But what is global civil society?

THE RISE OF GLOBAL CIVIL SOCIETY

Complex and contentious, Helmut Anheier, Marlies Glasius, and Mary Kaldor (2001) have noted that global civil society is an emerging paradigm tied in with the rise of globalization. Although contested, the rise of global civil society has enabled international networks of activists to hold states accountable in new ways, especially in the context of international law (Walker and Thompson 2008). Thomas Carothers (1999) offers an excellent take on civil society where he outlines and challenges mainstream views of how this sector functions. He notes that all civil society groups offer a space for political engagement outside the state. While the international arena has been dominated by governments, civil society networks like NGOs offer new avenues for individuals and groups to engage one another across boundaries. Yet it is important to remember that global civil society comprises more than just NGOs; rather, it also involves transnational criminal networks, multinational corporations, hacktivist networks, and those promoting political violence, such as terrorist organizations. All these groups challenge the state in some capacity, and they may not be democratic nor endorse the public good. Even NGOs hold narrowly focused agendas that often serve the interests of a few while claiming to hold the best intentions for all.

On the one hand, it could be argued that global civil society has enhanced the accountability of states, yet a strong civil society can also undermine it, since it exposes the weakness of governments. Meanwhile, it should be remembered that a strong civil society might not always be a requisite for developing a strong human security regime, as in the case of South Korea, which lived through a harsh authoritarian period. Today the country enjoys some of the highest levels of human security in the world despite years of suppression. Similarly, Sheri Berman (1997) has shown how strong civil society in Nazi Germany played a central role in subverting democratic institutions.

Ronnie Lipschutz (1992) has attributed the rise in global civil society to a "withering away" of international anarchy, which has seen the global arena dominated by self-interested states. For Lipschutz, new types of transnational nonstate political actors are set to "reconstruct, re-imagine or re-map" the global order. Civil society is challenging what he calls a "consumption space" that has been established through neoliberal planning. Lipschutz sees global civil society emerging in three ways. First is the taming of global anarchy through normative global governance frameworks rooted in consumer culture. Kenichi Ohmae (1999) has argued a similar point, referring to the growing influence of consumers over companies and states, which he sees as contributing to a "borderless world." Second, Lipschutz argues that states face an increasing inability to deal with issues at the macro-level, such as the environment and human rights, whereas global civil society is able to imagine and organize itself as a loosely structured network of transnational community activists seeking to bypass the state. Finally, globalization and neoliberalism has contributed to the softening of national identity and the promotion of transnational interconnectedness. Lipschutz proposes that state incompetence is a driver of greater civil associations, while a growing sense of societal competence has ensured legitimacy of nonstate actors. With the constant rollback of the welfare state through neoliberal planning, civil society will continue to grow dissatisfied with the state and emerge as an alternative sector to meet community needs that governments can't or won't address. Of course, global civil society must still recognize states as central players in the international order. While Lipschutz believes there is a shrinking of residual state power with political influence moving both upward to intergovernmental organizations (IGOs) and downward to NGOs, the state remains the principal actor of the international order.

Humanitarians as Global Nonstate Actors

One civil society group that has emerged over the past century are transnational humanitarian aid workers. Humanitarians are faced with complicated legal, moral, and ethical questions. Should they or shouldn't they enter war zones? How do international NGOs assure that they are not undermining local cultures by spreading their own values? What happens when governments refuse to let them in the country; should they enter illegally? Is there a possibility that NGOs are being manipulated by governments to continue their programs since they are doing the work of the state? Does this not provide state actors with an opportunity to ignore the development needs of their citizens?

Respecting national boundaries and the will of states has become a defining feature of international relations. Still, those who support humanitarianism are often challenging the traditional logic that has guided the laws of nations for centuries. By placing human rights and development at the center of sovereign responsibility, humanitarians are able to claim a collective obligation to intervene on the grounds that a regime has failed to protect human life and safeguard the well-being of its people. From this perspective, humanitarians place victims as opposed to sovereignty at the center of their work. For example, humanitarians may feel compelled to assist victims of conflict through charitable means, such as bringing much-needed medical supplies or emergency relief following a natural disaster. For many, intervention is about protecting the most vulnerable people on the planet.

Yet humanitarianism is an industry that has evolved into a highly public, hierarchical, and institutionalized movement devoted to helping strangers in distant lands. Individuals often join such efforts as a political act, even though the movement is meant to be nonpolitical. Thus, humanitarians struggle to differentiate themselves from those who use politics as a means for intervention (Barnett 2011). Still, humanitarians must work with governments and make deals with the very aggressors they are working against if they are to stay in conflict zones to create humanitarian space.

Although we intend to show the connection between civil society and human security, it's important to begin with a brief overview of why humanitarianism is so contentious. As some groups involve themselves with foreign democratization processes, they can be swiftly denounced by governments who see them as meddling in local affairs. Moreover, can these organizations even transfer their advocacy campaigns and strategies to communities in the developing world that have no history of such activism? These controversies offer good reasons why non-Western states may not trust foreign civil society groups who present themselves as transnational humanitarians.

But is this suspicion of Western humanitarians legitimate? We argue yes and suggest that it's impossible to understand the distrust that many in the developing world hold toward humanitarian interventionists without considering the relationship between colonialism and human insecurity. Though these groups may be acting with good intentions, foreign humanitarianism may well be perceived as paternalistic exploitation. It is therefore imperative that we begin with the history of Western intervention in the context of colonialism.

Colonialism, Philanthropy, and Insecurity

History tells us that intervening foreigners are usually motivated by their own self-interest rather than humanitarian objectives. The colonial explorers were no exception as they scoured the globe for resources in their quest to develop Western society. Europe's growth model demanded the extraction of gold and silver from South America, a developed spice trade in Asia, and a reliable supply of sugar and cotton from the Americas. A dominant merchant class emerged whose success was closely linked to **colonialism**. Europe's economic success required the exploitation of resources the world over. Five centuries later the colonial powers have left, but Western economic interests remain. To this day, questions concerning the motivation for intervention center on fears of foreign self-interest. After all, history presents little evidence that such interventionists place the well-being of strangers over their own opportunism. Therefore, it's no surprise that outside actors—including transnational civil society groups such as humanitarian aid organizations—are looked upon with suspicion when working in developing countries.

From the fifteenth century onwards, foreign intervention was more associated with the rise of industrial capitalism than humanitarian goodwill. Europe was undergoing a transformation, beginning with the Reformation and continuing with the Renaissance and early industrialization, during a period that was defined by discovery and revolution. It saw the European powers expand their empires to all corners of the Earth and place permanent colonies in the Americas, Africa, and Asia. Independent communities were now subject to the political and economic authority of Europe's monarchs, including the Dutch, English, French, Spanish, and Portuguese. European civil and military officials were dispatched to the colonies to govern the newly occupied territories while private merchants under the protection of the state managed the colonies' economic activities. Europe's economic prosperity became dependent on the exploitation of resources found within the colonies, including spices, raw materials, and labor. Thus, colonial economic models involved racist oppression that categorically denied the sovereignty and independence of weaker states.

All of Europe's monarchs had promoted intervention as a strategy for acquiring slaves in their efforts to develop economic growth. If it was not the Dutch in the Caribbean or the Spanish in South America, it was the British in North America or the Belgians in the Congo. **Slavery** was big business, with much of Europe's growth dependent on colonial expansion and the use of slaves to extract resources. For example, Britain's **triangular trade** system contributed to the enforced displacement of an estimated 6 million Africans between the seventeenth and early nineteenth centuries. The triangular trade system saw private merchant ships move slaves from Africa to the Americas. These ships would then transfer goods such as cotton, sugar, and tobacco to

Europe. Once leaving Europe, the merchant ships would return to Africa with cloth and weaponry. This system consolidated Europe's domination of the planet while entrenching uneven economic development throughout the colonies.

A telling example of European intervention became known as the **Scramble for Africa**, which occurred in the last quarter of the nineteenth century (1881–1914). The colonial powers rushed to gain control over every corner of the continent, raising fears of a European war in Africa. The Berlin Conference of 1884 was an attempt to mitigate the risk of conflict by dividing control of Africa among the Europeans, most notably Belgium, France, and Portugal. The conference was convened under the pretense of banning slavery, yet this was largely a public relations effort to gain acceptance for Europe's plan to regulate and control Africa. This late colonial push has been referred to as the era of "new imperialism" given the hyper-expansion of European states coupled with the rise of new actors looking to expand their overseas influence, such as Japan and the United States. Yet Europe's domination remained supreme, and by the early twentieth century it controlled roughly 90 percent of the African continent (David 2011).

Imperialist ambitions grew despite the colonial economic system losing support among industrialists, who saw the model as inefficient and unproductive. Europe was changing yet again, and an **imperialism of free trade** as opposed to direct colonial rule was endorsed by Europe's rising capitalist class, who needed to find new markets that could absorb the goods they were producing. Greater autonomy in the colonies was seen as a prerequisite for improving the economic development of new and emerging markets. The imperialist powers were able to maintain political control over the colonies yet force them to submit to unbalanced economic conditions and exploitative trade practices.

Occupation through colonial and imperial policies remained intact until the end of World War II, yet many of the colonial policies would be felt for years to come. For example, during Belgium's occupation of Rwanda the colonial government began documenting the ethnicity of Rwandans. The Belgian administrative system not only contributed to the ethnic divide of Rwandan society, but also to a newly emerging class structure. Rwandans were required to carry identification that stated their ethnicity, a policy that remained in place until the 1994 genocide. This is what made it so easy to determine who was Tutsi or Hutu during the genocide (Barnett 2011).

This brief discussion has thus far demonstrated the pressure and sheer violence associated with colonial interventionists, although much of this revolved around state policy. Yet humanitarians were actively involved in colonialism and fought to shape the imperialist mind through activist campaigns that focused on saving "the other."

Colonial philanthropy was seen by those espousing it as an alternative approach to the European occupation of foreign lands. They approached imperialism as a type of principled policy dedicated to civilizing the world and saving the human soul. Many activists came from Christian backgrounds and thereby rejected many of the violent colonial policies, like slavery; rather, they saw empire as having the potential for a progressive model of benevolent governance. As David Lambert and Alan Lester (2004) note, colonial philanthropists often held imperial ambitions that were framed within a paternalistic ideology:

> Colonial philanthropists were those people who believed, often passionately, that imperialism was about something more principled than the pursuit of military glory, personal riches or power, and who acted upon that belief in an attempt to influence official policy in the metropole and in the colonies themselves. The best known colonial interventions in the period with which we are concerned involved the abolition of the slave trade and then of slavery itself in the Caribbean, the Cape Colony and the rest of the British Empire; the "opening up" of India to Christian evangelization; and the appointment of "Protectors" and return or reservation of land to safeguard indigenous peoples from British settlers in the Cape, Australia, New Zealand and British North America. (323)

Colonial philanthropists worked to change the image of the colonies within elite circles to convince the homeland that there was a responsibility to care for the people throughout the empire. The idea that empire was an extended family began to take hold, and early humanitarians advocated for new policies around the respect and preservation of foreign cultures.

Two notorious examples of good intentions leading to disastrous results involved the Indigenous peoples in Australia and North America. In Australia, a policy of integration saw children stolen from their parents by the state and placed in white households where they were raised within a Christian tradition. Australia's "stolen generation," and similarly Canada's **residential school policy**, were both framed around paternalistic notions of saving souls and taking care of the weak. Another colonial policy designed to promote Indigenous culture in Canada was the reserve system, which forced Indigenous peoples into segregated communities with separate schools and hospitals. The oppressive system was established with the belief that this would help preserve Indigenous culture while European colonialists could exert direct control over all territory. Such policies would later be referred to by some scholars as cultural genocide and serve as a glaring reminder that good humanitarian intentions can produce the most appalling of outcomes (Neu and Therrien 2003).

The interventionist policies of the colonial powers were based on racism, ignorance, exploitation, and violence. Colonial philanthropists campaigned to change the mindset of European occupiers by rejecting slavery, endorsing limited independence of local populations, and preserving some elements of Indigenous cultures. While early civil society movements did bring meaningful change to European thinking, such as the rejection of slavery, many of the good intentions were fronts for "civilizing" and "developing" the colonies within a European worldview. **Eurocentrism** dominated, with Western notions of religious and economic supremacy driving the humanitarian discourse. The West's dark history of colonialism offers context as to why contemporary interventionists are so often met with suspicion when operating in foreign states.

THE RISE OF HUMANITARIANISM

Resistance to the politics of empire and exploitation would soon take hold in Europe. In what would later become known as the humanitarian movement, individuals and associations throughout Europe started to question the ethics of **imperialism**. As mentioned above, new demands were placed on governments to end oppressive colonial practices such as slavery, war crimes, and economic exploitation. For example, the anti-slavery movement was the first time individuals became angry over foreign human rights violations, although some of the activists were more interested in educating slaves about Christian values than actually fighting for their emancipation. Regardless, the rise of humanitarianism involved an emancipatory spirit that was able to cut across borders (Barnett 2011, 55).

In the UK, new movements emerged demanding rectification for the wrongs of the colonialists. A policy of atonement was promoted where "colonial rulers should act as benevolent leaders, do good works that the doer may benefit" (Barnett 2011, 55). In essence, a humanitarian coalition emerged that demanded compassion in the form of public works. The British colonial effort was pitched by authorities as charity. This, coupled with the rise of an evangelical humanitarian movement, brought new perspectives on charity and social reform. Of course, many humanitarian groups remained secular but still held strong social justice convictions, while some organizations claimed that religious groups themselves were the problems.

Imperial Humanitarianism

Contemporary humanitarianism did not happen overnight. Michael Barnett (2011) identifies three stages. First, imperial humanitarianism can be understood as the first modern approach to intervention, which lasted from the early nineteenth century to World War II. These years were marked by the first wave of humanitarian organizations, including the International Committee of the Red Cross (ICRC; see the box below). The ICRC advanced the humanitarian cause by positioning itself as an independent, neutral, and impartial organization. The group's founder, Swiss businessman

Henry Dunant, had witnessed firsthand the horrors of war. He decided to take on a personal mission to change the attitudes and behavior of combatants toward the injured during conflict. Dunant's vision has been called a "moral breakthrough" in a time when war and peace remained the domains of the state (Barnett 2011, 80). Nonetheless, this era was also dominated by Western ideologies and a view that Christian understandings of the world should be expanded in the form of international justice.

The ICRC and the Birth of Humanitarian Law

The rise of **humanitarian law** has been a long and complex history. The movement's beginnings are often traced to the experience of a Swiss businessman named Henry Dunant. In 1869, Dunant had been traveling for work when he came across a violent conflict in northern Italy. The Battle of Solferino had seen the French Piedmontese army defeat Austrian forces in a conflict so brutal that Napoleon III moved to sign a peace accord with Austrian Emperor Francis Joseph I. Following the conflict, Dunant toured the battle field to gain a firsthand look at the violence and the reality that there was no glory in war. He would later write a book about the incident entitled *A Memory of Solferino*, where he described the pain and suffering experienced by all sides of the conflict, especially injured combatants.

The experience motivated Dunant to start an organization dedicated to helping victims of conflict and establishing a set of rules for governing war. Launched in 1863, the International Committee of the Red Cross lobbied governments to develop international humanitarian law (IHL), arguing that if the rules of war were not endorsed authorities would lose public support for endorsing military action as a political act. The ICRC also called for national relief societies to provide medical services to militaries. Then, in 1884, the ICRC persuaded governments to adopt the first Geneva Convention that demanded militaries care for injured soldiers regardless of the side they were fighting for.

The ICRC began as a coordinating agency rallying around its red cross emblem, which would eventually become recognizable within the theater of war. For the next half century, the Red Cross worked to establish other conventions, including those that banned chemical weapons, and advocated for rule of war at sea. The organization continues to promote humanitarian law and has actively participated in further reforms of IHL, including the post–World War II conventions that focused on civilians and prisoners. Operating under the principles of impartiality, neutrality, and independence, the ICRC has defined the modern notion of humanitarianism and will continue to do so, since it sits as the only nongovernmental organization designated with official observation status at the United Nations.

The imperial stage of colonialism also saw the emergence of new types of media, with explicit descriptions of war enabling anyone with access to a newspaper the ability to visualize the terrors of conflict. War reporting took on new meaning, with correspondents actively seeking out conflict and detailing the not-so-honorable aspects of war. Imagery of young men being left for dead on the battlefield was becoming a tough sell for nation-states that had assured the public it took care of those who sacrificed their lives for their country. A humanitarian discourse emerged where political leaders voiced interest in the movement outside the formal channels of governance. The ICRC's proposed vision to operate as an independent, impartial, and neutral organization that could offer medical assistance within the combat zone was becoming a reality. Ironically, political endorsement of the ICRC's humanitarian mission in many ways helped governments continue to legitimize the tool of war as a manageable act that could be conducted ethically with the assistance of independent medical observers.

Neo-Humanitarianism

The second era of humanitarianism as outlined by Barnett (2011) can be called *neo-humanitarianism* and occurred between World War II and the end of the Cold War. This period is defined by decolonization coupled with the rise of the United States and the Soviet Union as superpowers. A political vacuum had been left throughout much of the world when the Europeans left their colonies. For example, in 1948 the British abruptly left Ceylon (modern-day Sri Lanka) after 133 years of colonial rule; many believe, however, that the British colonialists did not adequately prepare the Sri Lankans to transition from a colonial governance model to self-rule. Similar examples of abrupt colonial departures can be seen throughout the world, leaving some commentators to suggest this may explain why some states have struggled to develop politically. Neo-humanitarianism saw the emergence of new organizations that reinforced the traditional approach of neutrality. Organizations such as Save the Children, CARE International (the Cooperative for American Remittance to Europe), World Vision, and Oxfam began championing new approaches to aid and development.

One fundamental change that occurred during this period was that Western governments were becoming more active in funding the work of humanitarians. For example, the US government funded CARE because it believed the agency was constructing a positive overseas image of Americans. Moreover, aid agencies began demanding greater political intervention in some of the world's most dire conflicts. Many humanitarian activists took on paternalistic views within the societies they were working, adopting a philosophy that they had a duty to teach the developing world how to govern itself. Of course, some of these feelings may have been grounded in guilt, considering the destructive impact of the colonial era. Nonetheless, the newly established Western aid agencies began taking a less neutral role in their work. For example, the attempted succession of the Biafra region in Nigeria had a tremendous impact on the humanitarian movement, since the Nigerian government and the Biaf-ran authorities managed to turn humanitarianism into an instrument of war.

Despite the manipulation of humanitarianism in Biafra, the ICRC refused to com-ment and continued to carry out its work under the auspices of its mission of impartial-ity, neutrality, and independence. Such a stance proved highly controversial considering the ICRC was silent on other occasions of mass atrocity and political opportunism, including the Holocaust during World War II. The ICRC's refusal to take a public stand against the violence in Nigeria led a small group of physicians within the move-ment to break away from the organization and form their own group, which became known as Médecins Sans Frontières (MSF, or Doctors Without Borders in English; see the box below).

Médecins Sans Frontières and the War in Biafra

In the spring of 1968, a group of young doctors responded to an emergency appeal by the French Red Cross. The group set out to bring medical relief to the south-ern region of Nigeria where a war for independence had been waged by separat-ists looking to form the new state of Biafra. The region had been surrounded by Nigeria's military, who effectively cut the area off from outside supplies, resulting in a widespread famine. The violence was also being presented in Western media as "genocide" after a Swiss-based public relations outfit had been hired by Biafra's government to raise awareness of their plight. Subsequently, two physicians (Max Recamier and Bernard Kouchner), along with a team of clinicians and nurses, set out to aid the ICRC in their humanitarian effort.

However, the team of six soon found the ICRC principles of neutrality, impar-tiality, and independence to be problematic in war zones. The inability to speak out against the violence proved overwhelming, especially for Kouchner, who believed such principles were outdated and served narrow political interests. For Kouchner, the Hippocratic oath that doctors take required them to speak out on behalf of victims, regardless of political sensitivities. So in December 1971, Kouchner launched Médecins Sans Frontières as a new approach to humani-tarianism where aid workers would bear witness and document the atrocities of war. A group of 300 volunteers, including 13 founding doctors and journalists, launched MSF. Four decades later, MSF operates in 28 counties and employs over 30,000 humanitarians.

Liberal Humanitarianism

Barnett's (2011) third and final humanitarian era can be referred to as *liberal humanitari-anism*, or new humanitarianism. This period began with the end of the Cold War and continues until this day. For Aiden Hehir (2013), the post–Cold War humanitarian movement coincides with the rise of the international community, globalization, and the ease of transnational communication. Yet this era has also proved controversial, with the increased politicization of humanitarianism (Ferreiro 2012). Governments who reach out to aid agencies understand that there are significant public relations gains to be had if they are seen as partnering with civil society, especially in times of crisis. New humanitarians must often pick sides as they seek to remedy the underlying causes of conflict and catastrophe, such as ethnic and religious violence, poverty, and terrorism. In fact, in the post–9/11 world, engaging with and rescuing failed states has become of paramount concern to the international community.

Aidan Hehir (2013) organizes new humanitarians into three categories: those involved with **humanitarian intervention**, humanitarian action, and military action. These interventionists rationalize the legitimacy of their actions through a moralistic and nonpartisan framework. The right to intervene is based on normative claims grounded in objectivity. For example, a foreign government may turn to the United Nations in demanding a humanitarian intervention during times of **complex emergencies**. The World Health Organization (2015a) defines complex emergencies as the combination of "internal conflict with large-scale displacements of people, mass famine or food shortage, and fragile or failing economic, political, and social institutions . . . exacerbated by natural disasters." During such catastrophes, humanitarian interventionists see foreign assistance as a moral responsibility that is removed from any biased political agenda. Rather, they see themselves as outside parties willing to support a neutral political process that seeks a sustainable solution to the crisis. Hehir has written extensively on intervention and the responsibility to protect (R2P), recently making a compelling case along with Robert Murray for the need to reform the international order (Hehir and Murray 2015). They convincingly argue that states are not, and never will be, moral actors, suggesting that regimes need incentives and restraints grounded in international law. If we agree with Hehir and Murray, humanitarians will need to think long and hard before making any decision that would see them aligned with a potential amoral entity.

NGOs, DEVELOPMENT, AND SECURITY

Each year, over US$100 billion in **official development assistance (ODA)** flows from North to South (De Haan 2009). Some of this aid will never reach those in need on account of inefficiencies in the aid delivery system, corruption, poor governance, and resource mismanagement. When governments fail to ensure security, individuals look elsewhere for protection. Organized civil society groups have come to play an increasingly important role in peacebuilding and development. The United Nations Development Programme (UNDP) estimates there are roughly 37,000 international NGOs and millions of others operating at the domestic level in countries throughout the world. For example, India alone has over 20 million registered organizations! Many of these NGOs are small-scale ventures operating with a limited budget and a small team. Thomas Weiss (2013) identifies some of these groups as mom-and-pop aid deliverers, or MONGOs (my own NGO). They may work in communities offering support for rural development assistance, while others operate through specific government grants and honorariums to deliver community services in an efficient and cost-effective way. Yet larger NGOs operate with extensive budgets and may wield more political influence. For example, there are just over 3,000 NGOs that hold consultative status with the United Nations Economic and Social Council (ECOSOC). These select organizations have been identified as leaders in their subject area and are granted the right to speak and submit an annual report in front of the UN through a civil society participation program. Launched in 1946, the program allows voluntary organizations to register as either general, special, or roster consultative status groups, giving them direct access to government representatives and the international civil service.

Many of the highly organized NGOs operate similarly to successful multinational corporations while fiercely defending their independence from governments. For example, the Christian humanitarian aid organization World Vision has an annual operating budget of more than US$1 billion, allowing the organization to operate in nearly 100 countries and employ 46,000 staff. Founded in 1950, World Vision's organizational focus is children and families living in poverty in the Global South. They raise capital through a "sponsorship-centered" scheme that encourages individual donors to maintain long-term relationships with specific families in the developing world. In 2013, the organization sponsored 4.3 million children worldwide and responded to 88 humanitarian emergencies (World Vision 2013). The far reach of such a large organization has enabled World Vision to partner with governments in releasing humanitarian aid.

Partnership programs between governments in the Global North and large-scale NGOs are on the rise. Groups such as World Vision, CARE International, and the ICRC often have more resources in the field than governments. Indeed, roughly 15 percent of global ODA is channeled through NGOs (De Haan 2009). The outsourcing of ODA allows governments quicker access to crisis zones. For example, following the aftermath of Typhoon Haiyan in the Philippines, which killed over 6,000 people, the Canadian government announced it would enter into aid partnerships with seven approved NGOs on a dollar-for-dollar matching scheme—the government would match every dollar donated to the ICRC, World Vision, CARE International, Médecins Sans Frontières, Plan International, Oxfam, Save the Children, and the United Nations Office for the Coordination of Humanitarian Affairs.

Mercy Corps is another example of an organization receiving significant government funding from the state. The Portland-based NGO receives the majority of its revenue from the US government, which it then uses to deliver humanitarian relief around the world. NGOs who receive aid from the state are forced to confront the issue of independence in their work, especially when aid recipients ask where the money comes from. Even when independence and neutrality are in question, humanitarians working for aid groups such as Mercy Corps see themselves as just that: humanitarians. For the nearly 4,000 Mercy Corps staff dedicated to relief assistance, it is very much a nonpolitical endeavor, especially in times of crisis that require emergency assistance. Given that democratic governments receive their revenue and authority from taxpayers, there is an assumption that part of these funds should be used for humanitarian purposes. From this perspective, there is no conflict with the state since government aid is essentially taxpayer aid. Still, while partnership programs are important initiatives for getting aid on the ground, they are also controversial because they tend to favor certain groups over others.

Smaller NGOs are often left out of the partnership funding model simply because they do not have the big "household names" of some of the NGOs just discussed, even though their work may be just as important. Smaller organizations can range from a few hundred to only a handful of staff. These groups must raise capital though grassroots campaigning. While they often lack the reputational pull of the bigger organizations, smaller NGOs do not have as much red tape to go through as their larger counterparts, often giving them quick and direct access to the communities where they work. Although small NGOs may be versatile and efficient, there is a risk that they may be duplicating the work of other organizations. A lack of coordination between NGOs can lead to confusion and risks undermining the long-term trajectory of development work. In many cases, the confusion is extreme, with governments unaware of who works in their communities. What's more, there are sustainability questions regarding the work of NGOs, especially when their funding runs out. For example, when South African–based PlayPumps International began advertising a simple technology that claimed it would provide water for villages in rural sub-Saharan Africa by using roundabouts found on playgrounds as water pumps, the idea gathered international attention and funding poured in from foundations, celebrities, and governments. Yet the technology proved much more expensive than originally thought, and the company was marred by serious claims that the PlayPumps where being operated using child labor. Further, many villages had not asked for the devices to be installed and preferred using the traditional hand pumps found in the areas, so they had stopped using the PlayPumps, causing them to rust and break down (Hobbes 2014). This is one example of how seemingly good ideas put forth by development organizations can fail.

NGOs may also choose not to register with a local government office to avoid bureaucratic barriers and risk exposing their work, which may be deemed sensitive by the state, such as when NGOs are investigating police torture. Groups may also face the prospect of having to pay bribes to local officials to gain access to the work area. This is a common complaint of the estimated 3,500 NGOs in Cambodia, who see the government's proposed NGO Law as another outlet for official shakedowns by requiring organizations to pay a fee. At the time of writing, the law has yet to be finalized but will likely be met with skepticism from the international aid community. Rwanda is another country trying to regulate its NGO sector with the International Center for Not-for-Profit Law identifying only 319 registered civil society organizations in a country believed to be hosting another 37,000 unregistered groups. The lack of coordination and oversight within these groups has led the government to push for a two-tiered registration system to regulate both national and international organizations (International Center for Not-for-Profit Law 2015).

Although NGOs may have legitimate concerns about official registration, there are good long-term reasons why NGOs in post-conflict societies should register. First, it encourages transparency within the industry. Unaccountable NGOs risk turning into "for-profit" associations, as has been seen in Cambodia where international personnel receive disproportionately high salaries compared to locally engaged staff (Domashneva 2013). This is one reason why the government of Rwanda has proposed to set a 20 percent funding cap on what international NGOs can spend on administration.

Even with such challenges, there are successful examples of coordination and collaboration between NGOs. For example, the Alliance for Peacebuilding is a network of over 15,000 conflict resolution practitioners hailing from roughly 80 organizations in 153 countries. The organization facilitates networking events between members through training sessions, conferences, and online workshops. Another organization working to set up collaborative peacebuilding projects is the Global Partnership for the Prevention of Armed Conflict (GPPAC). The GPPAC is an association of 15 regional networks of civil society organizations working in collaboration with ODA agencies with a focus on peacebuilding and conflict prevention. In 2014, in association with the West African Network for Peacebuilding and the Human Security Collective, GPPAC launched a program in Mali to counter the international emphasis on "military interventionism" in the country. GPPAC's program seeks to support a strong Malian civil society network and enable them to implement a human security strategy for Mali, strengthen Malian's ability to counter violent extremism, and ensure security policies are developed with the engagement of and input from civil society groups (GPPAC 2015).

There is also debate about whether NGOs should focus more on an **actor-oriented approach** or adopt a **functional approach** to development. Actor-oriented approaches focus on the ability and expertise of civil society groups. Certain approaches to development by NGOs (actors) are seen as superior to others and are therefore promoted as best practice approaches to aid delivery. Actor-oriented approaches are therefore concerned with organizations developing technocratic skills that can consistently be applied in the field. This expertise gives actors an earned right to lay claims on how NGO programs should be managed since they allegedly "know best." From this perspective, NGOs provide top-down advice to civil society. On the other hand, a functional approach to civil society calls for a variety of models to be used in the field depending on the circumstances. There is no one-size-fits-all approach, and organizations must carefully weigh which options are best depending on programming goals. The focus is on the impact of programs and service delivery while placing a high priority on the NGOs accountability to donors (Paffenholz 2010). These two approaches signal the contested views on how civil society groups should operate in the community.

When placed in a human security context, organizations must ask if donor outcomes are more important than the organization's operational strategy. For example, should a human right's NGO take money from the US Central Intelligence Agency to help end torture in South Asia? What type of donor expectations would come with such funding, and would it compromise the NGO's work? What would the communities feel if they learned that the NGO sent to help them was funded by a foreign intelligence agency? These questions highlight just a few of the complexities behind each decision a civil society group must make when it considers its operational structure.

The Functions of NGOs

Christoph Spurk (2010) identifies three aspects of civil society during armed conflict. First, war contributes to the deterioration of civil society groups through the destruction of infrastructure that would otherwise allow NGOs to operate. The destruction of the state apparatus produces fear and insecurity driven by violence within communities, therefore causing many would-be activists to flee. Second, civil society groups will resort to primitive organizational structures during times of conflict. State decay in Bosnia-Herzegovina drove civilians into ethnic-based clusters that perpetuated the violence. Although "primary groupings" of society can resort to aggression toward others, they can also offer a sense of security when the social contract has collapsed. Finally, there is the possibility that international humanitarian organizations working in conflict and post-conflict zones may further destabilize the environment by creating a false sense of security while appeasing authoritarian state interests by rebuilding under the discretion of the local regime. When NGOs take on a dominant development position they risk marginalizing local actors while remaining more accountable to their international donors than the community they serve.

Civil society performs a range of functions in conflict zones. First, monitoring is done by an array of actors, including journalists, NGOs, and citizen activists. These nonstate actors can serve as invaluable watchdogs within their community. When the state cannot or will not report crimes committed by its agents or other actors within its borders, technology such as mobile phones and wireless Internet allows activists and groups to communicate information with the world. Civil society holds the state to account and challenges the power of the sovereign through documentation. The protection of journalists and activist citizens is paramount and highlights the critical importance of the right to freedom of speech in developing societies.

Second, civil society engages in a range of advocacy activities. By highlighting, documenting, and lobbying on behalf of those who cannot, NGOs are able to stand in solidarity with victims of state persecution while pressuring stakeholders to intervene. It is now common for governments to provide official responses to high-profile NGOs that critique the state's governance ability. For example, after Amnesty International accused the state of Eritrea, one of the world's most despotic regimes, for imprisoning over 10,000 activists, the government released an official statement citing Amnesty's "smug" and "self-righteous" approach to human rights (Government of Eritrea 2013). The Eritrean case is clear evidence that the influence of NGOs in the post–Cold War era is changing. Such examples of advocacy requiring governments to release official statements also raise the public profile of NGOs while simultaneously communicating the group's activities to donors.

A third function of NGOs in conflict zones is protection. These organizations often provide clothing, food, shelter, and psychological support for victims of state-directed violence. International NGOs are able to mobilize international networks through campaigning to secure the resources needed to help those experiencing conflict. For example, the Syrian Civil War, which began 2011, has resulted in nearly 2 million displaced persons. It is the largest refugee catastrophe the world has seen since the Rwandan genocide. In dealing with the crisis, UK-based Islamic Relief has launched high-profile funding campaigns. In 2013, the organization was able to provide the following:

- 73 ambulances and mobile health clinics
- Medical treatment for 46,889 injured and sick patients
- 664,340 food parcels and vouchers
- 125,199 blankets and mattresses
- Shelter (tents, caravans, and rent support) for 20,062 people
- 5,321,423 medical disposables and pieces of equipment (Islamic Relief 2016)

Organizations such as Islamic Relief are able to bypass governments and offer protection through direct people-to-people aid. In 2005, Islamic Relief, along with a host of other NGOs, played a critical role in Pakistan following a devastating earthquake, with some analysts suggesting these groups were more effective than the government's own response (International Crisis Group 2006).

A fourth function of NGOs involves socialization, or social reconstruction, which seeks to build the capacity of individuals through education and training programs. Victims of conflict are often traumatized, and there is a high sense of mistrust between citizens. NGOs focus on community building and reintegrating individuals into society while introducing organizational structures focused on democratic processes and human rights. In addition, by developing programs that are able to empower communities to take charge of their environment while introducing tools for holding states accountable, NGOS can bring long-lasting change in post-conflict societies. For example, International Bridges to Justice, a Swiss-based anti-torture organization, works to bridge gaps between society and the justice system. The group operates around the world and has managed a successful rule of law program in Burundi. The NGO provides citizens with training manuals on the law, connects communities with lawyers, and runs youth programs. In part this is accomplished through the following activities:

- Establishing relationships with key justice-sector partners
- Organizing pro bono lawyers to directly represent clients
- Bringing together lawyers, prosecutors, magistrates, police officers, and prison officials for joint training sessions on all aspects of the legal process
- Using rights awareness campaigns to demonstrate the importance of individual legal rights, such as the right to counsel, to a fair trial, and to be free from torture
- Distributing rights awareness posters in prisons, police stations, local government offices, and other public centers, sparking an overwhelming demand for legal assistance (International Bridges to Justice 2015)

A final function of NGOs in conflict zones involves facilitation. Acting as a bridge between governments and citizens not only helps increase trust in communities, it can help improve the capacity of service delivery. NGOs are able to mediate between government stakeholders and community leaders on humanitarian grounds. International groups are able to position themselves as nonpolitical entities looking to save lives. There are different methods of communication that NGOs can use, including facilitating demands, pure mediation, as well as other types of conflict resolution. For example, the NGO International Alert works in over 25 countries round the world promoting peace by acting as a neutral third party and offering mediated settlements. The group facilitates peace processes not only in war zones, but also within the private sector by offering services to firms and communities that become embroiled in violent conflict:

> We work with companies and associated organisations to ensure that they integrate a conflict-sensitive approach in the way they operate, so they contribute to peace. This work is tailored to the specific challenges companies face, using our knowledge and skills to maximum effect. These include expert technical analysis and advice, training, conflict-sensitive strategic planning, the development of methods and tools, as well as monitoring. (International Alert 2015)

Indeed, International Alert is able to fill a gap between the local authority's inability to resolve such challenges and the community's need for lasting peace.

Moreover, citizen-based movements often led to more formal associations such as NGOs. For example, India has seen a significant rise in anti-corruption groups developing innovative approaches to tackling the problem. Although India has ratified the United Nations Convention against Corruption, the government has struggled to minimize the practices. Corruption in India is endemic and impacts everyone, including the most marginalized. For example, one official noted that the practice was leading to the deaths of children because the state lacked resources to support communities. In 2010, the Asian Human Rights Commission (AHRC) spoke with a Justice Sheela Khanna, chairperson of Madhya Pradesh State Commission of Protection of Child Rights, who referred to corruption as "irregularities" that impacted the most vulnerable youth. The AHRC quoted her as follows:

> It is true that too many children die from malnutrition each year in this country. Some of their parents also die from starvation and hunger. But the children are more vulnerable . . . one of the reasons is the widespread "irregularity" in the state and central government services . . . the Chief Minister of Madhya Pradesh state is a very kind person . . . the Nutrition Rehabilitation Centers is not a solution for the millions of malnourished children. These centers are not cost effective. But now that the centers are there we must effectively use them. My suggestion is to appoint a Brahmin priest in each of these centers and require the priest to verify the horoscope of every child brought to the center. After studying a child's horoscope if the priest is of the opinion that the child will grow into a good citizen of this country, it must be provided treatment at the center. For the rest, I would say, let us just leave them to their fate . . . if not where do we stop? (Asian Legal Resource Centre 2011)

Not only does Justice Khanna's statement demonstrate a deep dysfunctionality of the state and a total failure in protecting children, it also points to the impact of corruption in the world's largest democracy. Examples such as this have forced the government to respond by developing stronger laws, such as the 2014 Jan Lokpal Bill, which calls for an independent anti-corruption investigative body and greater protection of whistle-blowers. The law is the result of mass public demonstrations that demanded the government improve its commitment to reducing official corruption. Public distrust of government in India is fierce, with activist Anna Hazare calling it the country's "second freedom struggle." The lack of transparency and accountability has led to grass-roots citizens initiatives, such as the "I paid a bribe" movement, which provides an outlet for victims of corruption to report the bribe they were forced to pay (Campion 2011). India's struggle against corruption demonstrates how civil society can push back against government dysfunctionality and work toward improving human security.

Human Security and the Limits of NGOs

The global proliferation of NGOs over the years has not been without its critics. Aid groups advocating human security have been accused of confusing the public over their objectives, whether through the launch of a funding campaign or to promote a vague organizational cause. There are skeptics who happily point out the challenges behind humanitarianism and development. Here, we wish to highlight three areas of common critique directed at NGOs operating in the Global South. First, there is a risk that actor-oriented approaches and narrow self-serving interest do little good for the long-term development needs of communities in crisis. Second, the NGO world is largely unregulated, with organizations competing for funding that ends up being administratively top-heavy. Third, NGOs may risk undermining government capacity since many take on responsibilities that are traditionally the realm of the state. Although NGO officials are often on the front line of humanitarian work, each of these critiques holds a certain truth.

The most obvious complaint is that NGOs are undemocratic agencies that claim to speak on behalf of a wide range of constituents. They run large-scale funding campaigns to gain public and political acceptance. As mentioned above, the Canadian government and public have warmly welcomed the work of CARE International and World Vision among others to deliver Canada's humanitarian relief. Yet as Ilan Kapoor (2012) has argued, some of these high-profile groups, such as Médecins Sans Frontières and Save Darfur, are in fact "spectacle" organizations that rely on celebrity endorsements and mass campaigns. By motivating people to give to humanitarian causes using celebrity images, and by placing a human face on the plight of the marginalized, charity organizations are ironically benefiting from an aid system that does not address the structural challenges of poverty and conflict. Such campaigns motivate the public to "give now" and "don't think" about the deeper crisis at hand:

It is important to note that the spectacularization of NGOs happens not just because NGOs need and use the corporate media, but also because the media need and use them . . . Humanitarian crises are eminently newsworthy; they offer sensational stories about destruction, suffering and triumph, with easily identifiable victim and heroes/heroines. (Kapoor 2012, 87)

In other words, there is a risk that the message of humanitarianism will be lost in the spectacle of celebrity, media, and mass appeal. From this perspective, NGOs have become celebrities that the public trusts, yet these organizations naively ignore the structural challenges associated with the very poverty and marginalization that they claim to confront.

Second, the NGO sector is largely unregulated, nontransparent, and can be aggressively competitive with one another over scarce resources provided by government and bestowed by the public. As Weiss (2013) notes, coordination between NGOs through federation and consortiums is weak, while resources to improve coherence between agencies operating in the field is low. Weiss notes, "Information is shared and guidelines are developed, but no authority can be exerted over such voluntary associations" (111). Moreover, NGOs compete for funding from government and business to ensure sustainable operating budgets. The humanitarian marketplace drives NGOs to engage in behavior that would otherwise run counter to their humanist objectives. Weiss points out that some organizations are afraid to be marginalized by the "gatekeepers" to victims. They will therefore "dine with the devil" to stay in the game. Furthermore, the age of liberal humanitarianism is just as concerned with market success and organizational branding; humanitarian NGOs are very much dependent on the capitalist economic order.

A final complaint leveraged against NGOs working on human security issues is concerned with foreign charities undermining the governance capacity of local authorities. A telling example involves the work of health-focused NGOs operating in the post-conflict societies of West Africa. The recent Ebola crisis that is ravaging parts of the region offers a glimpse into how global charities have paradoxically contributed to the weakening of national health systems yet also deliver critical care to countries that are too poor to develop their own centralized authorities. As Mary Moran and Daniel Hoffman (2014) write,

What is different about the Mano River countries is their recent history of war, state collapse, and crises of governmental legitimacy. In the case of Sierra Leone and Liberia, an additional factor may be the role of multiple and diverse external humanitarian organizations in managing health care in the post-war period, effectively removing more centralized local governments from the responsibility of monitoring and coordinating a single health care policy. This is not to say that humanitarian organizations have not been the heroic frontlines of the fight against the disease [Ebola], or that they have not fought for the world's attention, often ungranted until it was almost too late. However, the consequences of leaving the health care of millions of people in the hands of nongovernmental, private organizations is another lesson learned from this crisis.

Indeed, the situation in many of the Ebola-stricken countries is destructive and a direct consequence of an entrenched distrust between the public and government. With NGOs unable to cope and political leadership failing to ease fears, citizens have turned to each other for security. In Liberia, for example, Theresa Ammann (2014) notes "The failure of the GoL [Government of Liberia] not only reaffirmed distrust but also created a power vacuum in which communities are attempting to ensure security that the state fails to provide. Such actions include boy scouts awareness campaigns, self-quarantining, or vigilante groups that expel or quarantine infected people." Although the primary complaint is toward the Liberian government, observers of the aid versus trade debate will be quick to point out that NGOs operating in the country may have indirectly contributed to a weakening of the local health care system by removing the responsibility from government.

Although these challenges point to the limits of NGOs, humanitarian advocates should not lose perspective that these groups are on the frontline of aid delivery. While healthy skepticism toward these groups may be warranted, critics also need to remember that there is a market for such organizations considering many governments lack the capacity to provide security for their citizens. Aid groups play a critical role in promoting development, peace, and human security in environments where government is absent.

CONCLUSION

This chapter argues that civil society plays a critical role in contributing to human security in the developing world. By providing disaster relief, long-term humanitarian aid programs, and serving as champions of the marginalized, NGOs act as transnational advocates of human security. Often, NGOs provide much-needed aid under the harshest of conditions. In some cases, they act as the only life source for vulnerable populations long forgotten by the state, such as the stateless Rohingya people in Myanmar.

There is, however, major controversies around the role of NGOs, including the history of foreign intervention, NGO transparency and accountability, as well as the possibility that such groups undermine state capacity. There can also be distrust between governments in the South, who may fear NGOs represent the interests of the West, while North-based aid groups may hold contempt for governments in the South, who they perceive as corrupt. Moreover, it is not uncommon to hear NGOs being criticized for refusing to incorporate local advice into their operations; rather, some may insist on sticking to a rigid development strategy drafted by planners far removed from the local context.

Such criticisms are legitimate, and the aid versus trade debate will continue to shape the discourse around the role of NGOs in post-conflict societies. When the state does not or cannot provide the necessities of life, NGOs serve as important channels of aid delivery and advocates for human security. It is impossible to ignore the positive impact many international NGOs have in the developing world, especially in times of crisis.

KEY TERMS

Accountability; Actor-Oriented Approach; Advocacy; Colonial Philanthropy; Complex Emergencies; Cultural Genocide; Eurocentrism; Facilitation; Functional Approach; Global Civil Society; Humanitarian Intervention; Humanitarian Law; Imperialism; Monitoring; Nongovernmental Organizations; Official Development Assistance; Partnership Programs; Residential School Policy; Scramble for Africa; Slavery; Transparency; Triangular Trade

FURTHER READING

Anheier, H., M. Glasius, and M. Kaldor, eds. 2001. *Global Civil Society*. New York: Oxford University Press.

Berman, S. 1997. "Civil Society and the Collapse of the Weimar Republic." *World Politics* 49 (3): 401–29. http://dx.doi.org/10.1353/wp.1997.0008.

Carothers, Thomas. 1999. "Civil Society." *Foreign Policy* 117: 18–29. http://dx.doi.org/10.2307/1149558.

De Haan, A. 2009. *How the Aid Industry Works: An Introduction to International Development*. Boulder, CO: Kumarian Press.

Kapoor, I. 2012. *Celebrity Humanitarianism: The Ideology of Global Charity*. New York: Routledge.

Lambert, D., and A. Lester. 2004. "Geographies of Colonial Philanthropy." *Progress in Human Geography* 28 (3): 320–41. http://dx.doi.org/10.1191/0309132504ph489oa.

Lipschutz, R.D. 1992. "Reconstructing World Politics: The Emergence of Global Civil Society." *Millennium* 21 (3): 389–420. http://dx.doi.org/10.1177/03058298920210031001.

Paffenholz, T., ed. 2010. *Civil Society & Peacebuilding: A Critical Assessment*. London: Lynne Rienner Publishers.

Pakenham, T. 1992. *Scramble for Africa*. New York: Harper Collins.

Walker, J.W.S.G., and A.S. Thompson, eds. 2008. *Critical Mass: The Emergence of Global Civil Society*, vol. 5. Waterloo, ON: Wilfrid Laurier Univ. Press.

Weiss, Thomas G. 2013. *Humanitarian Business*. Cambridge: Polity Press.

WEBSITES

Centre for Humanitarian Dialogue: www.hdcentre.org

European Peacebuilding Liaison Office: www.eplo.org

Incore: International Conflict Research Institute: www.incore.ulst.ac.uk

International Alert: www.international-alert.org

International Committee of the Red Cross: www.icrc.org

International Rescue Committee: www.rescue.org

Médecins Sans Frontières/Doctors Without Borders: www.msf.org

SIPRI: Stockholm International Peace Research Institute: www.sipri.org

Transparency International: www.transparency.org

War Child: www.warchild.org

World Social Forum: www.fsm2016.org/en

Chapter 6

INTERVENTION AND
POST-CONFLICT STRATEGIES
IN HUMAN SECURITY AND
PEACEBUILDING

On 20th July 1995, young survivors from other villages came to our town. They told us they had seen rivers of blood, and piles of human bodies. We did not want to believe them. Two days later, on 23rd July, the Serbian army came to our village, and began their killing spree. They started from the first house on the road, and continued until they had burnt every house to the ground. In the first hour, they massacred 214 people. Then they arrived at my house. First, they shot my dog. Then they killed our horses. It all happened so quickly—one minute we were sitting peacefully at home, and the next our village was being destroyed. After that, they arrested my brother and me. Then they threw my mother and two sisters out, and set the house alight. My father had gone to visit friends, but because we lived in such a small town, the news spread quickly. Unbeknown to me, my father and his friends had rushed home thinking we were still inside. Just as they arrived, the Serb army soldiers shot them dead on the spot and threw their bodies in the water reservoir outside our house. Our neighbour, Hawa, suffered even greater loss. The Serbs massacred her husband and six sons on that day . . . It is astounding to me that a mere 20 km from me lies a border to a European Union country. And yet, we were subjected to the most brutal kind of torture under the watchful gaze of Europe and the world.

Sudbin Musić, Survivor Testimony from the Srebrenica
Genocide (Remembering Srebrenica 2014)

INTRODUCTION

In 2011, NATO forces acting under the authority of UN Security Council Resolution 1973 carried out a strategic military intervention in North Africa. Western governments, along with a handful of allies, set out to establish a "no-fly zone" over Libya to end a brutal assault by that country's leader, Muammar Gaddafi, against his own people. Fears that the Libyan government was carrying out war crimes against its citizens prompted a fierce and swift international response to end the conflict. Lasting just over seven months, the intervention was hailed as a model for future humanitarian military missions. Yet some would argue the intervention in Libya brought long-term consequences, including a deep sense of human insecurity and disunity while exposing the country's eastern borders to outside terrorist forces such as the Islamic State of Iraq and the Levant (ISIS). While it is too early to assess what lasting impact the Libyan intervention will have on the country and its people, questions surrounding the morality and ethics of intervention are worth serious consideration.

In this chapter we discuss humanitarian intervention and the responsibility to protect civilians and strangers in conflict and post-conflict scenarios from a human security perspective. We explore mitigation strategies such as conflict resolution and mediation and how these relate to the field and practice of human security. What about special victims such as women and children? How can restorative justice, reintegration, truth, and reconciliation play a role in peacebuilding and rebuilding communities? We begin by revisiting the concept of peacebuilding through a historical perspective while framing it within a humanitarian context.

THE RISE AND RISE OF PEACEBUILDING

The ideas and practice of **peacebuilding** do not have a long pedigree considering the amount of violent conflict we have witnessed over the last 100 years. The term itself emerged in the 1970s in the work of Johan Galtung (1969), who wanted to create peacebuilding structures aimed at sustainable peace by addressing the "root causes" of violent conflict. Furthermore, Galtung argued that we should support the internal home-grown abilities of those living within conflict zones rather than impose external capacities for management and conflict resolution. Galtung was one of the original proponents of the peace and conflict studies discipline, devoting all of his life to the field. Thereafter the term lost some of its coherence, covering many dimensions from disarmament to the restoration and rebuilding of institutions in strife-torn societies.

In the former UN Secretary-General Boutros Boutros-Ghali's 1992 report, "An Agenda for Peace," peacebuilding was redefined as a way to solidify peace and avoid backtracking into violent conflict. The UN Brahimi Report of 2000 continued in this theme, defining the term as "activities undertaken on the far side of conflict to reassemble the foundations of peace and provide the tools for building on those foundations something that is more than just the absence of war" (UN Peacebuilding Commission

2015b). By 2007, the UN had changed its views again (or made them more coherent, depending on your point of view), referring to it as

a range of measures targeted to reduce the risk of lapsing or relapsing into conflict by strengthening national capacities at all levels for conflict management, and to lay the foundations for sustainable peace and development. Peacebuilding strategies must be coherent and tailored to specific needs of the country concerned, based on national ownership, and should comprise a carefully prioritized, sequenced, and therefore relatively narrow set of activities aimed at achieving the above objectives. (UN Peacebuilding Fund 2011)

Throughout this text we argue that peacebuilding is a crucial element in the post-conflict management process and is intimately linked to human security in restoring these societies. There are several aspects to consider here, including a transformation in terms of taking broken relationships and structures and changing them in an effort to limit and even end the conflict. Peacebuilding is also not only concerned with **post-conflict development** but also pre-conflict activities, which seek to ameliorate and resolve the issues between different parties. These measures can include reconciliation, **restorative justice**, and developing new institutions that have the capacity to govern effectively. Because of globalization we have seen a plethora of these kinds of programs develop in the post–Cold War period and increasingly the development of an industry committed to advancing humanitarian goals and protecting vulnerable people.

MILITARY INTERVENTION FOR HUMANITARIAN PURPOSES

Can a national military be used for humanitarian purposes? This question was posed by Eve Massingham (2009), who concludes that while **military intervention** will always be accompanied by political self-interest, the idea of foreign governments believing there is a responsibility to protect the vulnerable in far off lands is a positive development. The controversy around intervention came to prominence in the 1990s, specifically in the period after the end of the Cold War. The term *intervention* is used to describe the exercise of authority in the territory of one state by another, usually without the consent of the latter. It's a much stronger term than simply interfering in another country's affairs. When we refer to **humanitarian intervention** we are providing the concept with a set of normative values. In this sense, we agree with Stephen Roach, Martin Griffiths, and Terry O'Callaghan (2014, 160) who write, "Humanitarian intervention refers to (forcible) action by one state or a group of states in the territory of another state without the consent of the latter, undertaken on humanitarian grounds or in order to restore constitutional governance." Of course this is a very broad definition, and many states might and will use it to justify intervention in violating the sovereignty of another state, and those states on the receiving end certainly do. In other words, it could have a political rationale. The important point is that just before the end of the Cold War humanitarian intervention was still regarded as an unlawful form of intervention and outlawed under the United Nations Charter because it undermined state sovereignty. Sovereignty or the idea that the state maintains control over its territory and affairs was at odds with this new doctrine, which argued that people had the right to be protected if their own government could not or was not willing to do so. It was effectively prompted by increasing levels of violence and hardship in the developing world.

After the end of the Cold War, the rationale for viewing this intrusion on sovereignty as an illegal type of intervention began to dissipate. As old regimes and authoritarian governments broke up in Eastern Europe (specifically the former Yugoslavia) and many conflict-ridden developing states, the international community began to demand more aggressive humanitarian interventions to resolve these difficult issues. Peacekeeping missions sponsored by the UN were seen as weak and vacillating in the use of force to solve problems.

But humanitarian interventions seemed to be on the increase in the post–Cold War period. One of the most often cited is the Australian-led intervention during the 1999 crisis in East Timor, which has been considered a success story in responding to a massive humanitarian emergency. It has been seen as part of the wider acceptance by the international community of the duty to protect innocent civilians suffering major human rights violations. We are not saying that countries do not intervene in other countries for purely altruistic reasons, which would be the ideal case for involvement in foreign conflicts, but many countries act on their national interests. Nevertheless, military intervention for humanitarian purposes has become more acceptable over time.

The Rwandan Genocide: A Case Study

All over the world, there were people like me sitting in offices, day after day, who did not fully appreciate the depth and the speed with which you were being engulfed in this unimaginable terror.

Former US President Bill Clinton (1998)
on the Rwandan genocide

The Rwandan genocide clearly stands as the main example of how this type of weak response in the post–Cold War period failed, and it led to enormous criticism of the UN. The rationale for humanitarian intervention needed to become more legitimate and stronger in terms of what it could solve. It needed teeth, and the failure of the UN in this case showed that while the rhetoric was there the political will to intervene was absent.

The background is fairly well known now, but worth repeating for context. On 6 April 1994, a plane carrying Rwandan President Juvénal Habyarimana was shot down above Kigali (the capital of Rwanda). Habyarimana's death sparked a vicious campaign by extremist Hutus to exterminate Rwanda's Tutsi minority. The differences between the Hutus and Tutsis are historical, stemming from Belgian colonial rule in Rwanda, and have been subject to manipulation by various powers over time, even by President Habyarimana to strengthen his position among fellow Hutus. The Hutu killing campaign that occurred after the president's death lasted three months, until the Rwandan Patriotic Front, under the leadership of now-President Paul Kagame, captured the capital in July 1994. The Rwandan genocide became known as one of the most ruthless and violent episodes of the late twentieth century.

In a period of just over 100 days, roughly 800,000 Tutsis were slaughtered by machete-wielding Hutu extremists who were targeting them and any other political opposition. Neighbors attacked neighbors; families massacred one another as the degree of bitter fighting escalated. UNICEF estimated that at least 300,000 of these victims were children, with at least 95,000 children orphaned by the killings. Moreover, roughly 250,000 women were raped within the three-month period. In addition, tens of thousands of Tutsi women were kidnapped for sex slavery. Rape and sexual humiliation were used as a tool of war against Tutsi women, Hutu wives of Tutsi men, and Hutu women who were suspected of aiding Tutsis. The tactics included rape, various forms of genital mutilation, the hacking off of breasts, sexual slavery, forced abortion, and forced marriage.

These atrocities were compounded by the fact that nearly 2 million refugees were created following the genocide, displaced to surrounding countries such as Burundi and the Democratic Republic of the Congo. The savagery of the genocide was seen as something from the dark ages, since it contained all the elements of barbarism and showed the depth of ethnic and tribal loyalties still engrained in the African context. While the conflict had roots in colonial times and practices of ethnic power imbalances, there was little effort made to prevent it or stop the killings when they got underway. Most UN peacekeepers along with the Belgians (the former colonial power) were evacuated when 10 Belgian military personnel were killed. The bottom line was that the UN gave no mandate for the peacekeeping forces to intervene and stop the killing. There was a severe lack of political will, and this remains a problem that the UN has in any humanitarian intervention it undertakes to this day. Canadian General Romeo Dallaire was in charge of a small peacekeeping mission in Rwanda from 1993, and he warned the UN in 1994 that mass murder was imminent. His warnings and pleas for an increase in forces to prevent the tragedy unfolding went unheeded. As Dallaire stated later in his biography,

> I know there is a God because in Rwanda I shook hands with the devil. I have seen him, I have smelled him and I have touched him. I know the devil exists and therefore I know there is a God.

Dallaire's life work is an indictment of the failure of humanitarian intervention in places like Rwanda and the need to strengthen the international community's response to these kinds of crime.

The genocidal implications went well beyond Rwanda's borders, spilling over into neighboring states seriously and destabilizing the Congo. As a result nearly 5 million people died in the conflict. The Rwandan government, run now by the Tutsis who formed the Rwandan Patriotic Front in 1959, has invaded the Congo several times on the basis of the alleged collusion of the government with the Hutu militias. President Paul Kagame has also been accused of waging a program of assassination against his political enemies inside and outside of Rwanda.

More than 20 years after the Rwandan genocide the conflict has been transformed and changed, but not ended. Hutu combatants in the Congo have formed the Democratic Forces for the Liberation of Rwanda (FDLR), a rebel group that remains a serious threat to security and stability in the region (Global Security 2015). What's more, as the International Criminal Tribunal for Rwanda carries out its mandate, the horrors of the war live on in the minds of both perpetrator and victim, who are now living side by side in the community. The conflict will haunt Rwandan society for generations to come.

RESPONSIBILITY TO PROTECT

I also believe that, if we are to take human rights seriously, we must embrace the concept of "the responsibility to protect" as a basis for collective action to prevent and stop instances of genocide, war crimes, and crimes against humanity. This is not meant as a way to bypass sovereignty, since each State remains, first and foremost, responsible for protecting its citizens. But when national authorities are unwilling or unable to do so, the international community, through the Security Council, should be able to act, and must be ready to do so.

Message to the Council of Europe Summit, Warsaw, 16 May 2005,
delivered by **Veira Vike-Freiberga** (2005), President of Latvia
and Envoy of the Secretary-General for the World Summit

When we discuss humanitarian intervention, we are discussing different levels and aspects that may be happening in close connection with each other. Until the late 1980s the most important doctrine in international relations was based on respect for state sovereignty; in fact, the UN Charter established that force could only be used in cases of self-defense. By the early 1990s, however, human rights had become, at least for a short time, the focus of attention in international relations, strengthening the case for humanitarian intervention and the protection of civilians in conflict.

Thereafter we see the development of an emerging norm that countries had a moral **responsibility to protect** (which is often shortened as **R2P**) the security of populations who were in grave danger elsewhere. Humanitarian intervention was seen as instrumentally important in two scenarios: (1) in failed states where the disintegration of government and society places the population in danger, and (2) in the case of dictatorial, unjust governments that are guilty of gross violations of human rights against their populations. In both cases public opinion, stunned into action by media depictions of human slaughter and suffering, was used to push governments to proactively provide some resolution to these difficulties.

Today, there are many international law experts and politicians who think it is more appropriate to talk about the "right to protect" rather than the "right to intervene," especially after the lack of action to impede the massacre in Rwanda and the military actions undertaken by NATO in Kosovo and the United States in Iraq, both of which occurred without the approval of the UN Security Council.

The doctrine of R2P is connected to other ideas of humanitarian intervention and the protection of people who face grave risks where they live. From this point of view, we have scenarios where we care more about the stance of those needing help. It also helps to focus attention on why intervention only takes place when the state concerned is unable to protect its own population.

The Beginning of R2P

The norm of the responsibility to protect was borne out of the international community's failure to respond to tragedies such as the Rwandan genocide in 1994 and the massacre in Srebrenica in Bosnia-Herzegovina the following year. Kofi Annan, who was assistant secretary-general at the UN Department for Peacekeeping Operations during the Rwandan genocide, was frustrated with the international community's failure to respond in an adequate and preventative way. In 2000, and in his capacity as UN secretary-general, Annan wrote the report "We the Peoples: The Role of the United Nations in the 21st Century," in which he posed the following questions: "If humanitarian intervention is, indeed, an unacceptable assault on sovereignty, how should we respond to a Rwanda, to a Srebrenica—to gross and systematic violations of human rights that offend every precept of our common humanity?" (Annan 2000b, 48).

Let's review the facts in the Srebrenica massacre, which is considered Europe's worst atrocity since World War II. In 2014, a Dutch court ruled that the Netherlands was liable for the killings of more than 300 Bosniak (Bosnian Muslim) men and boys at Srebrenica in Bosnia-Herzegovina in July 1995, when a battalion of Dutch peace-keepers was stationed there. The men and boys were among 5,000 Bosniaks, mostly women and children, sheltering with Dutch UN peacekeepers. At the same time the Dutch state was cleared over the deaths of more than 7,000 other men killed in and around Srebrenica.

A case was launched by relatives of the victims under the name "Mothers of Srebrenica." The Hague district court said that the Dutch peacekeeping forces, Dutchbat, did not do enough to protect more than 300 of the Bosniaks and should have been aware of the potential for genocide to be committed. It made the point that the Dutch state must accept some degree of responsibility for what happened and pay compensation to the families of the victims.

But the court stopped short of holding the Netherlands liable for the fate of the majority of men killed in Srebrenica, saying that many of the male refugees at the time had not fled to the UN compound but "fled to the woods in the vicinity of Srebrenica."

During the 1992–95 war, Bosniaks from the surrounding area sought refuge in the town of Srebrenica as the Bosnian Serb army carried out a campaign of ethnic cleansing, expelling non-Serb populations. The UN declared Srebrenica a "safe area" for civilians in 1993. It fell in July 1995, after more than two years under siege. Thousands of Bosniaks went to the UN base just outside Srebrenica at Potocari. However, the Dutch soldiers told them they would be safe and handed the men and boys over to the Bosnian Serb army. The massacres destroyed a great deal of faith in the ability of the UN to protect innocent civilians in times of conflict.

ICISS (The International Commission on Intervention and State Sovereignty)

The Canadian state has invested heavily in the human security nexus from the beginning and was keen to expand humanitarian values. In September 2000 the **International Commission on Intervention and State Sovereignty (ICISS)** was established to try to answer these issues and questions. In February 2001, at the third round table meeting of the ICISS in London, prominent figures suggested the phrase *responsibility to protect* be used instead of *right to intervene* or *obligation to intervene* to maintain a degree of duty and responsibility to act to resolve humanitarian crises.

In 2001 the commission released a report titled *The Responsibility to Protect.* In a radical reformulation of the meaning of state sovereignty, the report argued that sovereignty not only entailed rights but also responsibilities, specifically the state's responsibility to protect its people from major violations of human rights. The ICISS report further asserted that where a state was "unable or unwilling" to protect its people, the responsibility should shift to the international community and "the principle of non-intervention yields to the international responsibility to protect" (Evans and Sahnoun 2001). This meant that "sovereignty" was moved from being a "right" to a "responsibility" and in effect a dual responsibility shared by the state and the international community. The report concluded that there were six criteria that needed to be reached before any intervention on this scale could be implemented (see the box below).

Six Criteria for Justifying Intervention

1. **Just cause**—Is the threat a "serious and irreparable harm occurring to human beings?"
2. **Right intention**—Is the main intention of the military action to prevent human suffering, or are there other motives?
3. **Last resort**—Has every other measure besides military invention been taken into account? (This does not mean that every measurement has to be applied and failed, but that there are reasonable grounds to believe that only military action would work in the situation.)
4. **Legitimate authority**—Do the interveners have a legal right to decide the proportionality of intervention and what means should be applied?
5. **Proportional means**—Are the minimum necessary military means applied to secure human protection?
6. **Reasonable prospect**—Is it likely that military action will protect human life, and are the consequences of this action certain not to be worse than no action at all?

The responsibility to protect has a recent historical pedigree. It is seen as an emerging norm that sovereignty is not just an international right that states can hide behind. States are seen as ultimately responsible for protecting their populations from mass-atrocity crimes—namely genocide, crimes against humanity, war crimes, and ethnic cleansing, among others. And if they cannot secure their populations it falls to the international community to complete the task. R2P rests on three foundational "pillars":

1. A state has a responsibility to protect its population from genocide, war crimes, crimes against humanity, and ethnic cleansing.

2. The international community has a responsibility to assist the state to fulfill its primary responsibility.

3. If the state manifestly fails to protect its citizens from the four crimes cited previously and peaceful measures have failed, the international community has the responsibility to intervene through coercive measures, such as economic sanctions. Military intervention is considered the last resort.

While R2P is a norm and not a law, it is grounded in international law, especially the laws relating to sovereignty, peace and security, human rights, and armed conflict. It provides a framework for using tools that already exist (i.e., mediation, early warning mechanisms, economic sanctions) to prevent mass atrocities. Moreover, states are not alone—civil society organizations, states, regional organizations, and international institutions all have a role to play in the R2P process. The authority to employ the last resort and intervene militarily rests solely with the United Nations Security Council. So really R2P means that states should show the moral courage and political will to protect human security and act upon this responsibility. The consequences of such failure are too difficult in this version to contemplate. If we assess the doctrine of R2P from a conceptual viewpoint, we can argue that it is congruent with traditional security perspectives. It's not really displacing the role of the state or the military to oversee the protection of human security. Indeed, it's like pouring new wine into old bottles, the new wine being human security (and its protection), and the old bottle representing traditional state practice.

Criticisms of R2P

Criticisms of R2P include the view that interventions are often used in an alarmist and political manner that seeks to conceal the real strategic motives, thus simply becoming another name for proxy wars. Interventions, this version argues, are selective and based on preconceived strategic interests rather than genuine humanitarian grounds. Alex Bellamy (2008a, 2008b) argues that the prevention of conflict before it begins and the rebuilding of countries after they have endured war and other conflict have been neglected in favor of the focus on the reaction to the initial political violence at the start of the conflict.

The ICISS R2P report states that "the primary purpose of the intervention must be to halt or avert human suffering." To allow for this, the report provided certain criteria that must be met before military intervention should be used:

1. Military intervention should always take place on a collective or multilateral rather than single-country basis. This helps to provide it with legitimacy and credibility.

2. An assessment of whether and to what extent the intervention is actually supported by the people for whose benefit the intervention is intended should be completed. Are the recipients supporting the intervention?

3. An assessment of whether and to what extent the opinion of other countries in the region has been taken into account and is supportive should also be completed.

As discussed, there are multiple intentions and mixed motives on all sides. The critics have been fairly relentless in questioning the nature of R2P, asking if it is really designed to protect human security.

Lou Pingeot and Wolfgang Obenland (2014) have concluded that R2P does not provide a good answer to the central question it is supposed to address: How best to prevent and, if prevention fails, respond to large-scale human rights violations and killings? They argue that it is particularly difficult and dangerous as an idea because it combines arguments and proposals that mix widely accepted notions (that states have a responsibility toward their citizens) with more contentious views (that military intervention is an appropriate tool to protect civilians). Moreover, it ignores the real need to devote attention and time to prevention. They stress that legal instruments and institutions already in place for crisis prevention and management are being underused and clearly would benefit R2P without undermining the basic peaceful dispute settlement or sovereignty of individual states. They are skeptical of R2P as a fail-safe mechanism, easily called on when any crisis threatens to get out of hand and easily abused by the powers that be as a political tool to further their interests.

The Rationale for Intervention

In practical terms at least three aspects of humanitarian intervention are worth noting, in terms of rationale:

1. The interventions are not intended to be long term, but to respond to an emergency/crisis in human security by providing a quick solution to a potential disaster. In that sense they can be distinguished from long-term colonial ventures. They are not designated to solve the basic root social, political, and economic causes of the conflict, but rather fix an immediate problem in the conflict. This differentiates them from long-term interventions and allows them to be seen as a more rational solution. If we look at the Libyan intervention, it directly fits with this explanation.

2. There are multiple and complex goals in the decision to intervene on a humanitarian basis. Finding out these goals and separating them (if they can be separated) underscores the difficulty of the task. And as we have seen in the case of

nonintervention as in the case of Rwanda, there are many other long-term side effects, like major displacement of people.

3. The interventions are particularly connected to severe violations of human rights, and these can typically be distinguished by political motivations and rationales. Failed states that cannot protect their own populations might be the targets for humanitarian intervention, and often are; Libya was a good example of such a selective intervention. Countries where poverty, economic stagnation, and severe conditions exist are not prime targets of intervention per se. There has to be a political and human rights rationale (the use of chemical weapons in Syria, for instance, though in that case political pragmatism won over intervention). In Syria the complexity of the regional and global players taking part, with Russia still seeking to influence Middle East policy, and the United States and the West in general trying to maintain its position of dominance means that innocents get caught in the geopolitical crossfire.

In the late 1990s Kofi Annan, recognizing the failure of doctrine, placed at least three conditions for the legitimacy of intervention: (1) acts of genocide, (2) authorization by the UN for action, and (3) multilateral participation. By then it was too late to turn back the clock on Rwanda, but slowly the UN began to recognize the mistakes it had made that led to the deaths of hundreds of thousands and the continuing desperate insecurity of many more.

Today there is a fairly wide consensus (at least in the West) that humanitarian military intervention is justified, though real politicking by major powers still has an important effect. The question is, when and for what reasons? There are some clear-cut examples where intervention has been seen to be justified. Some have also pointed to the **just war theory**—it is the right thing to do—which is especially espoused by those who are victims of an attack on their soil. Here are a few examples of situations where intervention was deemed justifiable:

1. In 1979, Tanzania invaded Uganda to bring an end to the murderous regime of the dictator Idi Amin. Amin was responsible for killing nearly 300,000 real and imagined political opponents between 1971 and 1979. In 1978, after almost a decade of increasing hostilities, Uganda invaded Tanzania in an effort to annex the Kagera region. The war, which is typically known as the Liberation War in Uganda and the Kagera War in Tanzania, was fought between the two countries between 1978 and 1979 and resulted in the final overthrow of Idi Amin.

2. Between 1978 and 1979, Vietnam intervened in neighboring Cambodia to try and end a genocide started by the Khmer Rouge in 1975. This genocide killed 3 million people according to the Vietnamese, though at the time other estimates

put the figure lower at around 1.7 to 2 million. There is little doubt, however, that the Cambodian "killing fields" represented one of the great tragedies of the 1970s, and people are still being brought to trial today for these heinous acts. In 1991, the conflict finally came to an end and authority in Cambodia was divided between the UN Transitional Authority in Cambodia (UNTAC) and various political factions. Finally, in 1993, after overseeing elections, UNTAC saw the completion of the transition to a new Cambodian government.

3. Following the Cold War in the 1990s, NATO conducted humanitarian interventions in Bosnia and Kosovo, which had been subject to ethnic cleansing by Serbia. In the town of Srebrenica, for instance, which was lightly protected by Dutch soldiers, the Bosnian Serb forces killed 7,500 Bosnian Muslims in what was essentially a UN safe zone. By 1997, the NATO bombing of Serbia had produced high numbers of civilian casualties, which called the practice into question. However, it was through incidents like this that humanitarian intervention was initiated to avoid more massacres and civilian casualties.

It should be emphasized that R2P is seen in many ways as a last resort to protect human security, and the military (a traditional guarantor of state security) is seen as indispensable in providing people with human security. Some have even argued that it provided Canada with the opportunity to rethink the traditional role of its military and enable it to work in these new emerging norms on a global basis.

HUMAN SECURITY, INTERVENTION, AND SYRIA

One of the cases for humanitarian intervention that has been controversial is whether the international community (or indeed the United States) should intervene in the civil war in Syria, which has been going on since 2012. With over 100,000 people killed since the fighting began, and hundreds of thousands of refugees fleeing war-torn areas, the question remains of why the conflict in Syria has lasted so long without some intervention. The answer, to some extent, lies in the volatility of the situation, the fact that Russia has lost most of its influence in the post–Cold War period and still sees Syria as part of its sphere of influence, and the sheer complexity of the ethnic mixture. Syria has always been a crossroads in the Middle East for traders and different groups. Syria, which had been under French control, stepped out of the imperial shadow in 1946 and gained its independence. But instability was still prevalent. For a brief period in the late 1950s it joined with Egypt in a union, but an army coup put an end to this, and the pan-Arab Nationalist Ba'ath group took power in 1963 (this was the same kind of party/organization that ruled Iraq for decades). The Alawites, a subset of the Shia group, assumed power, and in 1970 President Hafez al-Assad ruled with an authoritarian fist in what was essentially a police and military state that liked to be anti-Western at home and interfere in neighboring Lebanese politics.

The Assad government dealt ferociously with any political opposition, killing thousands of opponents and dissidents from the regime. After the death of Hafez al-Assad in 2000, the anticipated liberalization failed to occur, despite some cosmetic political reforms. Syria's most recent political history has seen the trend of strong male rulers continue, which has initiated a family dynasty. Hafez's son, Bashar al-Assad, a Western-educated doctor, took over and followed in his father's footsteps. The Arab Spring in 2012 took everyone by surprise, and many saw their chance to challenge the government. The resulting heavy-handed put-down of demonstrators and protesters only encouraged the many different opposition groups to organize their fight against the Ba'athist regime. As of 2015, the conflict has developed into a civil war with over a hundred opposition groups organizing themselves along military and paramilitary lines to fight the regime.

Does the international community have a responsibility to intervene in conflicts such as those raging in Syria? On the one hand, military intervention has the ability to bring an end to hostilities, or at least create conditions of calm while combatants work toward a peaceful settlement. Foreign intervention can also target the expanding role and influence of ISIS, which has wreaked havoc on the region. On the other hand, it may be unrealistic to assume a sustainable peace can be achieved with such a diverse range of actors fighting each other, and there is also the serious risk of destabilizing the country even further, as was witnessed in Libya. What's more, a foreign intervention could prove disastrous for relations on the Security Council, since China and Russia have categorically rejected such an option.

In the end, it's impossible to predict what long-term, unintended consequences can emerge from intervening in Syria's civil war. Yet as will be discussed below, political posturing by members of the UN Security Council and their continued failure to find a solution to the violence has completely shattered any hope of achieving human security in Syria.

The Politics of Stalemate: How Not to End Conflict

As noted by former UK Foreign Secretary David Miliband, President Assad's forces and rebel fighters are locked in a destructive stalemate. The country is now in political, social, and ethnic chaos with many of the opposition's political leaders hopelessly divided. Key world and regional players, such as the United States and Russia, have been unable to move beyond Cold War posturing and have found themselves in a stalemate over how to approach any resolution to the crisis. Within this, Islamist and jihadist fighters took advantage of this power vacuum, enabling President Assad to portray himself as the last hope for stability. ISIS, for instance, now controls large parts of Syrian territory.

Monzer Akbik, chief of staff to the head of the opposition Syrian National Coalition, was highly critical of what he sees as the West's impotence over the crisis. "You could have saved tens of thousands of lives if the international community had taken action, either in 2011 or in 2013 when the chemical weapons were used," he says. "Today, Assad is still carpet-bombing. He is still torturing people to death. He is still committing war crimes. And still there is no action whatsoever from the international community" (quoted in Robbins 2014).

Some politicians following the Syrian crisis have now decried the decision to not intervene. "If a policy of non-intervention produces what we've seen in Syria, is that genuinely better than the consequences of intervention?" asked Alistair Burt, British foreign office minister responsible for Syria until October 2013. And yet who knows? We have seen interventions in many places that have not produced the desired results and indeed have exacerbated the conflict.

Syria represents a nightmare for observers of its human security situation. Wracked by civil war and political violence in the last several years and with the body count now over 100,000, it is a humanitarian crisis that will be difficult to control even if intervention happens now. In fact, it is likely that intervention would exacerbate the conflict. Syria's economic situation is becoming dire as it appears to disintegrate. The international community's failure to act, followed by the resignation of its peace envoy, Kofi Annan, is simply another sign of the desperate situation that has developed over a conflict that appears unsolvable in the immediate future and may be intractable in the long range. Annan's replacement, Lakhdar Brahimi, a former foreign minister for Algeria, is speaking from experience when he describes Syria as "a civil war." And in civil wars in the developing world, rarely is there a happy ending, particularly when those wars tend to have ethnic and sectarian dimensions.

Three things are really at stake in the crisis and how it will affect human security: (1) the protection of vulnerable individuals and civilians in the war, (2) the dire consequences for regional instability as a result, and (3) the risks for minority and ethnic groups who are caught up in the conflict, both within the country and across the Syrian border. All of these facets are increasingly overlapping with one another.

The real problem is the fact that thousands are fleeing Syria to neighboring countries, putting enormous strain on their already weak resources and fragile economies. There are no real safe zones within Syria anymore. Hundreds of thousands of Syrians have fled their homes looking for shelter from both the government and rebel forces who desperately seek to control the large cities of Damascus and Aleppo among others. The repercussions for regional stability here could be complex and dramatic. Some think the war is becoming a proxy struggle between Shiite Iran and the Sunni states of Turkey and the Arab Middle East, if respective weapons flows are anything to go by. If the Sunnis came to dominate a post-Assad Syria, for instance, it might result in the exodus of a large number of Christians who fear such a scenario. The problematic situation of the Kurds, who could control their own areas, would exacerbate tensions with Turkey. For decades Turkey has been fighting a Kurdish insurgency that has left at least 40,000 dead on both sides. Turkey would be upset to see the Kurds gain more territory in the north, such as that they claimed in the autonomous zone in northern Iraq, creating new regional tensions. The political fallout could be disastrous. All the regional actors involved have to take some responsibility for the fault lines that are developing in this Syrian end game, but none appear willing to do so as Russia, China, and the West are still divided over the peace process and the outcomes.

Further complicating matters, ethnic and sectarian tensions are reaching a boiling point in Syria. The divisions between the ruling Alawite sect and the Sunni Muslims (the majority of the population) grow more intense and bitter every day. These sectarian clashes and divisions are already spilling over into Lebanon, which is hardly known for its levels of stability over the years. The result will be a terrible sectarian mess fueled by political and social insecurity. These lines are becoming harder and messier as the war drags on. Syria continues to sink into chaos. The stakes are enormously high for all concerned, but it's the individuals on the ground—the women and children and the weak—who will suffer the most.

There is also the severe problem of the new jihadi group, ISIS, who now occupy large swathes of Syrian territory and seek to establish an Islamic caliphate (an ancient form of Islamic government that emerged after the death of the Prophet Muhammad) in the region. These jihadist fighters have been known for their brutal and barbaric tactics, such as beheadings, crucifixions, and other measures to ensure fear in the local populations. The Syrian situation at the time of writing represents a highly volatile human security crisis with many actors (internal and external) all having a stake in the outcomes. It is also important to note that the crisis has had severe implications beyond Syria's borders, creating instability and chaos in the region with the outflow of refugees and displaced people and the fact that the conflict has spilled over borders. As of the time of writing it's hard to see how this situation will be resolved with any clarity in the immediate future.

The topic of "Why Libya and not Syria?" has been argued extensively in the popular media and news circles. Why are we selective about intervention when peoples' lives are at stake? Libya saw widespread international support behind an early response, but in the case of Syria regional and international organizations have been more hesitant in responding to the crisis, despite an independent UN inquiry finding "that crimes against humanity have been committed in different locations" and repeated censures by the UN Human Rights Council. Why did the crisis in Libya captivate the attention of the international community and quickly become labeled as a clear case for a timely and decisive response to uphold R2P? The wide range of economic, political, and military measures that were taken to try and protect the local population can be cited as the main factors leading to the end of that conflict.

Failing to Protect: Canadian Troops Withdraw from Afghanistan

Canadian troops began their withdrawal from Afghanistan in 2014, but this came as no surprise—from a political perspective, it was always in the cards. Support for the war in Afghanistan had declined dramatically over the last 10 years, partly because it was the longest foreign conflict Canada had been involved in since the end of World War II. Canadians were tired with the loss of life, the slow and halting progress, the financial burdens, and the venal corruption of what some term a "narco-state," all of which ensured that this exit strategy was not one that caused great criticism. The reasons for getting into the conflict seem to have disappeared altogether. With Osama bin Laden dead and the Taliban diminished, the argument that leaving Afghans to run their own affairs and assume responsibility for their security held strong currency in the minds of politicians and voters. Stephen Harper, Canada's prime minister at the time, had already stated that "the longer a foreign intervention stays, eventually the less likely its success becomes."

From a human security perspective, however, the withdrawal was highly problematic. Canada, which has always been one of the strongest proponents of the concept of human security, must hope that freedom from fear and freedom from want, the two pillars of the perspective, have been strengthened in Afghanistan with our presence. However, there is little evidence to support this view on the ground. On the positive side there were some gains: Women are now represented in Parliament, girls are attending school, and the economy seemed to be improving. Yet these gains are overshadowed by many elements of what still remains a "failed state." The tribal social structure has changed little, and the government is not seen as widely legitimate and is heavily involved in corruption. President Hamid Karzai's recent, strange pronouncements that the burning of Korans by US officials were satanic acts that will never be forgiven by apologies didn't bode well for the development of a rational state structure. And his description of the Taliban and NATO as "two demons; let's Pray for God to rescue us from these two demons" did nothing to instill faith in his leadership abilities and only served to undermine the planned withdrawal. Most military officials seem to doubt whether the Afghan army is capable of maintaining and protecting the security of the Afghan people or even containing an anticipated resurgence of the Taliban. There is still the problem of its neighbor Pakistan, which has provided safe haven to Afghan insurgents and has been accused of "passive acceptance" in the conflict. Canada's contribution of $110 million a year to support the military and police appears generous, but one wonders how much it will assist in protecting the vulnerable or if it will instead line the coffers of state officials.

It was a risky strategy to aggressively retreat, because it sends the wrong message. When the Soviets withdrew from Afghanistan, leaving a weak government, the country disintegrated into civil war that left thousands dead and led to the Taliban assuming control. The strategy by NATO aimed to avoid that scenario by fostering reconciliation between enemies and arming and training proper security forces to take over. If this happens and chaos is avoided it would be some sort of victory. However, the signals are mixed and complicated. It didn't help that a deranged American army sergeant killed 16 civilians (nine of them children) and was then shipped off to the United States to face justice. Burning the Koran in public has not helped the case either—waves of violent protest followed, and Afghan soldiers attacked NATO troops. Levels of distrust are at an all-time high.

The traditional conservative structure will take years to erode in Afghanistan, and while NATO missions here may have eroded some aspects it will take much longer to dismantle many of the attitudes that are engrained in the local population. As just one example, on 22 May 2015, 125 girls and three teachers were admitted to hospital because of a suspected poison attack by conservative radicals on a school in the Takhar province. This was the second attack of this kind in two months and does little to instill faith in the governance or security structures.

Unless Canada and its NATO allies find increasingly innovative ways to protect such vulnerable individuals from fear and want, it appears likely that Afghanistan will self-destruct once more, and the implications will simply be more conflict, more death, and the absence of genuine human security.

CONFLICT RESOLUTION AND MEDIATING CONFLICTS IN HUMAN SECURITY

In this section we will focus on some of the trends in resolving post-conflict situations where societies find themselves in political and social transition. In the 1970s many countries began to institute **truth commissions** and inquiries into the past as a way of dealing with and moving forward to democratic structures.

On a global basis, state- and nonstate-sponsored inquiries into the past are becoming commonplace and are intimately linked to the ongoing human security of these states. Revisiting the past is not simply confined to countries making political and social transitions, either. From the developing world to the developed, governments are actively looking back and considering their historical roles in problematic policies instituted by their predecessors. Truth commissions in particular are aimed at inquiries into the recent past, a history that is more often than not filled with misdeeds, atrocities, and gross human rights violations. Recognition, acknowledgment, and some sort of closure on the problematic events of the past are necessary in some cases for the new government to legitimize itself politically and move on. They are thus faced with a paradox: How is this legitimacy established? Should they take a hard line, attempting to prosecute the perpetrators of misdeeds through their criminal justice system? Or should they offer unconditional amnesty to the former, a willed amnesia to simply forget the past, let bygones be bygones, and plan for the future.

Truth Commissions and the Case of South Africa

Dictatorships have frequently come and gone over the last 100 years, but **apartheid** in every way represented an affront to the basic concept of human dignity. Few prolonged conflicts of the twentieth century could match the terror and pain that apartheid caused its victims. In part the state claimed to be fighting a war against communism (seen as terrorism) to justify their policies. This resulted in the wide-scale militarization of the state apparatus and the creation of secret security mechanisms that did not adhere to the rule of law in any form. Apartheid was regarded as a crime against humanity. Some have likened the policies to the Israeli occupation of Palestine (including senior political figures in South Africa). The levels of human insecurity in South Africa were grave and disturbing. In the 70 years that the Pass Laws were in force, nearly 16.5 million black South Africans were treated as criminals and discriminated against; several million people were forcibly removed from their land and homes; 300 laws were placed on the statute books to ensure that black people were treated like second-class citizens for all of their lives. In 1994, after the end of apartheid and the first democratic elections, South Africa instituted a truth and reconciliation commission.

We might be surprised if the social fabric could be ripped any further apart than it already was under the old South Africa, but the truth was that there was no social fabric for the vast majority of the population. They had always lived in a society that excluded the very core of their being and created a total condition of human insecurity.

Two crucial objectives have been achieved through the South African Truth and Reconciliation Commission. The first is that it has achieved a remarkable and far-ranging public exposure of the human rights violations and crimes committed under the apartheid regime. In this sense it has created a record of the crimes of the past so that they will not be forgotten. It has significantly reduced the number of lies in circulation by forcing people to admit to crimes against the broad mass of the South African population. This is an important and necessary exercise in itself. In 10 or 20 years' time, there can be no denial that these things happened. It has forced a previously reluctant population (though of course there is still denial at one level) to see that apartheid was morally (and politically, economically, etc.) bankrupt—that it was a crime against humanity. It has produced an archive that allows people to examine their past and hopefully learn from it.

Second, it allowed ordinary people to find expression for their suffering under the regime. It had a completely cathartic function for many of the victims. The truth commission provided people with a voice where previously there only existed silence and rage. In this sense there has been a therapeutic conversation taking place in South Africa. Of course, as with all forms of therapy, there is a great deal of pain involved and some people have argued that it might be better if the cupboards of apartheid had not been opened and laid bare. However, this is problematic. There will be pain in the short run, but we would argue that in the long run South Africa will benefit tremendously from the process of airing the truth about victim experiences. At the same time it is clear that the truth, the whole truth, and nothing but the truth has not fully emerged, but this is only to be expected given the clandestine nature of the regime.

Finally, the commission has provided the foundation for societal transformation and the beginnings of a common identity. In terms of coping and going forward, this is the same for individuals as well as aggregates of individuals who eventually develop a national identity and common goals. In some ways the commission has allowed the development of common bonds through a shared truth. This is not to say that this leads to perfect peace and harmony, but it's a process that has started. There are other mechanisms designed to forge bonds and create common goals of transformation, but the commission can play an important part in making people acknowledge the past, remember it, and ultimately and hopefully "get over it." Truth, then, and the recognition and acknowledgment of it help provide the basis for a workable political community; it will also help provide it with legitimacy and durability.

The majority of South Africa's people who were so long excluded from their system are now incorporated into a democratic dispensation; it will take some time for them to learn, as well as the previous advantaged minority, how democracy works. Democracies require habituation; they require time to forge the common understandings that allow their institutions to work in a free and open manner. Ernest Renan (1990) has argued that nation-building demands that history be forgotten for the past to be remade in the image of the present. But the denial of the past and the impunity of those who held the reins of power needs to be challenged to begin rebuilding the social fabric of this multiracial society. While there is still a long way to go, peacebuilding and human security have to some extent been served by the examination of the past. To do nothing would have been a grave misdeed. Truth commissions might be compromises, but within the political landscape of South Africa and other countries in transition they have affected positive change.

Reintegrating Child Soldiers in Uganda

The case of child soldiers in Uganda is one of the worst examples of crimes against children and horrific abuses of their human rights. It started with the rebel Lord's Resistance Army (LRA), led by the charismatic but psychopathic Joseph Konya, abducting more than 30,000 boys and girls as soldiers. Attacks against Uganda's Acholi people in the north resulted in severe trauma to civilians from extreme violence and abduction. Girls were typically forced to be sex slaves to the LRA. The Uganda People's Defence Force also recruited small numbers of children into its forces as young as 13, including local defense units.

The use of child soldiers is strategic. Traditionally, societies have aimed to protect children during war. In Uganda, the Acholi people would avoid attacking children to facilitate post-conflict reconciliation. And according to international law, special treatment is given to children who are under 15 years of age, and these children should not be killed, maimed, or tortured. Moreover, there are cases when children were intentionally targeted, used as human shields, or killed by terrorists. Roughly 90 percent of the victims of wars are civilians, and estimates have claimed that half of these are children (see the box "Children in Conflict").

Children in Conflict

One of the most disturbing aspects of post–Cold War conflict and violence has been the increasing use of children as active participants in the conflict and as victims. Recent conflicts have seen increased involvement of children both as perpetrators of violent crimes and also as victims of war atrocities. UNICEF (2013) has compiled some disturbing statistics about children in conflict:

- More than 2 million children have died as a direct result of armed conflict over the last decade.
- At least 6 million children have been permanently disabled or seriously injured.
- More than 1 million have been orphaned or separated from their families.
- Between 8,000 and 10,000 are killed or maimed by landmines every year.

Similarly, UNICEF states that an estimated 300,000 child soldiers—boys and girls under the age of 18—are involved in more than 30 conflicts worldwide. Child soldiers are used as combatants, messengers, porters, cooks, and to provide sexual services. Some are forcibly recruited or abducted; others are driven to join by poverty, abuse, and discrimination, or to seek revenge for violence enacted against themselves and their families (UNICEF 2013).

It is believed that children associated with fighting forces have been severely manipulated to perpetrate heinous crimes. This is possible largely because of a lack of education, which makes these children highly vulnerable to recruitment. Most of these kids are often neglected street children or those with minimal parental care, sometimes due to poverty.

Many child soldiers are found in Africa, but there are no geographical boundaries to this crime. From Afghanistan to Iraq, Ethiopia to Yemen and the Congo, child soldiers have been used extensively in countries where there is poor economic development, failing states, and vicious internal conflict.

Reintegration programs should target education and reorienting child ex-combatants to peaceful living in order to avoid a relapse to conflict. This education can be both formal and informal. The International Labour Organization argues that skills training should not be conceived of as a quick fix to get rid of ex-combatants or to fulfill some international funding requirements; rather it should be genuinely crafted to ensure sustainability. In post-war countries, education can be a vital tool for social transformation, which is one reason why the nongovernmental organization War Child is investing in the lives of children affected by war. Their view is that this is a genuine way of fostering peace and stability.

Some people believe it is an integral part of the reintegration and rehabilitative program for child ex-combatants to genuinely accept their role in the destruction of these post-conflict societies. Hence reintegration programs should be perceived of as an opportunity for their restoration to normal societies and an attempt to prevent a relapse to conflict.

CONCLUSION

This chapter has focused on humanitarian intervention as a way of making the international community respect and deal with human security issues. It has also focused on the multifaceted work of peacebuilding in restoring and healing societies after major conflicts. What we have seen is that intervention and the responsibility to protect doctrine have been used like many other instruments available to states—as a selective tool to sometimes further their own interests.

In the end, many of the decisions made around these instruments still come down to politics and the agendas of the important and powerful nations who can exercise these choices. The question of why some interventions happen and not others will always be an important one. Why did the West intervene in the Libyan conflict after the Arab Spring and not in Syria? The answers are complex because they involve opportunities and costs as well as taking into account the diversity of influences in the Middle East, such as Western, Russian, and Chinese interests. None of these aspects are likely to be resolved any time soon. R2P is still emerging as a norm and will continue to evolve over time.

We also noted there are other mechanisms for resolving conflict that have developed. In the case of transitions from a past often imbued with traumatic conflicts for ordinary civilians, truth commissions have allowed people to deal with the past and explore new avenues for reconciliation. Restorative justice in Africa has had some success and has allowed societies and individuals to move on.

KEY TERMS

Apartheid; Genocide; Humanitarian Intervention; International Commission on Intervention and State Sovereignty (ICISS); Just Cause; Just War Theory; Last Resort; Legitimate Authority; Military Intervention; Peacebuilding; Post-Conflict

Development; Proportional Means; Reasonable Prospect; Responsibility to Protect (R2P); Restorative Justice; Right Intention; Sovereignty; Truth Commissions

FURTHER READING

Abiew, F.K., ed. 1999. *The Evolution of the Doctrine and Practice of Humanitarian Intervention*. Netherlands: Martinus Nijhoff Publishers.

Boutros-Ghali, Boutros. "An Agenda for Peace: Preventative Diplomacy, Peacemaking and Peacekeeping." *International Relations*, 11: 201–18.

Brahimi, Lakhdar. 2000. *Report of the Panel on United Nations Peace Operations*. http://www.un.org/en/events/pastevents/brahimi_report.shtml.

Chandler, D. 2004. "The Responsibility to Protect? Imposing the 'Liberal Peace.'" *International Peacekeeping* 11 (1): 59–81. http://dx.doi.org/10.1080/1353331042000 228454.

Dallaire, Romeo. 2003. *Shake Hands with the Devil: The Failure of Humanity in Rwanda*. Toronto: Random House.

Evans, G., and M. Sahnoun. 2002. "The Responsibility to Protect." *Foreign Affairs* 81 (6): 99–110. http://dx.doi.org/10.2307/20033347.

Galtung, Johan. 1975. *Peace: Research, Education, Action*. Copenhagen: Christian Eljers.

ICISS. 2001. *The Responsibility to Protect*. Ottawa: IDRC.

Steenkamp, Christina. 2009. *Violence and Post-War Reconstruction: Managing Insecurity in the Aftermath of Peace Accords*. New York: I.B. Tauris.

United Nations. 1965. United Nations General Assembly Resolution 2131(XX). *Declaration on the Inadmissibility of Intervention in the Domestic Affairs of States and the Protection of Their Independence and Sovereignty*.

Wheeler, Nicholas J. 2000. *Saving Strangers: Humanitarian Intervention in International Society*. Oxford: Oxford University Press.

WEBSITES

Asia-Pacific Centre for the Responsibility to Protect: www.r2pasiapacific.org

International Coalition on the Responsibility to Protect: www.responsibilitytoprotect.org

International Crisis Group: www.crisisgroup.org

International Institute for Strategic Studies: www.iiss.org

International Peace Institute: www.ipinst.org

Organization for Security and Co-operation in Europe: www.osce.org

Peace Women: www.peacewomen.org

United States Institute of Peace: www.usip.org

PART THREE

Chapter 7

GLOBALIZATION, GOVERNANCE, AND FREEDOM FROM POVERTY

Overcoming poverty is not a task of charity, it is an act of justice. Like slavery and apartheid, poverty is not natural. It is man-made and it can be overcome and eradicated by the actions of human beings.

Nelson Mandela (United Nations Foundation 2013)

INTRODUCTION

The field of global governance has emerged as both an interdisciplinary academic discipline and an operational strategy for managing the global commons. Intergovernmental organizations (IGOs) work on a range of issues such as trade liberalization, human migration, and environmental protection, to name just a few. Yet do these global regimes enhance or hinder human security, especially for marginalized populations? In this chapter, we discuss the relationship between globalization, governance, and poverty in terms of the impact each is having on food security, a subsection of the larger concept of human security. Strong global governance is increasingly being viewed as a fundamental component of development and global security. Yet how can macro-level policy recommendations function effectively at a local community-based level, and what is their relation to human security? How does this impact the Millennium Development Goals (MDGs) and the post-2015 development agenda? What impact does poverty have on an individual's food security? Here we address several of these questions while critically exploring the impact of **trade liberalization** on food security, water, and other health issues. We argue that reducing poverty and moving toward the MDGs provides the best opportunity for creating increasing human security among vulnerable individuals as well as nation-states and regions, in a world that has become increasingly interconnected. Economic strategies should reflect the goals of human security and vice versa to create a more just, equitable, and fair world.

There is a clear relationship between poverty and bad governance. If we take a development perspective, violent conflict might be seen as the ultimate proof that governance has failed. Conflicts tend to flourish in weak or failed states, and we have seen that many in the development assistance community are reluctant to commit help and might even withdraw from countries where the physical and personal security situation is deteriorating. According to one source, a failed state is a state that

> can no longer perform basic functions such as education, security, or governance, usually due to fractious violence or extreme poverty. Within this power vacuum, people fall victim to competing factions and crime. However, states fail not only because of internal factors. Foreign governments can also knowingly destabilize a state by fueling ethnic warfare or supporting rebel forces, causing it to collapse. (Global Policy Forum 2005)

There is more to the idea than this, of course, and we will explore it throughout this chapter.

In the overall framework, security provides some stability for development. A common complaint is that its development becomes impossible in conflict-ridden communities because of the high degree of violence and tension. Fragile and failing states appear to be on the receiving end of this more than any other states and sometimes face imminent collapse into chaos and anarchy.

GLOBALIZATION'S ROLE

As discussed in Chapter 1, it might be argued that globalization has a discomforting and dislocating effect on individuals and states. While embracing the phenomenon (less a choice than a given in today's world), states have seen themselves destabilized and on the receiving end of things they can no longer control. It eats into fundamental aspects of statehood, such as sovereignty. Individuals have leapt in some ways on the bandwagon of global change and the speed of this change. This economic and social change is spurring political change. The economic instruments of globalization such as the state, multinational corporations, and institutions like the World Bank, International Monetary Fund, and World Trade Organization, among others, have had a tremendous impact on the forces governing people's lives.

The consequences of cultural globalization are numerous. It is clear that there have been trends toward a more uniform set of cultural and social norms that limits the scope for richness, complexity, and diversity. As a result, local social norms and cultural practices are being greatly influenced by Western ideals, creating social tensions in different sectors of society. Governments, political parties, civil society, and religious organizations in non-Western countries have tried to minimize what they perceive as the negative effects of globalization. The increasing strength shown by fundamentalist religious and ethnic-based groups represent a serious threat to human and national security.

Another consequence of globalization has been an increase in insecurity at the personal, family, and community level as a result of the profound changes in the role of the state and public institutions. In many Western countries the dismantling of the welfare state and the liberalization of international trade has seriously weakened family and public safety nets. Trade unions and institutions representing working people have been diminished, and we have seen that corporate-style managers have been elevated to important positions in society. Moreover, welfare institutions that seemed protective of their members have increasingly been weakened by the effects of globalization.

There have, of course, been positive aspects of globalization—we have seen advances in knowledge and technology that have benefited millions and helped lift people out of poverty. Nevertheless the serious uneven distribution of wealth, power among peoples and countries, as well as lack of access to universal health care and education continually threaten the social and economic well-being of many developing or undeveloped nations. Caroline Thomas and Peter Wilkin (1999, 1) argue that while human security entails "a condition of existence in which basic material needs are met and in which human dignity, including meaningful participation in the life of the community . . . poverty is the ultimate systematic threat facing humanity." This represents a fundamental barrier to human well-being and development.

The importance and economic power of **multinational corporations** (**MNCs**) has grown steadily over the last 30 years. In fact, many large corporations have total sales larger than the GDP (gross domestic product) of many individual countries. In 2012 Apple's net worth exceeded US$500 billion, more than the country of Poland (Alexander 2012). As Thomas and Wilkin (1999, 84–85) write, "In large part this can be attributed to the success of the G7, IMF and World Bank in promoting the development of a neoliberal global order in which the role of the state is redefined in support for the private sector." Meanwhile, US-based Apple is on track to become the first company to be valued at over US$1 trillion, giving the firm more economic worth than the GDPs of Indonesia, the Netherlands, and Saudi Arabia (Neate 2015).

The widening **wealth gap** between rich and poor countries and groups within society is another element that poses a potential threat to human security. A 2015 report by Oxfam International estimates that half of all wealth is held by 1 percent of the global population. What's more, the UK-based NGO estimates that "85 billionaires have the same wealth as the bottom half of the world's population" (Oxfam International 2015). As Thomas and Wilkin (1999) note, the inequality between states, within states, and between multinational corporations has grown. This is directly impacting the well-being of underdeveloped communities, who are finding themselves ever more marginalized from those that are benefiting from the neoliberal economic order. There are, however, economists and representatives of financial institutions who claim that the negative impact of globalization on global labor rights and the environment is a myth: "There is no indication that the reduction of controls on trade and capital flows has forced a generalized downgrading in labor or environmental conditions. If anything, the opposite has occurred" (Drezner 2000, 65). Still, as Thomas and Wilkin (1999, 160) argue, "Human insecurity is not some inevitable occurrence . . . Rather, human insecurity results directly from existing structures of power that determines who enjoys the entitlement to security and who does not." The widening gap between developed and underdeveloped communities is a direct consequence of these power structures.

Globalization and Development

Different people in different epochs have attributed various meanings to the concept of development. The analysis of these meanings helps us to understand how the ideological foundations of this concept influence the design and implementation of economic development policies and programs. In everyday language, the "common sense" meaning of "development" conveys the idea of progress (understood as progressive positive change). In the realm of the natural sciences it is used in its broader meaning to indicate transformation (a process) that can take either the form of "progression" (e.g., from an embryo to a grown human being) or "regression," as would be the case of a debilitating disease. As a concept, development has helped to characterize the gradual (always positive) progression from the lower steps of a hierarchy to its higher levels. In the domain of economic development, rural, traditional, or **"underdeveloped"** societies were to achieve industrialization (progress) by following the steps previously undertaken by the industrial nations.

When *development* ideas were unsuccessful in producing the desired growth effects and failed to explain the persistence of "underdeveloped" societies, the concept of **modernization** was brought into the discourse. As Arturo Escobar (2011, 383) writes,

> To understand development as a discourse, one must look at this system of relations, relations that define the conditions under which objects, concepts, theories, and strategies can be incorporated into the discourse. The system of relations establishes a discursive practice that sets the rules of the game: who

can speak, from what points of view, with what authority, and according to what criteria of expertise; it determines the rules that must be followed for this or that problem, theory, or object to merge and be named, analyzed, and eventually transformed into a policy or a plan.

Modernization is thus understood as the application of the principles of "objective scientific" rationality and "technology" within the context of a market economy to resolve the problems of the "lack of development" prevalent in less-industrialized areas of the world. According to modernization theory, the solution to lack of development is to be found not only in more growth, which by definition corresponds to progress, but also in the restructuring of the social and economic institutions of the country or region. These are the conditions necessary to accommodate the advent of the new modern era. Countries in the less-industrialized world need to "grow" and become "modern" (Escobar 2011). In the next section, we look briefly at some of these dominant views on development that have shaped our thinking.

The Dominant View: Growth and Modernization

The major advances of productive forces achieved by industry and technologies as a result of the accumulation of capital after the Industrial Revolution in England led economists to conceptualize development as "progress." Consequently, from the beginning of the eighteenth century to the present, Western industrialized countries have taken for granted the need for a continuous capitalist development, mainly understood as material progress (Larrain 2013). Development theories centered on economic growth dominated Western international "aid" policies through the 1960s. From then on, international "aid" and national, regional, or sector-specific development programs that emphasized "progress" through scientific rationality and technology were implemented to promote the expansion of those areas that lagged behind. Following the logic of "development" as sustained economic growth, the so-called "aid" programs were aimed at promoting the continuous industrialization and urbanization of society and the restructuring of the social and economic institutions of the country. "Progress" is something to be measured in terms of its contribution to material well-being and profit maximization at the microeconomic level, and to maximization of the gross national product (GNP) at the macroeconomic level.

The consolidation of capitalist expansion after World War II manifested itself in increased wealth in the northern industrialized countries that sharply contrasted with increasing poverty in the southern regions. The awareness of the increasing disparity between the benefits of development that accrued to North and South forced Western scholars, administrators, and international **technocrats** to search for a new "logical" explanation. Western economic sciences found the answer to the unequal growth between the northern and southern regions in the concept of modernization. Modernization and the modern/non-modern dichotomy allowed technocrats and politicians in Western industrialized countries to define "other" countries, regions, and ethnic groups as deficient in terms of what they (the self-named "developed" nations) regarded as the right standards. Today, the idea of development as progress has been linked to the existence of a liberal democratic political system and a free market economic system as the guarantors of the concretization of the "innate" human desire for personal success.

Governance, Ungovernability, and Development

After the collapse of the Soviet Union in 1991, President Bush announced a **New World Order** where free trade and free markets would bring economic growth, prosperity, and peace to the whole of humanity. While the new neoliberal economic system has brought prosperity for a minority of nations, it has failed to bring a more equitable and ecologically sound development for the vast majority of the world's population. Furthermore, the powerful nations and business corporations of the industrialized world have been implementing international terms of trade that have brought stability to their economies, while **structural adjustment programs**, imposed by the IMF and the World Bank on less-industrialized countries, have greatly contributed to exacerbating poverty levels and unequal income distribution. As the UN's 2013 report on the World Social Situation notes,

> Globally, the distribution of income remains very uneven. In 2010, high-income countries—that accounted for only 16 per cent of the world's population— were estimated to generate 55 per cent of global income. Low-income countries created just above 1 per cent of global income even though they contained 72 per cent of global population. (United Nations 2013, 25)

As a direct result of the conditions emanating from the New World Order and the transition in international relations from a bipolar world to one of unilateralism or, depending on the circumstances, multilateralism under the mandate of the United Nations Security Council, new threats to the security of industrialized countries and power elites elsewhere in the world have been generated. The unequal distribution of wealth, among countries and among social groups, generated by the New World Order has created a profound sense of alienation from Western modernization in the less-industrialized and poor regions of the globe. Indeed, 15 years since the launch of the MDGs, an estimated 836 million people continue to live in absolute poverty.

The perception that the imposition of Western liberal democracy is a direct threat to their traditional cultural, religious, and local political structures has been feeding extreme nationalistic and religious sentiments among the population in these regions. This, in turn, has resulted in new security threats. These new threats are mainly coming from nation-states whose internal governance institutions have collapsed as a direct consequence of social unrest derived from extreme poverty conditions and from the intervention of multinational corporations from the old colonial powers, who are mainly interested in exploiting the nation's natural resources. When the conditions are such that governance institutions can no longer guarantee law and order, these "failed states" have, in some cases, become the command center for drug dealers and terrorist groups, and the incubator for extremist groups advocating nationalistic, ethnic, and religious extremist ideals.

It must be remembered that "failed states" do not refer only to those that cannot maintain functioning governance institutions, such as education and health care. The term also refers to states that cannot maintain their borders and the rule of law. Susan Rice (2008) identifies failed states as "countries in which the central government does not exert effective control over, nor is it able to deliver vital services to, significant parts of its own territory due to conflict, ineffective governance or state collapse." Moreover, the United States Agency for International Development (USAID 2005) distinguishes between **fragile states**, **vulnerable states**, and **crisis states**:

- *Fragile states* refer generally to a broad range of failing, failed, and recovering states. However, the distinction among them is not always clear, since fragile states rarely travel a predictable path of failure and recovery, and the labels may mask sub-state and regional conditions (insurgencies, factions, etc.) that may be important factors in conflict and fragility. It is more important to understand how far and quickly a country is moving from or toward stability than it is to categorize a state as failed or not. Therefore, the strategy distinguishes between fragile states that are vulnerable from those that are already in crisis.
- *Vulnerable states* refer to those states unable or unwilling to adequately assure the provision of security and basic services to significant portions of their populations and where the legitimacy of the government is in question. This includes states that are failing or recovering from crisis.
- *Crisis states* refer to those states where the central government does not exert effective control over its own territory or is unable or unwilling to assure the provision of vital services to significant parts of its territory, where legitimacy of the government is weak or nonexistent, and where violent conflict is a reality or a great risk.

The definitions offered by USAID provide a helpful typology for distinguishing among failed states. While all provide a subtle yet clear distinction, a common theme that runs through each is a dysfunctionality of government that leads to human suffering caused by such things as violence, disease, or poverty. Here we turn to poverty, which we see as both a contributing factor to and a consequence of state failure.

GLOBAL POVERTY AS A THREAT TO HUMAN SECURITY

Poverty is one of the great scourges of the global conditions we live in. Many people feel trapped and impoverished by poverty, which prevents them from leading real and fulfilling lives. While some institutions like the World Bank define poverty in terms of statistics and how much is needed for people to exist on a daily basis, the United Nations takes a multifaceted approach. This approach shows that poverty encompasses not only very low income but also themes such as malnutrition, education, health, water, and general economic vulnerability. By using this multipronged and dimensional approach to poverty, the UN hopes to get at the underlying factors and how they are interconnected, rather than simply looking at statistical wealth indicators. Poverty is cyclical, in other words, with these different factors feeding into one another and creating more poverty.

We begin with the reality that there has always been economic inequality among people. What has happened in the era of globalization is that these disparities have increased dramatically, and there appears little hope that the situation can be reversed in the short term. The differences are staggering between the *North* (generally seen as the rich, Western, industrialized countries of the Northern hemisphere) and the *South* (generally seen as the poor, underdeveloped countries of the Southern hemisphere); this disparity is often referred to as the **North–South divide**. With roughly 17 percent of the global population living on roughly $1.25 a day, we know that nearly 1 billion people live in extreme poverty (World Bank 2015b). Although improving since the early 1980s, when 52 percent of the planet lived in scarcity, much of this number is skewed considering China's massive accomplishments in lifting 300 million people out of deep depravation.

What Is Poverty?

There are generally three classifications for poverty: absolute poverty, moderate poverty, and relative poverty. The question of absolute poverty is still one of the most serious facing the planet, and it is linked to serious issues of economic inequality and environmental disasters, among others. Getting rid of absolute poverty is not a new idea and has been around at least since the end of World War II. But with increasing levels of poverty it has become established as more of a priority for the international community, although we're still not seeing the positive impact many would like. Hunger as a result of famine remains one of the most crucial issues; because it is a result of human-made and environmental problems, it is a highly contested area.

Absolute poverty can be defined as those living on less than US$1.25 per day. In 2011, there was another 2.2 billion people living in *moderate poverty*, which is living on less than US$2.00 per day. While these indicators are used by the World Bank, organizations have a more difficult time identifying those living in *relative poverty*, which compares levels of inequality between groups and over time—that is, relative to their positions over time in terms of economic wealth. Those living in relative poverty are generally not considered to be facing threats to their basic survival; rather, they experience a general sense of insecurity by not having access to things available to others. For example, they may lack access to education or the Internet. Such poverty has also been referred to as *social exclusion* since the individual is not able to participate fully in the community on account of economic barriers.

Even with these definitions, there are challenges in gaining a complete understanding of poverty. Caterina Laderchi, Ruhi Saith, and Francis Stewart (2003) identify several barriers in defining poverty. First, what is the space for thinking about poverty? For example, should measuring poverty be confined to material characteristics, such as income and possession, or should we expand this understanding to include social and political features? Second, can we universally apply a one-size-fits-all definition to poverty? We are confronted with the problem of only thinking about poverty within a developing world context. For example, while Hong Kong may be one of the wealthiest countries in the world, it typically holds the largest **Gini coefficient** of all OECD (Organisation for Economic Co-operation and Development) jurisdictions in terms of wealth gap. With over a million people living on less than US$2 per day, should the country not be considered in a definition of poverty?

Another challenge is identifying the **poverty line**. The threshold can change over time, and it can change from one jurisdiction to another. Moreover, what is the unit of poverty? Should it be the individual or the household? There are surely wealthy households who neglect members of the family. Is it not fair to say that a child who is neglected by affluent parents is not living in some type of poverty? Finally, there is the issue of **multidimensionality** within the poverty sphere. That is, poverty has many dimensions, such as education levels, access to health care, and nutritional levels of the population. Do societies then need multiple metrics to understand how these themes impact communities? Indeed, there are many sides to poverty that applying a single definition to try and explain the human security implications of depravation is problematic.

Laderchi, Saith, and Stewart therefore present four approaches to measuring poverty. First, the *monetary approach* focuses on income levels to establish basic thresholds of an individual's financial well-being. Questions on the ability to procure nutritional food and household resources also come into play while theorists seek to identify a measurable poverty line. For example, the World Bank identifies anyone earning less than US$1.25/day as an individual living in absolute poverty as opposed to relative poverty.

A second approach to measuring poverty is the *participatory approach*. This approach encourages populations to assess their own poverty levels. This allows for internal rather than external assessment, thereby promoting self-determination and empowerment to improve locally driven anti-poverty initiatives. This is the method that is most often used by the World Bank. Of course, there are challenges with this approach, especially when one asks who has the right to participate and speak on behalf of the community?

A third approach identified by Laderchi, Saith, and Stewart is the *social exclusion approach*, which explores marginalization and depravation within industrialized societies. It focuses on relativity, agency, and the future dynamics of poverty. This approach considers the dynamics of group marginalization to identify the *excluders* and the *excludees*. The purpose is to consider the multidimensionality of depravation within affluent societies.

Finally, developed by Nobel Laureate Amartya Sen, the *capabilities approach* measures the individual's capacity to achieve "the good life." Themes such as freedom and human well-being are considered of primary importance. In 1990, this approach would become operational and consolidated into the United Nations Human Development Report, which was designed by Sen and Pakistani economist Mahbub-ul-Haq with the goal of identifying the structural elements of poverty. The approach argues that since traditional agendas do not adequately deal with the structural sources of poverty, development agencies needed to shift focus toward the symptoms rather than the root causes. The bottom line from a human security perspective is that addressing the symptoms of poverty is akin to placing a bandage over the problem and hoping it will go away. Deep-seated structural roots of poverty need to be dealt with to create a better and fairer world. There are at least three structural areas cited by the UNDP in the Human Development Report 2013 (UNDP 2013). These are an unequal access to assets, unequal participation in the market, and weak or unjust governance.

First, the UNDP identifies the *unequal access to material assets*. If you are poor and have no access to wealth and knowledge it is unlikely that you will be able to change your human security situation. A lack of access to land, water, and resources mires people in structural poverty, making it even more difficult to escape. In the developing world, income inequalities have increased, as have all other indicators of inequality. Land ownership by a few continues to perpetuate this inequality; in urban areas property ownership continues to exacerbate inequality.

Second, a *lack of access to the marketplace* can contribute to poverty. The UNDP report also cites unequal participation in the marketplace, meaning that people with few resources are unable to compete in more dynamic market areas. Wealthy people who live in cities and towns that have these kinds of assets are able to exclude just about everyone else. Powerful corporations can effectively squeeze out the basic producers and wage earners so they feel they have no stake.

Finally, *a sense of unjust governance,* in which there is a prevailing sense of unfair treatment by those left outside the mainstream economy and political development, impacts poverty levels. Politicians and leaders of state still tend to be wealthy individuals who often perpetuate and maintain their power by excluding others from the process. Most politicians in the West tend to come from wealthy backgrounds, and even poor people who rise in the developing world to become political figures in their own countries tend to perpetuate their own new wealth and power.

On the other hand, we could change these aspects by promoting fair and good governance and allowing people to own their land and properties, which would in turn benefit them and provide them with a stake in the local community.

Food Security

All three types of poverty lead to serious threats to an individual's ability to achieve **food security**. In 1996, the World Food Summit declared food security as existing only "when all people at all times have access to sufficient, safe, nutritious food to maintain a healthy and active life." It is therefore understood as holding both economic and physical dimensions that not only require access to food but also healthy food that prevents malnutrition. The World Health Organization (WHO 2015b) identifies the three pillars of food security as:

- Food availability: sufficient quantities of food available on a consistent basis.
- Food access: having sufficient resources to obtain appropriate foods for a nutritious diet.
- Food use: appropriate use based on knowledge of basic nutrition and care, as well as adequate water and sanitation.

Still, there is much debate around how to interpret each of these points. Issues of globalization, food supply chains and distribution, as well as agricultural policy on support for green technologies like genetically modified organisms (GMOs) have led to fierce debates within the food security world. Indeed, questions around how food security should be measured within households once food is distributed as well as the impact of trade liberalization on farmers in the developing world have proved contentious.

Human Security and Drought: A "Slow, Creeping Natural Disaster"

Drought has both direct and indirect implications for food security. Land erosion, increased likelihood of fires, and reduced water levels are among a few of the many direct consequences of drought-like conditions. All of this can have a negative impact on human security, leading to economic instability, increased food prices, and a greater human migration. The United Nations Food and Agriculture Organization (FOA) has referred to drought as "the slow, creeping natural disaster." For example, the FOA (2013) has noted the following:

- Since 1900, more than 11 million people have died as a consequence of drought, and more than 2 billion people have been affected by drought, more than any other physical hazard.
- Droughts are the primary cause of most illnesses and death because they deny access to adequate water supplies and often trigger or exacerbate malnutrition and famine.
- The duration and intensity of droughts have generally increased. While regional droughts have occurred in the past, the widespread spatial extent of current droughts is broadly consistent with expected changes in the hydrologic cycle under warming.
- Current IPCC (Intergovernmental Panel on Climate Change) projections of rising temperatures and sea levels and increased intensity of droughts and storms suggest that substantial population displacements will take place within the next 30–50 years, particularly in coastal zones.

Debate surrounding top-down policy decisions made behind closed doors at the World Trade Organization have food security specialists looking to understand the impact of trade on local food producers, especially considering that the majority of agricultural trade is managed by multinational corporations. The WHO (2015b) has identified this as a problem, and questions what the net impact of trade liberalization will be on those suffering from food insecurity, and how international policies can help offset these impacts.

Famine

Some of the worst threats to basic human security are **famines** and natural disasters, where people are at their most vulnerable in terms of lack of access to basic life-preserving goods. In this section we examine the relationship between famine and human security and how they exist within a complex, multifaceted relationship. The way in which famine has been used as a political weapon to achieve certain ends also speaks to the need to increase development and stability in many developing countries, particularly in the African context.

Famines are dramatic and sudden, leading to increases in death caused by a shortage of food. They are controversial because their causes are debated by academics and politicians. It is part of the function of a government to declare famines, for instance, but where there are "failed" states without centralized functioning governments, often the United Nations will declare famines and humanitarian emergency situations, as was the case in Somalia in 2011. Here, we borrow Jenny Edkins's (2000, 20) definition of famine, which can be described as "a socio-economic process that causes the accelerated destitution of the most vulnerable and marginal groups in society." In this sense, famine is one of the worse types of insecurity an already vulnerable population can experience.

In many ways it is the lack of governance that plays an important role, as authorities simply do not have the resources or capabilities to deal with the crisis that food shortages cause. Moreover, states and governments are hesitant politically to describe their situations as "famine" because they fear the effect it will have on their reputation: It is seen as a mark of failure and has caused the collapse of governments and institutions within a famine-stricken country at times. However, we can see that famines are generally caused by both natural and human-made factors. Three elements seem common to all famines:

1. A decrease in the food supply
2. An increase in the demand for food
3. Changes and deviations in the way food is normally distributed

There is no doubt that these three factors play a large part in determining the levels of suffering and hunger during famines, and they also increase mortality rates as a result. But food security in general has become increasingly important as populations are faced with environmental threats and catastrophes as well as internal civil wars and conflict. There have been some efforts to describe the levels of food security, ranging from good, positive evaluations to disastrous, negative levels of food security. The reality of global development is that we live in an unequal world where some states have more resources and more access to resources than others. A crucial element in human security is the ability to gain access to those resources.

Stages of Food Insecurity

Stage 1: Overall secure food supplies; high level of food security
Stage 2: Moderate to borderline insecurity
Stage 3: Development of food and livelihood crisis, creating insecurity
Stage 4: Beginning of humanitarian emergency
Stage 5: Fully fledged famine conditions/humanitarian disaster

Famine and Insecurity in Somalia

In 2011, the United Nations declared a famine in parts of Somalia, one of the world's failed states where a lack of central government and political, social, and economic conflict had reached crisis levels. Two years of drought displaced 25 percent of Somalia's population, while other countries in the region suffered from spillover effects.

The Problem

Extended drought—the worst in 60 years, according to the UN—caused a severe food crisis in the Horn of Africa, which includes Kenya, Ethiopia, Djibouti, and Somalia. An estimated 12 million people in the region were affected by the drought. The UN declared a famine in six areas of southern Somalia, where it said 750,000 people were in danger of dying without international aid. A lack of rain and the inability of governments to adequately finance agriculture and irrigation schemes were seen as the major causes. Somalia was the worst hit, with at least 6 out of 10,000 children dying each day. In addition, farmers who were unable to meet their basic food costs were abandoning their herds. High cereal and fuel prices had already forced them to sell many animals before the drought, and their smaller herds were now unprofitable or dying.

The humanitarian problem was made worse by conflict. Since its last national government collapsed in 1991, Somalia has become a classic failed state. The UN-backed government is only in charge of parts of the capital, Mogadishu. After two decades of nonstop fighting, most of Somalia's people were already living close to the edge when the drought hit.

The militant group al-Shabab, which has links to al-Qaeda, controls many southern and central areas, including those where famine was declared. But al-Shabab argued that there was no famine in the country, making relief efforts all the more difficult. They also argued that Western aid workers were linked to intelligence services, increasing suspicion and distrust. Even though militants lifted a ban on aid agencies operating in parts of southern Somalia when the drought hit, soon after they accused Western groups of exaggerating the scale of the crisis and again limited access. Politically, al-Shabab, an East African version of the Taliban, wanted to control the aid supplies and forced most Western aid agencies out of the areas they controlled in 2009, which prevented the aid effort in much of Somalia from succeeding.

The result of these factors was that millions of people in Kenya, Ethiopia, and Somalia were forced to live on food rations. Since the beginning of 2011, around 15,000 Somalis each month fled into refugee camps in Kenya and Ethiopia looking for food and water. And while the refugee problem may have been preventable, the violent conflicts in the region had deterred international investment in long-term development programs, which could have reduced the effects of the drought. Development aid would focus on reducing deforestation, topsoil erosion, and overgrazing and improving water conservation. New roads and infrastructure for markets would help farmers increase their profits.

Can Peace Be Restored to Somalia?

Restoring peace to this conflict-ridden nation is the only long-term way to solve the hunger crisis, but it is not easy. Since Somalia descended into anarchy, there have been lots of peace talks but precious little peace. More than a dozen initiatives—spearheaded by the African Union, the UN, and regional countries— have collapsed. Military intervention by foreign countries has also failed.

In addition, economic uncertainty exacerbates the problems. The lack of ways to earn a living and the absence of any government to enforce laws also explain why so many young Somali men have taken to become pirates in the Indian Ocean.

There are now African Union peacekeepers in Somalia, but only 9,000 troops of the promised 20,000 have been deployed, and they are confined to a small part of Mogadishu. Al-Shabab controls the rest of the capital and most southern and central areas. The prospects of a peaceful resolution in Somalia are looking grim at the present time.

Source: BBC News 2011.

Why Are People Hungry?

There has been some success in recent times in alleviating and preventing the number of famines that take place. Through its World Food Program (WFP), the United Nations and groups such as Oxfam and CARE have acted to prevent such human-made and natural disasters. However, this does not mean that hunger has decreased in a global sense. There are still more people dying from starvation because of impoverishment than from the problems created by disasters, although we still see the latter widely used in the media. The WFP estimates that roughly 25,000 people die every day from hunger and associated problems, and that at least a billion people worldwide suffer from malnutrition at any given time. These figures indicate that such problems pose a far greater threat to human existence than wars or terrorism.

The problem is not about supply and demand. We know we have enough food to feed everyone the minimum nutritional intake. Why we have hunger can commonly be attributed to weak or poor governance. Governments that fall into these categories are often highly corrupt, diverting essential resources from their populations to further their own interests, and are often undemocratic in nature. These are political failings and are solvable, but they require political will and social change.

Beyond the basic dysfunctionality of governments, the WFP (2015) further identifies six major factors that contribute to food insecurity:

1. *The poverty trap:* Poverty and hunger are cyclical and repetitive. People who are poor are hungry, and people who are hungry tend to be the poor. They are linked, and the cycle continues until they can break free of the poverty trap, a trap that keeps them confined by their poor circumstances.

2. *Lack of investment in agriculture:* Many developing countries "lack key agricultural infrastructure," preventing them from growing food. If there were more investment in land management, effective use of water, and creating more resistant seed types, poverty and hunger would be drastically reduced. Investment in agriculture is five times more effective in reducing poverty and hunger than any other kind of investment.

3. *Climate and weather:* Natural disasters and changing weather patterns both have an effect on poverty and hunger, but not so much in terms of a lack of food; instead, it is more about the distribution and control of the food supply. These are human-made phenomena and can be rectified given the political will.

4. *War and displacement:* Conflict is an ongoing source of hunger, deprivation, and poverty since it creates instability as people are forced to flee their homes and livelihoods for an uncertain future. In areas where there is relative stability and peaceful circumstances, poverty appears as less of a problem than where there is strife-torn, conflict-ridden communities such as Somalia and the Congo.

5. *Unstable markets:* Food is regarded as a commodity, and the price of food in all its varieties tends to rise and fall. This produces instability for people in the developing world and does not provide them with decent and consistent access to the nutrition they need to survive. Again this is clearly linked to the levels of poverty. If prices of basic nutritional foods are high, poor people cannot afford them. There are many instances of people eating cheaper food, which lacks high nutritional quality, but this can lead to all sorts of problems.

6. *Food wastage:* One-third of all food produced (1.3 billion tons) never gets eaten. This is also linked to energy wastage and ineffective use of resources because it costs money and resources to dispose of the food. It also adds to the environmental problems we see through climate change.

But what drives each of these six factors that result in such extreme poverty? Paul Collier (2008) argues that the poorest countries on the planet are diverging away from other poor states that are experiencing slow growth and raising their living standards. Roughly 70 percent of people living in bottom-billion countries are in Africa, while examples of countries outside the continent that are experiencing such economic crises are Bolivia, Haiti, as well as Laos, Yemen, and Burma. While the world seems to be progressing, conditions in bottom-billion societies are worsening. According to Collier, there are four reasons, or **poverty traps**, that can explain why bottom-billion societies continue to experience extreme depravation.

First, Collier's conflict trap argues that countries experiencing protracted conflicts struggle to lift themselves out of poverty. This group of countries experiences political instability that deters investment on account of continuous civil wars or military coups. The results are extreme social and trade disruption, slow growth, the destruction of infrastructure, and an economic dependency on the sale of primary resources for revenue as a consequence of warlord governance. According to Collier, the average civil war costs approximately US$64 billion.

The second trap is the natural resource trap, which occurs when governments are excessively dependent on their resources sector. When leaders exploit the state's natural resources, they ignore other modes of development, resulting in periods of boom and bust. Such economies fuel corruption, which often leads to dysfunctional governments who fail to invest in their economies. Since revenue is stolen by the state, there is little economic trickle-down to the people. Such states have been referred to as **kleptocratic regimes** since leadership siphons off resource revenue and moves capital outside of the country.

The third trap is referred to as the geography trap and argues that landlocked states that have unfriendly relations with their neighbors will struggle to access global markets. Over 40 percent of the world's poorest societies are landlocked. They must negotiate with their neighbors to access waterways to export materials and also import goods. Some neighbors do not have strong infrastructure while others are war-torn societies, significantly impacting the growth capacity of landlocked states.

Collier's final trap is the governance trap, which argues that dysfunctional democracies and authoritarian states are squandering state resources and mismanaging the economy. Corruption and patronage is endemic in these types of regimes, where political elites manipulate populations to secure power. The result is a lack of investment since official corruption cuts into private-sector costs. Weak taxation systems also emerge since citizens are more likely to hide their income from the state since there is little payoff in the form of social services.

The Post-2015 Development Agenda

The Millennium Development Goals were a set of goals designed to meet certain targets by 2015. While many saw them as a successful initiative at enhancing human security in the Global South, they have also been criticized for leaving out key elements, such as democracy and human rights. Some have even argued that the MDG data are not that impressive when China is removed from the equation, since the goals consider the global average (MacFarquhar 2010). Nonetheless, the MDGs are not simply some "pie in the sky" list designed in some idealistic way. They are actually measurable outcomes in terms of how we can pursue policies to achieve these goals. They can be summarized as follows:

- Goal 1: Reduce extreme poverty and hunger by half.
- Goal 2: Achieve universal primary education.
- Goal 3: Promote gender equality and empower women.
- Goal 4: Reduce child mortality by two-thirds.
- Goal 5: Reduce maternal mortality by three-quarters.
- Goal 6: Reverse the spread of HIV/AIDS, malaria, and other diseases.
- Goal 7: Ensure environmental sustainability.
- Goal 8: Develop a global partnership for development (fair trade and more aid).

While many of the goals were not achieved between 2000 and 2015, the UN has been working to establish a new set of targets. The post-2015 goals will focus on development objectives over the next 15 years and are being drafted as we write this book. They are expected to have more of a focus on sustainable development, trade, and good governance.

While the MDGs may have been a contentious issue for some, few can deny that they have the political world thinking about development. Indeed, the post-2015 development agenda is central to socioeconomic goals in the field of human security.

Solutions to Poverty

While Collier's explanation offers some understanding of why the poorest societies are staying poor, his theory does not offer clear-cut remedies. However, Collier has put forward some ideas for reducing poverty, as have other development economists, including William Easterly and Jeffrey Sachs. These scholars each offer a unique approach to understanding poverty while providing controversial solutions.

For William Easterly (2006), aid workers are usually guilty of the headless heart syndrome, or thinking with their emotions rather than evidence. He criticizes development agencies run by bureaucrats in the West who act as **planners** and design grand aid delivery systems that have a high rate of failure. He sees this type of aid as problematic because it is endorsed and organized by foreigners who have little understanding of the negative effects of aid, which can backfire. He therefore calls on *searchers* to find solutions based on incentive regimes. Easterly's solution to fight endemic poverty is therefore based on developing democratic institutions and free markets within the spirit of entrepreneurialism. Empowering local communities is critical, while foreign intervention is disastrous since it undermines local development initiatives.

According to Jeffrey Sachs (2006), the major barrier to development is poverty itself, which can only be overcome through a major increase in foreign aid. He calls on "planners" to introduce stronger policies that promote trade liberalization at the local level, to engage in **technology transfer**, and to forgive debt of poorer countries. He attacks the World Bank and IMF for failed development policies. Arguing that poor infrastructure, health, and geography have exacerbated the problems in the poorest countries, these economies need a "clinical" approach to development where an increase in capital is prescribed as the best way to reach the MDG goals.

Collier (2008) argues against both Easterly and Sachs by suggesting that aid has contributed to the problem of poverty in bottom-billion societies. Still, he does concede that some aid can work, especially in the context of health. For Collier, aid needs to be strategically repositioned while calling for political, economic, and social reform at the local level. He endorses entrepreneurialism and free markets, as well as the rule of law, charters, and long-term military intervention in failed states. He suggests that stronger laws and regulations leveraged against despotic regimes will minimize the efforts of corrupt leaders to steal state revenue and move it overseas. For Collier, the solution therefore is a multidimensional approach to development through strategic aid, since misguided development assistance contributes to the depravation in bottom-billion societies.

CONCLUSION

We have seen throughout this chapter that globalization is a process that involves the integration of markets on a worldwide basis. Since the end of World War II, this process has accelerated at a rapid scale with the development of new technologies and the reduction in transportation and transaction costs, while tariffs and other human-made barriers to international trade have been lowered. The results have been remarkable. Increasing numbers of developing countries have been experiencing sustained growth rates of 7–10 percent; 13 countries, including China, have grown by more than 7 percent per year for 25 years or more. And the impact of this growth and the emerging economies on the global economy is increasing.

Yet the overall picture is not good. In 2012, a tiny minority (0.6 percent) of the world's population collectively owned 39.3 percent of global assets (Durden 2013). And 1 percent of the world's top wealth holders live in North America, Europe, and the Asian-Pacific countries. All of the indicators point to India, China, and countries in transition as the ones that will become wealthier over time. At the bottom of the pyramid of wealth, Africans will continue to be immersed in poverty, along with parts of Latin America and Asia (Davies, Sandström, Shorrocks, and Wolff 2009).

A recent study entitled "Ethnic Inequality," by Alberto Alesina, Stelios Michalo-poulos, and Elias Papaioannou (2012), found that many underdeveloped countries tend to have wider income disparities across regions, and that ethnic inequality has a strong negative correlation to economic development. Not only is there an unequal distribution of wealth globally, but there is also inequality within countries. According to York University professor Amy Chua (2004), "market dominant minorities," defined by ethnicity, enjoy a distinct economic advantage over the poorer majorities of the population.

There is little doubt that the gap between the rich and the poor continues to grow over time. This is not only in terms of individual wealth but also the divide between rich and poor countries. The relationships are clear. Poor countries and failed states suffer from tremendous levels of human insecurity. We know from history that divisions in wealth are a prime motivator for conflict.

We have also seen, as Nelson Mandela so wisely pointed out, that "poverty is not natural." For every human problem there is a solution. Looking at human security in a more holistic and analytical way is the first step in moving toward solutions to these human-made problems.

KEY TERMS

Absolute Poverty; Capabilities Approach; Conflict Trap; Crisis States; Famine; Food Security; Fragile States; Geography Trap; Gini Coefficient; Governance Trap; Kleptocratic Regimes; Moderate Poverty; Modernization; Monetary Approach; Multidimensional; Multinational Corporations; Natural Resource Trap; New World Order; North–South Divide; Participatory Approach; Planners; Post-2015 Development Agenda; Poverty; Poverty Line; Poverty Trap; Relative Poverty; Social Exclusion; Structural Adjustment Programs; Technocrat; Technology Transfer; Trade Liberalization; Underdeveloped; Vulnerable States; Wealth Gap; Welfare Institutions

FURTHER READING

Collier, Paul. 2008. *The Bottom Billion: Why the Poorest Countries Are Failing and What Can Be Done about It.* Oxford: Oxford University Press.

Easterly, W. 2006. *The White Man's Burden: Why the West's Efforts to Aid the Rest Have Done so Much Ill and so Little Good.* London: Penguin.

Edkins, Jenny. 2000. *Whose Hunger? Concepts of Famine, Practices of Aid*, vol. 17. Minneapolis: University of Minnesota Press.

Freeman, Richard B. 2011. "Globalization and Inequality." In *The Oxford Handbook of Economic Inequality*, edited by Brian Nolan, Wiemer Salverda, and Timothy M. Smeeding. Oxford: Oxford University Press. http://dx.doi.org/10.1093/oxfordhb/9780199606061.013.0023.

Hope, Kempe Ronald. 2005. "Child Survival, Poverty, and Labor in Africa." *Journal of Children & Poverty* 11 (1): 19–42. http://dx.doi.org/10.1080/1079612042000333036.

Keane, J. 2004. "Introduction: Surplus Violence." In *Violence and Democracy* (pp. 1–14). Cambridge: Cambridge University Press. http://dx.doi.org/10.1017/CBO9780511756023.001.

Rotberg, R. 2002. "The New Nature of Nation-State Failure." *Washington Quarterly* 25 (3): 83–96. http://dx.doi.org/10.1162/01636600260046253.

Sachs, Jeffrey. 2006. *The End of Poverty: Economic Possibilities for Our Time*. New York: Penguin.

Therien, J.P. 1999. "Beyond the North–South Divide: The Two Tales of World Poverty." *Third World Quarterly* 20 (4): 723–42. http://dx.doi.org/10.1080/01436599913523.

Thomas, C. 2001. "Global Governance, Development and Human Security: Exploring the Links." *Third World Quarterly* 22 (2): 159–75. http://dx.doi.org/10.1080/01436590120037018.

United Nations Development Programme. 2013. "Human Development Report 2013: The Rise of the South: Human Progress in a Diverse World." http://hdr.undp.org/sites/default/files/reports/14/hdr2013_en_complete.pdf.

Visser, E., and M.O. Van Dijk. 2006. "Economic Globalisation and Workers: Introduction." *Tijdschrift voor Economische en Sociale Geografie* 97 (5): 463–9. http://dx.doi.org/10.1111/j.1467-9663.2006.00356.x.

WEBSITES

Food and Agriculture Organization (FAO): www.fao.org/statistics/en/
Freedom from Hunger: www.freedomfromhunger.org/world-hunger-facts
Human Development Reports: http://hdr.undp.org/en/
Integrated Regional Information Networks (IRIN): www.irinnews.org
International Institute for Sustainable Development: www.iisd.org
Millennium Development Goals: http://undp.org/mdg/
Oxfam International: www.oxfam.org
World Food Programme: www.wfp.org

Chapter 8

BUSINESS AND HUMAN SECURITY
IN FRAGILE ENVIRONMENTS

We have discovered that there is water in Chile, but that the wall that separates it from us is called "profit" and was built by the water code, the constitution, international agreements like the binational mining treaty and, fundamentally, the imposition of a culture where it is seen as normal for the water that falls from the sky to have owners . . . This wall is drying up our basins, it is devastating the water cycles that have sustained our valleys for centuries, it is sowing death in our territories and it must be torn down now.
Chilean demonstrators, Santiago, 2013 (Jarroud 2013)

INTRODUCTION

The impact of business actors on human security is one of the most under-researched fields in the discipline. While a tremendous amount of literature on multinational corporations (MNCs) has emerged in development studies, business ethics, and other fields such as sociology and anthropology, human security specialists often focus on the role of the state, intergovernmental bodies like the United Nations, and NGOs.

This chapter discusses the connection between human security and the private sector. It will explore the impact of MNCs in the Global South and discuss the dynamics of corporate social responsibility within the context of human security. It will present the debates behind environmental protection, climate change, and sustainable development. It will introduce key voluntary initiatives designed to hold business accountable, while presenting case studies surrounding the extractive industry sector. Finally, this chapter will explore corporate social responsibility as a major tool for promoting human security and labor rights.

One of the more controversial themes raised in development studies is the aid versus trade debate. While it is not our intention to revisit this debate, we draw attention to the underlying argument that free trade and investment can enhance the economic security of communities. A principal method for achieving growth is investment, which often comes through the work of transnational business actors. Many of these multinational corporations consider their investments as providing much-needed opportunities throughout the developing world.

Through job creation, skills training, and technology transfer, business actors have much to offer, especially in the context of poverty alleviation and human rights. The growing literature around **corporate social responsibility (CSR)** has called on industry to take on development responsibilities. CSR can be defined as a business strategy that seeks to incorporate economic, social, and environmental policy in the day-to-day operations of a company.

The World Bank defines corporate social responsibility as "The commitment of business to contribute to sustainable economic development, working with employees, their families, the local community and society at large to improve their quality of life, in ways that are both good for business and good for development" (World Business Council for Sustainable Development 2015).

John Elkington (1997) has referred to this approach as the **triple bottom line**, a model that is often used in sustainability reporting by thousands of firms around the world. Yet decades of path-breaking scholarship, such as that by Howard Bowen ([1953] 2013), Robert Ackerman (1973), Archie Carroll (1979), and Duane Windsor (2006), still points to a debate about how a company should behave if it is to be considered socially responsible, let alone as a contributor to development and human security.

Indeed, over the past half century CSR has become an important management issue. Yet business has only recently begun drafting corporate policy around human security themes such as operating in conflict zones, corruption, human rights, and environmental sustainability. Such themes have increasingly become important for business, especially in the post–Cold War era with the downfall of the Soviet Union and the rapid opening of new markets. New opportunities have brought new risks that require industry to think outside its traditional profit-maximization paradigm to minimize operational liabilities brought on by negative environmental and social externalities. As a result, human security themes are now regularly featured in CSR reports, while industry leaders seek out the advice of a wide range of stakeholders, including NGOs, academics, and intergovernmental organizations. Civil society organizations are now considered key stakeholders that have both direct and indirect impacts on the business community.

Calls for industry to use their **sphere of influence** and **sphere of responsibility** to improve the human security of workers and communities has long been considered a practical approach to improving labor rights and environmental degradation in places where regulations are weak. It is also claimed that foreign direct investment (FDI) can help contribute to governments reaching their Millennium Development Goals. CSR programs can help improve human security by targeting child literacy, encouraging microfinancing, promoting best practice labor standards, and ensuring human rights are upheld.

Governments of all types value FDI because it can often bring long-term commitments from the private sector to help improve infrastructure, increase the tax revenue base, and help build the capacity of local industry by providing access to global markets. Business leaders acknowledge the role industry plays in the Global South with many choosing to promote their commitment to development. Multilateral CSR initiatives are increasingly common, such as the United Nations Global Compact, the Equator Principles, the Voluntary Principles on Security and Human Rights, the Global Reporting Initiative, among many others.

On the other hand, there is skepticism about the efficacy and long-term benefits of FDI. A common argument is that FDI only benefits elites and has little economic impact on the poorest communities. Contracts developed between local elites and transnational business actors increases the risk of corruption, especially in the extractive industry where high-level negotiations behind closed doors are common. There is also concern about the cultural impact on communities when MNCs enter an economy. Sociologists have long studied the influence of globalization on non-Western and traditional societies, leading to such concepts as the "McDonaldization" or Americanization of culture. There is also evidence that MNCs bring insecurity and can destabilize communities.

For example, the Coca-Cola Company has been accused of contributing to water insecurity in India. In 2014, local officials in the state of Uttar Pradesh ordered a bottling plant closed for using too much groundwater and causing excess amounts of pollution (Associated Press 2014). While the US-based company has challenged the government's order, controversy over the firm's use of water has long been a grievance of communities and organizations who suggest the company contributes to water shortages and labor rights violations. Yet Coca-Cola has also worked to develop high-profile CSR programs involving primary school education as well as community-based rainwater harvesting projects. The company has also invested heavily in its due diligence program in sourcing materials from its supply chain (Hills and Welford 2005).

Business actors like Coca-Cola undeniably play a role in development. Whether one supports or rejects neoliberal economic growth models, the actions of MNCs deeply impact the security of communities in the developing world. As will be discussed below, there is mounting evidence that business can be a force for good, especially when catastrophe hits. Providing much-needed investment where communities experience economic hardship is an important component of peacebuilding.

Traditionally, MNCs have relied on the **precautionary principle** to ensure they conducted **due diligence** throughout their operations. The concept called on business to reject operations that could damage the environment or cause human harm. Hence, the do-no-harm ethos can be called an early risk assessment to ensure companies did not bring insecurity to the communities where they worked. But as Shawn MacDonald (2013) notes, the do-no-harm principle may do little to advocate peacebuilding initiatives since it does not sway industry to act as a proactive peacebuilder.

This chapter focuses on many of these themes, including the controversies behind profit making in conflict zones, private-sector development in post-conflict societies, as well a discussion on how industry can reduce its nonfinancial risk by integrating CSR strategies into its business model. To begin, we first explore the controversy and human security implications of business operating in conflict zones.

BUSINESS AND CONFLICT ZONES

It is no surprise that the private sector is out for profit, nor should business apologize for protecting its interests and maximizing revenue. After all, this is the nature of business. So long as industry operates within the confines of the law, profit making is both morally and ethically encouraged within the entrenched global economic order. But what happens when business decides to operate in war zones? Is it possible for private-sector actors who benefit from war to be socially responsible? Can business actors promote peace in conflict zones?

Jennifer Oetzel and her colleagues (2010) addressed several of these questions in a recent study by mapping out the business decisions behind the promotion of peace. They outlined numerous ways industry can contribute to peace by fostering economic development, adopting strict codes of conduct, contributing to the community, engaging in track-two diplomacy, and performing risk assessments. The authors note that firms that act ethically may already be contributing to peace through principled behavior, with some companies going as far as strategically promoting it. After all, war is generally bad for business. Yet some companies benefit from conflict, especially firms that are able to secure military contracts that have been outsourced to the private sector. In this section, we highlight the range of actors operating in conflict zones, including multinational corporations, private consultants hired by aid agencies and combatants alike, as well as private military companies.

Making a Profit in Conflict Zones

We have identified five high-risk areas where profit maximization crosses into active conflict zones. First, companies are at risk of contributing to political conflict to protect their resources. The civil war in Angola is one example of a conflict being funded by the exploits of the international mining industry. The international NGO Global Witness estimates that the National Union for the Total Independence of Angola (UNITA), a guerilla group engaged in conflict with the government since the 1970s, had paid for its campaigns through the sales of nearly US$4 billion in diamonds. UNITA controlled close to 70 percent of Angola's diamond deposits, which the group then sold to foreign multinational corporations that would take the goods to market. One of the companies involved was the South African and British–based diamond company De Beers. The company was able to operate in Angola despite a UN Security Council embargo since little enforcement or monitoring was in place. By the turn of the century, campaigns for more accountability and transparency in the diamond sector gained ground, leading to a multilateral effort to end the trade of "blood diamonds" or "conflict diamonds." The result was a certification scheme that became known as the Kimberly Process (Global Witness 2013; see the box below).

The Kimberley Process

The **Kimberley Process** (or KP) is an international governmental certification scheme that was set up to prevent the trade of diamonds that fund conflict. Launched in January 2003, the scheme requires governments to certify that shipments of rough diamonds are conflict-free.

How Did the Kimberley Process Begin?

In 1998, Global Witness launched a campaign to expose the role of diamonds in funding conflict as part of broader research into the link between natural resources and conflict. In response to growing international pressure from Global Witness and other NGOs, the major diamond-trading and -producing countries, representatives of the diamond industry, and NGOs met in Kimberley, South Africa, to determine how to tackle the blood diamond problem. The meeting, hosted by the South African government, was the start of an often contentious three-year negotiating process that culminated in the establishment of an international diamond certification scheme. The Kimberley Process was endorsed by the United Nations General Assembly and the United Nations Security Council and launched in January 2003.

How Does It Work in Practice?

The KP is an import–export certification scheme that requires participating governments to certify the origin of rough diamonds and put in place controls to prevent conflict stones from entering the supply chain. Participant countries enact domestic legislation to implement the scheme and can only trade rough diamonds with other members. The KP's technical provisions are implemented by governments, and NGOs and the diamond industry hold official observer status.

Is the Kimberley Process Working?

The Kimberley Process has chalked up some notable achievements in the past 10 years, including pioneering a tripartite approach to solving international problems and helping some of the countries that were worst hit by diamond-fueled wars to increase their official diamond revenues. However, member governments have repeatedly failed to deal effectively with problem cases such as Zimbabwe, Côte d'Ivoire, and Venezuela. Despite the existence of the Kimberley Process, diamonds are still fueling violence and human rights abuses. The KP's refusal to evolve and address the clear links between diamonds, violence, and tyranny has rendered it increasingly outdated.

Source: Global Witness 2013.

Second, foreign investment in fragile states could lead to divided communities, resulting in ethnic violence and increased insecurity. The oil and gas sector has also been accused of fueling violence in resource-rich economies in the developing world. For example, Royal Dutch Shell was accused of complicity in the violence carried out in Nigeria against an ethnic minority group that had been protesting a company pipeline. In 1993, roughly 300,000 ethnic Ogonis demanded an end to the firm's operations in southeastern Nigeria, claiming that oil production would bring irreversible environmental damage to the region. A series of protests led the Nigerian government to crack down on the protesters, and several activists were shot by police while others were illegally detained. When Royal Dutch Shell complained that the protests continued and had cost the company upwards of $200 million, the government responded by arresting and eventually executing the protest movement's leader. In 1994 Ken Saro-Wiwa, leader of the Movement for the Survival of the Ogoni People (MOSOP), was sentenced to death along with eight other accomplices. When Royal Dutch Shell was publicly criticized for complicity in the outcome, a company spokesperson was quoted as saying the event was "not an appropriate subject for private companies ... to comment on" (Bennett 2001).

Third, the private sector risks **corporate complicity** in human rights violations when they are politically exposed. As mentioned earlier in this text, one of the more infamous cases involved Anvil Mining in Kilwa, a town in the Democratic Republic of the Congo (DRC). In October 2004, the Australian–Canadian mining firm provided company equipment to the DRC government so that it could suppress a local uprising that had put the company's assets in jeopardy. Company officials asked the government to protect its mining interests in the region by flying Congolese soldiers into the community along with military equipment to end the hostilities. Once the soldiers arrived, they quickly ended the small-scale rebellion by killing over 100 people. The soldiers had also used Anvil vehicles to reach Kilwa. Following an investigation by the United Nations Organization

Stabilization Mission in the Democratic Republic of the Congo (MONUSCO), officials accused the company of complicity in rights violations for providing equipment to the government. The incident was later brought to a Quebec civil court by a group of NGOs, but the case was thrown out on jurisdictional grounds by the Supreme Court.

Fourth, business increases its corporate complicity risk when entering joint partnerships with governments engaged in war. Profit seeking in conflict zones can range from weapons manufacturers to Internet service providers. Engineering firms and the food service industry may also operate alongside combatants, as has been the case in Afghanistan. Foreign business actors have been involved with the conflict in that country since the United States launched Operation Enduring Freedom. Private contracting has seen multinational firms partner with US forces as well as the NATO-led International Security Assistance Force. The Swiss firm Supreme Foodservice is estimated to have received over US$5 billion worth of contracts for providing provisions to the US military. American firms have also reaped the benefits of the conflict, including DynCorp International, KBR, and Fluor Corporation. Billions of dollars in contracts have been awarded to these firms through controversial no-bid contracts to carry out a range of activities from construction to logistics (Beaucar Vlahos 2014). Chain restaurants such as Burger King, TGI Fridays, Tim Hortons, KFC, and Pizza Hut have also acted as contractors serving military personal in Kandahar.

Finally, doing business in a fragile post-conflict society can exacerbate peacebuilding initiatives. As Afghanistan transitioned to a post-conflict state dealing with an ongoing insurgency, other multinationals expanded their operations into the country. In 2006, Coca-Cola opened a US$25 million production plant that was awarded to a Dubai-based Afghani entrepreneur. Telecommunications contracts were given to United Arab Emirates (UAE)–based firm Emirates Telecommunications Corporation and South African firm MTN, while financial service providers from Europe and North America launched branches in key cities throughout the country (Garwood 2006). One of the more recent sectors to expand into the country is mining, with Canadian companies taking part in the exploration. MNCs have become a central part of Afghanistan's reconstruction strategy. But can the private sector be integrated into peacebuilding initiatives? After all, it is well known that political and ethnic wars are often fought over resources.

In conflict zones, the most pressing issue for most business actors is profit maximization and maintaining investor confidence. Supremacy is given to meeting financial targets while social and environmental concerns are placed lower on the corporate priority list. The risk is that managers may perceive human security as an immaterial concept falling outside the scope of business. While business actors may not work to directly undermine human security, they may dismiss the concept as a political issue that should be left to government. The conceptual disconnect between human security and business is a dangerous phenomenon in conflict zones.

With heightened security risks, business will often hire **private military companies (PMC)** to protect their assets. The International Code of Conduct for Private Security Service Providers (ICoC) defines PMCs as "guarding and protecting of persons and objects, such as conveys, facilities, designated sites, property or other places (whether armed or unarmed), or any other activity for which the Personnel of Companies are required to carry and operate a weapon in the performance of their duties" (Geneva Academy 2013). In other words, PMCs can be referred to as nonstate armed groups (NSAGs) that provide a range of services in high-risk situations. Often associated with military contractors, PMCs are used by many outfits, including NGOs. As Tim Cross has argued, the hiring of PMCs by humanitarian organizations has "taken place under a veil of silence, in an ad hoc way" (quoted in Perrin 2012, 135). For example, CARE International and the World Food Programme (WFP) have both used PMCs to protect their humanitarian aid missions, while groups such as Médecins Sans Frontières (MSF) have adamantly refused to use them, saying it would compromise their neutrality.

The point that MSF raises is important. As Benjamin Perrin (2012) posits, can PMCs be neutral? After all, they are for-profit actors often operating outside the scope of international law. Infamous violations of humanitarian law involving the now defunct PMC Blackwater raised all sorts of questions concerning how NSAGs operate in conflict zones. But as Perrin points out, the use of PMCs is likely to increase as clients seek protection to operate in the world's most violent conflict zones. This is a telling example of the changing nature of conflict in the post–Cold War era.

A final point worth mentioning is the often overlooked connection between legitimate business interests, human trafficking, and the arms trade. While the criminal element to trafficking and weapons procurement is discussed in the following chapter, there are active transnational firms participating in and profiting from these areas. Global recruitment companies move labor across borders, while a diverse range of legal arms suppliers are found throughout the world. While many of these companies have developed CSR programs, there is a lack of transparency around how these firms operate in conflict zones and perform their due diligence.

War is a profitable enterprise, and business actors will continue to operate in conflict zones so long as there is a market available for them to access. Although most of these firms are acting in their own self-interest, they are also in some ways contributing to long-term peacebuilding objectives by developing infrastructure, creating economic stability, and providing skills training. Of course, as discussed above, MNCs can also bring an array of problems when they profit from war. This section has outlined five concerns about business operating in war-torn societies. We now turn our attention to the relationship between human security and multinational corporations in the Global South.

CAPITALISM AND HUMAN SECURITY

Belief systems on how to improve human security in the developing world are often contentious. With some advocating for greater trade and access to markets, others see debt forgiveness and humanitarian assistance as important strategies for reducing poverty and improving human security. Amid the thousands of studies, data, and opinions on how best to approach the issue, a fundamental question remains on what role, if any, the private sector should play in improving the lives of billions of people.

With nation-building and security traditionally being the responsibility of governments, it is not surprising that industry has been reluctant to join in the development debates. After all, business is not government. The private sector speaks to a whole different set of constituents, including shareholders, employees, and customers. For some, the idea of business performing the tasks of development is misguided because it weakens state capacity by shifting the government's responsibility to unaccountable corporate entities.

Milton Friedman (2002) famously argued that such a system would lead to an unaccountable corporatized world where MNCs would steal from their shareholders to implement public projects that they know nothing about. From this perspective, MNCs pursuing development work to improve human security are buying into a dangerous proposition that sees profit move away from shareholders. It could result in a company losing its competitive edge since the firm might become unable to perform its fiduciary duty to its shareholders by maximizing profit. As Friedman argued, "There is only one social responsibility—to use [a business's] resources to engage in activities designed to increase its profits so long as it stays within the rules of the game, which is to say, engages in open and free competition, without deception or fraud" (Friedman 2002, 133).

Historically, such ideology was entrenched in business school teachings, which could explain why so few companies saw human security themes as a business issue. Bowen ([1953] 2013, 3) recognized this problem early on and wrote "The individual businessman often fails to apprehend fully the connection between his private decisions and the public welfare." Rory Sullivan and Nina Seppala (2003) have made similar arguments and suggest that industry tends to approach issues such as human rights retroactively and typically will only perform a rights audit as a legal defensive mechanism. It is important to remember that there are legitimate arguments as to why business should stay out of the area of human security. For example, business actors do not make laws nor do they develop government institutions. Remaining neutral in the eyes of the state has been a cornerstone of **best practice**.

Critics have accused the private sector's apolitical approach as being damaging and having social and environmental implications because of a global system of unregulated capitalism, especially in the Global South. Business is able to remove itself from the ethical dimension of entering new markets since dysfunctional legal systems and authoritarian regimes fall outside the scope of private-sector duty. Issues such as human rights and corruption are perceived as too politically sensitive for management to discuss; industry perceives itself as a weak link that is unable to make change.

For Janet Dine (2005), this is the result of a dysfunctional market system that leads to a "**race to the bottom**" that is structurally designed to exploit workers and oppress the marginalized. Since private firms operate in this system, there are serious limits to how effective industry can be when it comes to enhancing human rights if they subscribe to profit-maximization theory. For Dine, business interests do not reflect societal interests since management must make decisions based on shareholders rather than the community. Even with such challenges, progressive firms are implementing CSR strategies that reflect human security themes.

The Impact of Multilateral Initiatives

In this section we identify three initiatives being driven by progressive members of the business community that are changing the way MNCs operate in the developing world. First, the post–Cold War era has seen the proliferation of multilateral regulatory initiatives that seek to influence the behavior of the private sector. While many of these regimes remain voluntary global governance initiatives, they have the ability to change the mindsets of industry while providing practical guidance on how to implement accountability mechanisms into a business model. As globalization has increased the power of MNCs, the international community has looked to industry for leadership and innovation. The United Nations no longer speaks only to governments. Regular consultations between the business community and the UN occur to not only seek donor assistance, but also to call for corporate advocacy on issues such as human rights, anti-corruption, climate change, and transparency.

The glut of human security issues facing billions of people who live in communities frequented by MNCs has resulted in the rise of multilateral initiatives. Schemes such as the United Nations Global Compact, the Global Reporting Initiative, and the International Organization for Standardization's recent ISO 26000 all focus on strengthening codes of conduct and enhancing due diligence in terms of social and environmental issues. One of the early multilateral business regimes that addressed such themes was known as the Sullivan Principles. This 1970s initiative was the work of a board member of General Motors (GM), Leon Sullivan, who believed GM could use its corporate influence to help bring an end to apartheid in South Africa. Sullivan would later explain his goal as follows: "Starting with the work place, I tightened the screws step by step and raised the bar step by step. Eventually I got to the point where I said that companies must practice corporate civil disobedience against the laws and

I threatened South Africa and said in two years Mandela must be freed, apartheid must end, and blacks must vote or else I'll bring every American company I can out of South Africa." The principles influenced over 100 companies to leave South Africa in protest and demonstrated how the private sector could mobilize itself around human security issues. It proved so powerful that former UN Secretary-General Kofi Annan would later launch the "Global Sullivan Principles" that brought human rights to the forefront of corporate social responsibility.

The Sullivan Principles

Sullivan Principles (1977)	Global Sullivan Principles (1999)
1. Nonsegregation of the races in all eating, comfort, and work facilities.	1. Express our support for universal human rights and, particularly, those of our employees, the communities within which we operate, and parties with whom we do business.
2. Equal and fair employment practices for all employees.	2. Promote equal opportunity for our employees at all levels of the company with respect to issues such as color, race, gender, age, ethnicity, or religious beliefs, and operate without unacceptable worker treatment such as the exploitation of children, physical punishment, female abuse, involuntary servitude, or other forms of abuse.
3. Equal pay for all employees doing equal or comparable work for the same period of time.	
4. Initiation of and development of training programs that will prepare, in substantial numbers, blacks and other nonwhites for supervisory, administrative, clerical, and technical jobs.	3. Respect our employees' voluntary freedom of association.
	4. Compensate our employees to enable them to meet at least their basic needs and provide the opportunity to improve their skill and capability in order to raise their social and economic opportunities.
5. Increasing the number of blacks and other nonwhites in management and supervisory positions.	5. Provide a safe and healthy workplace; protect human health and the environment; and promote sustainable development.
6. Improving the quality of life for blacks and other nonwhites outside the work environment in such areas as housing, transportation, school, recreation, and health facilities.	6. Promote fair competition, including respect for intellectual and other property rights, and not offer, pay, or accept bribes.
7. Working to eliminate laws and customs that impede social, economic, and political justice (added in 1984).	7. Work with government and communities in which we do business to improve the quality of life in those communities—their educational, cultural, economic, and social well-being—and seek to provide training and opportunities for workers from disadvantaged backgrounds.
	8. Promote the application of these principles by those with whom we do business.

Source: Marshall University, 1977. University of Minnesota Human Rights Library, 2015.

The **United Nations Global Compact (UNGC)** is another key multilateral initiative that seeks to promote human rights, labor rights, sustainable development, and anti-corruption policy. The UNGC is a voluntary global governance initiative that calls on the private sector to respect human rights and the environment, and not engage in corrupt practices. The UNGC serves as a strategic policy initiative that sees business as the primary driver of globalization and an agent capable of ensuring market growth, technology transfer, and economic prosperity (United Nations Global Compact 2015).

On the other hand, critics have accused the UNGC as being a weak governance mechanism since adherence to the UNGC's principles is voluntary and the organization does not monitor the actions of its members. Rather, the UNGC flags companies that fail to meet a certain standard of CSR reporting. Still, the UNGC's influence is rapidly expanding; there are more than 10,000 business participants involved with the scheme, and it has served as a public policy platform for international organizations looking to engage the private sector through a social and environmental framework. For example, in 2003 the UNGC delivered a report entitled "Norms on the Responsibilities of Transnational Corporations and Other Business Enterprises with Regards to Human Rights." The UN suggested that the business community should endorse codes of conducts that were similar to those being adopted by international agencies like the International Labour Organization. The norms were to be modeled after the Universal Declaration of Human Rights so that business would reflect international custom.

However, this model was problematic for industry since it blurred the lines between state and corporate responsibility. As Denis Arnold (2010) notes, although corporations can be implicated in human rights abuse, business lacks the authority to develop and implement laws. The proposal also failed to set basic standards that corporations needed to adhere to, making for weak guidelines. Finally, the norms were not considered voluntary and thus required business to report on human rights themes that they did not fully understand. Industry pushback against the document led the UN secretary-general to reject the proposal and appoint a special rapporteur to make clear the UN's position on business and human rights.

The Ten Principles of the United Nations Global Compact

Human Rights

- Principle 1: Businesses should support and respect the protection of internationally proclaimed human rights; and
- Principle 2: make sure that they are not complicit in human rights abuses.

In 2008, the UN's Special Rapporteur John Ruggie launched a proposal framework for business and human rights that outlined the following responsibilities:

1. The state duty to protect against human rights abuses by third parties, including business
2. The corporate responsibility to respect human rights
3. The need for greater access by victims to effective remedy, both judicial and nonjudicial (Business and Human Rights Resource Centre 2015b)

This framework would become known as the "protect, respect, remedy" approach and was unanimously approved by the UN Human Rights Council. In 2011, the special rapporteur introduced a report entitled "Guiding Principles on Business and Human Rights: Implementing the United Nations 'Protect, Respect and Remedy' Framework," which would provide further direction on how industry could better work with states to protect human rights.

Two other reporting initiatives worth mentioning that influence the behavior of business in the context of human security are the **Global Reporting Initiative (GRI)** and the ISO 26000. The GRI is a Dutch-based sustainability organization that collaborates with the United Nations Environment Programme to provide explicit instructions on how a business may audit, draft, and implement CSR strategies. Founded in the United States in 1997 by the Coalition for Environmentally Responsible Economies and the Tellus Institute, the original aim of the GRI was to ensure responsible environmental conduct and reporting. Since the GRI's inception, however, the initiative has evolved to cover a range of social and environmental concerns. The GRI's fourth generation, or G4, was launched in 2013 and provides specific instructions on how a company can enhance its transparency through reporting on issues such as human rights, corruption, sustainability, labor rights, and management's approach to sustainability reporting. The GRI is meant to complement other voluntary reporting regimes such as the UNGC, the UN's Guiding Principles on Business and Human Rights, as well as the OECD Guidelines for Multinational Enterprises.

Launched in 2010, **ISO 26000** is an initiative of the International Organization for Standardization that offers guidance for organizations looking to develop standard social responsibility practices such as community outreach and **stakeholder engagement** developed around a CSR framework. The purpose of the tool is to move business beyond basic compliance with the law toward thinking about how a firm impacts the community around it. Themes emerging from the standard include transparency, accountability, human rights, business ethics, international norms, respect for the rule of law, as well as stakeholder interest. ISO 26000 is yet another example of a business-driven multilateral stakeholder initiative that offers guidance on how a company can ethically operate in environments where it may encounter human security threats on a day-to-day basis.

A second shift in business ideology that has taken place over the years is the growing support for **public–private partnerships** (**PPPs**) to help alleviate development challenges like poverty. Craig Zelizer (2013, 44) writes "a growing number of businesses have been involved in international development, especially as donors push for increased public/private partnerships." The United Nations defines a true PPP as follows:

- Voluntary and builds on the respective strengths of each partner
- Optimizes the allocation of resources
- Achieves mutually beneficial results over a sustained period
- Involves written agreements that specify the purpose and duration of the partnership, governance, as well as exit arrangements (United Nations Foundation 2002)

The idea of partnering is both publicly appealing and operationally efficient for aid agencies. It also appeals to governments and businesses alike who benefit from a shared responsibility and self-interest for the delivery of public goods and services. While

PPPs may be attractive for aid agencies looking to increase their capacity for delivering aid and building resources, the business community has other motivations that may entice partnership agreements. According to Blowfield and Murray (2008), PPPs must provide some type of alternative public relations gains that would not otherwise be available to the business. Second, the company has to see a strong **business case** for a PPP, such as access to a new market or branding opportunities. Finally, the company may be actively pursuing PPPs in an effort to voluntarily regulate itself and comply with government demands. Although each motivation listed above is shaped by corporate self-interest, it is not to say that PPPs cannot play a positive role in building security.

For example, the United Nations Development Programme (2014) manages the Public–Private Partnerships for Service Delivery (PPPSD) program that "seeks to increase the access of the poor to basic services such as water, waste, energy, education and health by promoting inclusive partnerships between local government, business and communities." The program operates within the context of the Millennium Development Goals that seek to reduce poverty while connecting with civil society and the private sector. By drawing investment from the private sector, the PPPSD moves development strategy beyond the traditional realm of public-sector initiatives. The program also hosts a Global Learning Network that offers a space for stakeholders to come together and pool their resources when building partnerships. Partners can range from individuals, NGOs, and also industry.

Private–public partnerships are indeed on the rise, with industry seeing reputation gains and new market access through such partnerships. Business is moving beyond the traditional one-off philanthropic donation model and is now providing wide-ranging material support for public outreach campaigns that deal with human security issues. For example, the Norwegian oil giant Statoil has developed partnerships with Amnesty International, the United Nations Development Programme (UNDP), the International Crisis Group, and the Red Cross, among others. Part of Statoil's CSR policy has been to integrate human rights themes into its business model. In Venezuela, for example, the company helped finance efforts by Amnesty International and the UNDP to modernize the country's judicial system in an effort to improve the country's human rights record.

In the area of public health, PPPs are emerging to address the scourge of infectious disease worldwide. In 1996, the Rockefeller Foundation launched the International AIDS Vaccine Initiative, which works with governments, foundations, MNCs, and NGOs. The project develops advocacy networks, runs educational campaigns, and develops vaccine candidates along with administering drug trails. Another multistakeholder coalition is the Global Fund to Fight Aids, Tuberculosis and Malaria, launched in 2002, which was to act as a "war chest" of funding to fight three of the world's deadliest diseases. The Global Fund began as a commitment from governments but has since involved the participation of private-sector actors. In 2008, for example, Chevron donated $30 million to the fund and committed an additional $25 million two years later.

The Equator Principles are another multilateral initiate championed by the financial industry to manage economic, environmental, and social risk associated with lending. The initiative was developed under the guidance of the World Bank and called on financial institutions to not lend money to projects that violated UN conventions. In 2013, Equator Principles III was launched, where the 80 member-institutions rank potential clients based on social and environmental risk. Specific attention is placed on human rights and the environmental impact of large-scale infrastructure projects.

A final banking scheme worth mentioning is the Wolfsberg Group, which serves as a multilateral monitoring initiative that focuses on anti-money laundering and terrorist financing. It is well established that many terrorists move money using the global banking system. The Wolfsberg Group have committed themselves to perform "enhanced due diligence" when operating in high-risk environments or with suspicious clients. Although both are voluntary, the Equator Principles and the Wolfsberg Group will continue to play an important role in encouraging transparency and accountability within the financial sector throughout the post–Cold War era.

BUSINESS AND HUMAN SECURITY IN THE GLOBAL SOUTH

Thomas Weiss (2013) has accurately pointed out that principles of neoliberalism and those of humanitarianism may seem to controversially juxtapose each other. In fact, aid workers may take offense to having the terms *business* and *humanitarianism* in the same sentence. Whatever your feelings may be about this issue, private-sector actors *are* championing human security issues, and many aid agencies and governments are starting to see the financial support and corporate influence of business as pillars in development.

One multi-stakeholder business-driven organization is the Business and Humanitarian Forum (BHF). The BHF was founded in 1999 and is designed to bring industry, NGOs, and government together. It has been involved in organizing funds for humanitarian relief in Afghanistan and the Balkans, and in 2014 the BHF held a joint conference with the human security and business unit of the Swiss Federal Department of Foreign Affairs entitled "Responsible Growth Paths: Policies and Practices from the Extractive Sector." The two-day workshop looked at how to develop CSR strategies in the mining sector. Participants from major multinational corporations such as De Beers, Norsk Hydro, and Addax Petroleum met with humanitarian groups ranging from UNICEF, World Vision, and the World Wide Fund for Nature. Representatives from the World Economic Forum, the International Labour Organization, as well as several academics also attended.

Corporate Humanitarians in the Philippines

In November 2013, one of the world's strongest typhoons on record made land-fall in the small Southeast Asian country of the Philippines. Typhoon Yolanda/Haiyan brought widespread devastation to one of the region's poorest countries, killing over 6,000 people. More than 1 million homes were destroyed, displacing over 4 million people. Nearly 6 million workers lost their livelihoods with no work available because of damaged infrastructure and little market access. Health facilities were destroyed, schools were annihilated, and sanitation infrastructure was leveled. The tragedy in the Philippines offers a solemn reminder that there are unforeseeable natural events that cause pervasive human insecurity.

International donors rushed to the Philippines's assistance in building an integrated recovery effort. This involved foreign government assistance, international NGOs, humanitarian appeals, fundraising events, as well as a strong United Nations response. Over the next two years, donors would give nearly US$800 million and counting. While traditional donors have been critical in coordinating and rallying the international community's disaster response effort, the business community has played a quieter role as an important stakeholder in the recovery.

Asian, European, and North American MNCs have contributed millions to the relief effort while partnering with NGOs to deliver the funding. For example, PepsiCo donated $1 million and partnered with the American Red Cross, Give 2Asia, Save the Children, and Habitat for Humanity. The global logistics firm UPS launched its "Global Humanitarian Relief Program" by offering $1 million in aid as well as technical expertise in distributing relief material. Other companies, such as JPMorgan Chase, Walt Disney Company, Toyota, IKEA, Sony, Nikon, and Royal Caribbean Cruises, all contributed substantial donations.

The humanitarian motivation of the private sector is debatable, with many of the donor corporations having significant business ties with the Philippines. Firms that did not provide any humanitarian relief would risk being labeled a "bad corporate citizen" for failing to support the community in a time of crisis. Still, CSR advocates would quickly point to a clear business case for humanitarianism that appeals to the self-interest of industry. Indeed, self-interested MNCs are becoming an important ally of humanitarian relief campaigns.

Source: Business and Human Rights Resource Centre 2013.

In fact, humanitarianism has been on the corporate agenda for decades. According to Michael Hopkins (2012), there are three types of activities that business has traditionally engaged in to carry out development work. The first type is charitable donations given by a company within the context of philanthropy. Interest in giving monetary donations has been on the rise since the early 1990s, with industry supporting causes that are in line with their respective business interests. Powerful individuals, such as Warren Buffett and Bill Gates, are now leading the charge to give and engage in humanitarian causes. For example, the Bill & Melinda Gates Foundation alone has contributed over US$30 billion in funding to public health initiatives in the developing world. The foundation provides vaccines, medicine, and diagnostics to combat diseases such as HIV, polio, and malaria. To put this in perspective, the Gates Foundation's aid budget is larger than the World Health Organization's. Billionaire investor George Soros is another philanthropist who has contributed extensive funding to human security causes. In 2010, Soros gifted US$100 million to New York–based Human Rights Watch to help increase the capacity and global reach of the organization.

The second type of business and development activity performed by MNCs is operating in the Global South. Hopkins (2012, 9) notes, "Development inside the company that initiates new products for developing countries, or invests in a developing country to take advantage of cheap labour or special skills or natural resources such as oil . . . directly impacts upon the profits of the whole organization." This type of humanitarianism is ideological and endorses a certain type of business model. Still, there are many examples of MNCs developing local products that have contributed to building state capacity. For instance, in 2005 Oxfam worked with Unilever Indonesia to assess the societal impact of the MNC's operations. The report concluded that Unilever helped create jobs, kept capital in the country, transferred technology, and improved local job skills. In addition, there were lessons learned by each partner, with Oxfam acknowledging that not all business decisions made by Unilever were about profit, while Unilever gained insight into how the company's value-chain policies can help reduce poverty by creating new jobs (Oxfam 2005).

Hopkins's third type of development work involving MNCs is the promotion of **sustainable development**. Such programs can help build a company's reputation as well as profitability. Sustainable development encourages businesses to reduce their energy consumption, use materials more efficiently, and produce less waste, all of which contributes to the bottom line while reducing the business's footprint. The past half century has seen greater public demand for environmental accountability from the private sector. The relationship between business and ecosystems in the developing world is of increasing importance since regulatory regimes are weak. In 2006, the Stern Review (an independent review of the effects of climate change undertaken by UK government) confirmed that the developing world would suffer more than advanced economies on account of climate change (Stern 2006). The IMF and World Bank estimate that $100 billion will be needed each year from the advanced economies for climate mitigation and adaptation infrastructure investment (World Bank 2015a). But business has been late to the debate, with some industries explicitly denying that climate change is occurring.

For example, the former CEO of Exxon Mobil, Lee Raymond, publicly questioned the science behind global warming while the company donated over $15 million to right-leaning think tanks that sought to challenge climate science and lobby government policy. Today, Exxon Mobil, along with other oil MNCs such as BP and Shell, all acknowledge the existence of climate change. BP, for instance, has undertaken a greening strategy to brand itself as a champion of sustainable development, while Shell's (2015) climate change policy reads as follows:

> Population growth and economic development are driving up energy demand. All energy sources will be needed, with fossil fuels meeting the bulk of demand. At the same time CO_2 emissions must be reduced to avoid serious climate change. To manage CO_2, governments and industry must work together. Government action is needed and we support an international framework that puts a price on CO_2, encouraging the use of all CO_2-reducing technologies. Shell is taking action across four areas to help secure a sustainable energy future: natural gas, biofuels, carbon capture and storage, and energy efficiency.

Apart from the oil and gas sector, other business organizations are actively involved in sustainable development initiatives. The World Business Council for Sustainable Development (WBCSD) is one of the better-known organizations, with offices in India, Switzerland, and the United States. Following the Earth Summit held in Rio de Janeiro in 1992, the WBCSD emerged as a CEO-led group committed to sustainability and the environment. There are 200 member companies operating throughout the world whose combined revenue tops US$7 trillion. The WBCSD works to disseminate best practice environmental policy throughout its network. Overall, the three types of development aid—philanthropy, internal development of corporate capacity, as well as sustainable development—all play a role in improving livelihoods in the Global South.

HUMAN SECURITY, CORRUPTION, AND CSR

Perhaps the most serious allegations levied against MNCs operating in the developing world concerns human rights. While touching on this issue in Chapter 3, it is worth revisiting at length given the close connection between human insecurity and illicit corporate behavior. As already discussed, corporations cannot commit direct human rights violations under international law since they are not nation-states. However, MNCs may be complicit in right violations, especially when they provide material support for governments that commit such acts. Complicity can range from bribing state officials to secure land concessions to lending company equipment to government forces to carry out state-sanctioned atrocities.

Still, indirect violations are much more common and often difficult to identify. One measure of assessing a company's human security impact is to consider the organization's legal compliance. There is a deep connection between human insecurity and **corruption**. Companies that ignore the rule of law or undermine it by cheating are weakening human security in developing states. One of the most frequent offenses committed by the private sector is bribery, which seriously impacts governing institutions such as the judiciary and police.

It is now widely accepted that societies struggling with endemic corruption are more likely to experience low levels of human security and rights violations. Corruption in the developing world contributes to human rights violations because it undermines the capacity of state institutions that are designed to protect citizens. When government agencies are compromised on account of bribery or patronage, society becomes a victim. When state funding is stolen by officials, critical services such as a country's health and security regime are impacted by a lack of resources. Professionals who are underpaid by the state are more likely to turn to bribery to supplement their income, contributing to a dysfunctional state. For example, when a company pays bribes to customs' officials to export goods out of a country, they are contributing to the destabilization of government and thereby the weakening of state capacity. Those who cannot afford to bribe are left without options and quickly become marginalized. When foreign MNCs enter weak markets and pay bribes to compete, they are silently endorsing a dysfunctional legal system that cannot ensure human security.

Corruption can be defined as "the abuse of entrusted power for private gain. It hurts everyone whose life, livelihood or happiness depends on the integrity of people in a position of authority" (Transparency International 2015). Endemic corruption exists in many emerging economies, with business actors seeing little choice but to pay bribes if they are to stay competitive. Indeed, management is often ill prepared to implement strong anti-corruption policies within their business model. We also know that anti-corruption and human rights strategies are rarely taught in business schools (Hanlon and Frost 2013). This has contributed to a managerial knowledge gap on how business can effectively operate in weak regulatory environments while protecting human rights.

Moreover, managers who are unwilling to perform social or environmental risk assessments may be undermining human security. For these types of operations, doing business with oppressive regimes is not a moral issue. Human security is to be left up to government since these firms follow the Friedman (2002) ethos that the "business of business is business." However, such firms will respond to a strong business case that centers on financial gains and corporate risk. Advocates for human rights and security must find ways to communicate nontraditional financial risk to these so-called hardnosed businesspeople. Focusing the business case on financial loss, corporate liability, and criminal negligence can serve as a powerful motivator to even the most skeptical agents. For example, in 2008 a shockwave of fear was sent through industry when Europe's largest engineering firm, Siemens, was fined nearly US$1.4 billion for bribery by US and German regulators. The specter of the US Department of Justice was felt by firms whose stock is traded on US stock exchanges since they are bound by the US Foreign Corrupt Practices Act. The long reach of the US anti-corruption authorities was recently witnessed with a crackdown on FIFA executives accused of receiving bribes in exchange for supporting votes for the 2018 and 2022 World Cups (Phipps, Hills, and Armen Graham 2015). Indeed, foreign bribe paying became a real financial and legal threat to any firm with ties to the US market. Although corruption in emerging economies has become a business issue, human rights have been slow to catch on in similar circles, although this is changing.

As former United Nations High Commissioner for Human Rights Mary Robinson (2003) has argued, the private sector now considers human rights as a business issue. Globalization has brought new technology that enables activist groups to document and disseminate irresponsible corporate behavior in real time. Civil society is challenging the private sector to take responsibility in their spheres of influence. An influential 2003 article in the *Harvard Business Review* by Elliot Schrage (2003a) sounded the corporate alarm by suggesting that business needed to adapt to changing societal expectations. Schrage (2003b) cites various human security themes that could place corporate interests in jeopardy. He then recommends that businesses establish clear guidelines on how to work with governments yet ensure the relationship remains separate from any dubious state activity. Many firms are now actively considering how they impact communities and what financial fallout will occur if the issue is not taken seriously.

Finance and Land Grabbing in Cambodia

One of the most controversial methods of development is the reclaiming of private land by governments to promote development. In Cambodia, the illegal seizure of land has been a common occurrence over the past few decades. Since 2000, the Cambodian rights group Licadho estimates that over 500,000 people have been forcefully evicted from their land. In 2011, the World Bank suspended loans to the country after complaints of violent evictions in the Boeung Kak Lake community in Phnom Penh.

Many of these evictions have been carried out on behalf of private business actors who have secured land concessions for development. One company at the center of the controversy was the Phnom Penh (PP) Sugar Company, which was accused of forcefully removing over 1,000 families from their homes to develop a sugar plantation. The crop was to be owned by a Cambodian tycoon who was also a senator with the country's ruling party.

Representatives from the evicted community noted that the land was seized by the military, and families were given US$100 in compensation, which did not cover the costs of rebuilding their livelihoods. The displacement resulted in greater poverty within the community and pressured some families to remove their children from school so that they could find work.

It was later discovered that the PP Sugar Company had received its financial backing from the Australian-based ANZ Bank. The company is a signatory to the

Equator Principles, which requires it to conduct extensive social and environmental audits on high-risk loans. In this case, due diligence failed and the bank was left with a public relations debacle. ANZ dropped PP Sugar Company as a client, which caused more controversy from local NGOs as well as Oxfam International, who argued that such an abrupt end to the relationship could negatively impact the communities that were benefiting from the sugar company's investments.

Although there is no easy solution in this situation, the ANZ controversy provides an example of the often complex and ethically uncertain world of finance in emerging economies. The bank may not have had an easy out, but it could have significantly minimized its risk by effectively carrying out its due diligence obligations and following its own corporate policies that were in line with the Equator Principles.

Sources: Oxfam 2014; Snowdon 2014.

Robert and Shannon Blanton (2007) also note that environments that enjoy strong human rights are able to develop sustainable conditions for business innovation and productivity while also promoting trade. They suggest that companies that operate in environments with poor human rights records are exposed to high risk, such as unpredictable taxation, political violence, and economic sanctions. From this perspective, MNCs that promote human security and operate in stable environments may lower their business risk—human security and CSR are good for business.

Nonetheless, there are many companies that hold different views of what CSR means. Companies that advocate responsible investment and endorse CSR as a community engagement strategy may be met by local resistance. Communities may be skeptical of MNCs that endorse human rights given the long imperial history of many Western states. While most routine business practices do not bring negative human security implications, community perceptions may differ. Given the high-level talks and closed-door meetings associated with business negotiations, communities may feel excluded and that their best interests are unrepresented.

Moreover, MNCs often operate within legal gray zones that may witness questionable corporate behavior that is not necessary illegal. As mentioned above, US companies operating in South Africa during the apartheid era were following the law; however, the ethics of profiting from a racist regime would be considered by many to be morally reprehensible behavior. Indeed, transnational markets have raised new questions on how MNCs should operate in the era of globalization. Here we hope to explore the intersection of globalization and human insecurity to gain a clearer understanding of how CSR can help enhance security in the developing world.

First, MNCs can advocate for the principles of sustainable development. The practice of outsourcing has allowed certain industries to externalize costs by moving production of goods and services to jurisdictions with weak environmental regulations and poor labor practices, resulting in pollution and low wages. The "race to the bottom," driven by neoliberal ideology, has led to serious health risks for workers and consumers buying ready-made products. Materials used in the production process of many goods often involve energy-generating raw materials. Mismanagement of finite resources such as oil, solid fuel, and natural gas can significantly damage ecosystems. There is a strong business case for protecting ecosystems since industry benefits from the natural environment. For example, the agribusiness industry depends on a stable freshwater supply and nature's pollination. The Millennium Ecosystem Assessment, a study concerned with ecosystem trends launched by former UN Secretary-General Kofi Annan, has suggested that the private sector can serve as a powerful force by promoting environmental protection and improving their operational strategies to reduce waste and endorse environmental regulatory regimes.

Second, business can take on humanitarian causes through fundraising and philanthropy. Yet industry can also respond to international crises by volunteering their services and providing expert skills during disaster relief efforts. Emergency microfinancing and local investment can help communities rebuild following tragedies such as natural disasters or violent conflict. Business plays an important role in rebuilding domestic economies, a point the UNDP has long recognized, which is why it works to connect stakeholders from the NGO world with industry. The need to rebuild local markets quickly is imperative to ensure livelihoods are sustained. For example, the UNDP's emergency response program endorsed a "cash-for-work" program following Typhoon Haiyan in the Philippines. Cash donations that were made to the UNDP were used to empower communities via financial incentives throughout the clean-up effort. Moreover, some corporate leaders are endorsing the concept of social enterprise as a self-sustaining for-profit business model to address humanitarian concerns the world over. Social entrepreneurism is on the rise as humanitarians look to move to a more financially secure organizational model.

A final humanitarian focus where business can play a direct impact involves labor rights. Business operations in weak legal jurisdictions can lead to lax rules and regulations in the workforce. Only through due diligence can companies ensure that workers' rights are respected and labor laws are not violated. Corporate leadership needs to regularly inspect its **supply chain** and ensure that human resource managers are well equipped for dealing with employee grievances. There must be clear policies in place to ensure child labor is rejected and that health and safety issues are a priority. This is especially true considering the complexity of most supply chains, which may have components buried throughout multiple tiers throughout the network. For example, while a manager may be able to investigate factory conditions at the point of assembly where a product is made, it becomes difficult to examine the factories where each component of the product originates; each of these parts also has their own supply chain.

Still, companies can improve the well-being of workers by endorsing best practice standards as set by the International Labour Organization (ILO). If a company is unsure how to proceed, they can consult the ILO, which offers training on how to transform dysfunctional work environments into models of professionalism. Moreover, companies can bridge cultural divides by offering employment to diverse groups of job seekers. For example, some companies in Northern Ireland intentionally hired both Catholics and Protestants to work together in an effort to bridge the religious divide. Another humanitarian effort might involve human rights training of police and corporate security officers, a move Freeport Mining in Indonesia undertook after violence had been reported at its mining operations. In 2011, the company had been accused of complicity in human rights violations for inadequately training security guards, while police officers protecting the mine shot and killed three workers who were protesting over a wage dispute. Due diligence and training may have reduced such violence.

CONCLUSION

There is no denying that multinational corporations can have a significant impact on an individual's human security. Historically, capitalist systems have been designed to maximize profit and exploit resources without considering the social and environmental costs of such behavior. This is changing with many leading business actors publicly endorsing the triple bottom line ideology and corporate social responsibility strategies while performing due diligence throughout their business models.

Industry cannot afford to ignore the human security risks associated with their actions. Corruption and corporate complicity in human rights violations directly undermine the rule of law, thereby weakening the very institutions designed to build human security. Moreover, firms who operate in conflict zones and profit from war stand to lose revenue while incurring damage to their reputation should they not adhere to strong codes of conduct. Although business actors are not bound by international law in the same way that states are, there are significant nontraditional risks and costs faced by firms that are noncompliant with best practice standards on how to manage their operations in conflict and post-conflict societies.

Although there is much debate surrounding the impact of MNCs in development and their relation to human security, transnational business actors operate in these environments whether we agree with it or not. This sector can hold powerful sway over state agencies tasked to deliver human security. From this perspective, MNCs can play an important role as advocates for human security by leading through example and contributing to the well-being of communities, especially when they face humanitarian crises. The private sector is a critical human security stakeholder that cannot be overlooked.

KEY TERMS

Best Practice; Business Case; Corporate Complicity; Corporate Social Responsibility (CSR); Corruption; Due Diligence; Global Reporting Initiative (GRI); ISO 26000; Kimberley Process; Philanthropy; Precautionary Principle; Private Military Company (PMC); Protect, Respect, Remedy; Public–Private Partnership (PPP); Race to the Bottom; Sphere of Influence; Sphere of Responsibility; Stakeholder Engagement; Supply Chain; Sustainable Development; Triple Bottom Line; United Nations Global Compact (UNGC)

FURTHER READING

Carroll, A.B. 1999. "Corporate Social Responsibility: Evolution of a Definitional Construct." *Business & Society* 38 (3): 268–95. http://dx.doi.org/10.1177/000765039903800303.

Hanlon, R.J. 2014. *Corporate Social Responsibility and Human Rights in Asia*, vol. 48. New York: Routledge.

Hopkins, M. 2007. *Corporate Social Responsibility and International Development: Is Business the Solution?* London: Earthscan.

Ruggie, John G. 2007. "Business and Human Rights: The Evolving International Agenda." *American Journal of International Law* 101 (4): 819–40.

Welford, R. 2002. "Globalization, Corporate Social Responsibility and Human Rights." *Corporate Social Responsibility and Environmental Management* 9 (1): 1–7. http://dx.doi.org/10.1002/csr.4.

Windsor, D. 2006. "Corporate Social Responsibility: Three Key Approaches." *Journal of Management Studies* 43 (1): 93–114. http://dx.doi.org/10.1111/j.1467-6486.2006.00584.x.

WEBSITES

Anti-Corruption Research Network: http://corruptionresearchnetwork.org

Ashoka Foundation: www.ashoka.org

Equator Principles: www.equator-principles.com

Fair Labor Association: www.fairlabor.org

Global Reporting Initiative: www.globalreporting.org

Global Witness: www.globalwitness.org

International Standardization Organization: ISO 26000: www.iso.org/iso/home/standards/iso26000.htm

Transparency International: http://www.transparency.org

United Nations Global Compact: www.unglobalcompact.org

Voluntary Principles on Security and Human Rights: www.voluntaryprinciples.org

World Business Council on Sustainable Development: www.wbcsd.org

Chapter 9

DISPLACED PEOPLE, TRANSNATIONAL CRIME, AND HUMAN SECURITY

We are entering a bifurcated world. Part of the globe is inhabited by Hegel's and Fukuyama's Last Man, healthy, well fed, and pampered by technology. The other, larger, part is inhabited by Hobbes' First Man, condemned to a life that is "poor, nasty, brutish and short." Although both parts will be threatened by environmental stress, the Last Man will be able to master it; the First Man will not.

Robert Kaplan (1994)

INTRODUCTION

More than 20 years ago, Robert Kaplan painted a picture of a descending anarchy that was going to engulf parts of West Africa with global consequences. Ethnic, tribal, and identity grievances reinforced by environmental disasters, economic despair, and the collapse of states reinforced these predictions of a bleak future. At the time, and now, we face the fallout of human security catastrophes, with millions moving across borders legally and illegally, drug wars, and massive criminal networks that feed off of and create these anarchic conditions, leading to cycles of violence and insecurity. The future seems exceptionally bleak from this perspective: Progress and the betterment of humanity seem like illusions, as does human security for individuals, groups, and many nations and nation-states. Shimmering in the distance but just out of reach are the promises of globalization, which appears to have left far more in the losing camp than the winning.

This chapter deals with some of the most pressing problems in human insecurity today in the sense that it examines the movement of people across borders, human trafficking, and transnational crime. These problems are largely human-made and take on special significance because with concerted political will they could be prevented or solved. Many of the people on the move (voluntary or involuntary) are some of the most vulnerable individuals and groups on the planet. They lack the empowerment and strength necessary to control the direction of their lives, and this places them in a vulnerable and disturbed state of human insecurity. They appear to be without the capacity to control or influence their political, social, or economic direction. What's interesting from a human security perspective is that many of these problems have strong links to organized transnational crime and global criminal networks. Due to globalization, consumerism, and the increasing interdependence of the world we live in this makes these difficulties far harder to eradicate and resolve. It also makes these desperate individuals so much more vulnerable to ruthless predators willing to exploit their circumstances and conditions. The fact that organized terrorist networks and groups like Al-Qaeda and ISIS are also heavily embedded in criminal activity is another worrying trend and even more difficult to eradicate in many ways.

This chapter also argues that although **refugees** and economic **migrants** are often perceived as contentious and seen as threats to state sovereignty, they are often the victims of oppressive national state policies that discriminate and condemn them to marginalized lives. These people typically fall within the ranks of the disempowered, only distinguished in their degree of choice in the matter. Much of this cheap migrant labor helps to sustain the economies of the Global North and South, yet the vast majority of these people are often on the receiving end of brutal hardship and grave human insecurity in living and employment terms. The case of migrant workers in the Arab Gulf states is a good example of people enduring severe hardship, alienation, and abysmal living conditions while working away from home. To state the obvious that they can earn more there than back home does nothing to diminish the sad state of insecurity and poor conditions they find themselves in where they can be deported on a whim. The case of the Rohingya people (Muslim refugees/migrants from Bangladesh into Burma) is also important because it combines aspects of refugees, youth, and children who are exploited by criminal sex traffickers.

Throughout this chapter the reader will be introduced to the key concepts, institutions, and definitions of migration and trafficking. More important, what does it mean to be stateless? What does the United Nations High Commissioner for Refugees do and why should anyone be concerned about migration patterns on the other side of the world? The role of transnational crime is also a topic covered in this chapter, including its deleterious effects on human security. The case of the Mexican drug war will be examined in some detail because it is a conflict that transcends borders and has implications for ordinary people.

Migration is one of the most important and difficult issues facing nation-states and the international community today. Globalization is transforming and accelerating the movement of people seeking new economic opportunities around the world. The push–pull figures are staggering: The number of labor migrants living outside their country of origin for a minimum of one year constitutes an estimated 3 percent of the global population. Conditions at home and a lack of economic opportunities (push factors) are coupled with incentives (pull factors) from receiving countries that contribute to skills-based labor or cheap manual labor. While neoliberalism and deregulation have encouraged mobility of capital across boundaries, restrictions on labor flows have remained intact and in some cases increasingly suppressive, impeding the efforts of migrants seeking more economically viable opportunities outside their home base. This protectionist response taken by receiving states contributes to the insecurity and vulnerability of migrants by limiting access to employment, protection, and social safety nets. These processes highlight what's missing in governance as a result of globalization. In this section of the chapter we will explore some of the ways in which globalization has contributed to increased rates in migration and the subsequent effects this has had on human security. Good governance should encompass reasonable protection for migrants. Unfortunately, in many states it seems that this is not the case.

Globalization's Effects on Migration

Globalization has had wide-reaching effects, going well beyond the exchange of goods and services as positioned by neoliberal economic models of capitalism. The transformation in communications and transportation has provided the global population with access to the rest of the planet. This has delivered not only an increased awareness of alternative and different worldviews and cultural norms, it has also shown the diversity in standards of living, income disparities, and differences in social and economic well-being. The globalization of employment opportunities and more sustainable livelihoods in other parts of the world has also provided incentive for migration. However, the minority of migrants who have real choices like this are in decline as more and more people are forced out of their home countries in search of work, through necessity, and through various push and pull factors.

In addition to this transformation in how people move, we see *transnational networks* emerging that attempt to provide migrants with information on employment, financing, housing, and access to intermediaries (both legal and illegal) who are capable of facilitating migration. Moving companies have become extremely large business organizations that operate on a multinational scale. People are constantly being encouraged to seek a better life elsewhere, whether for work or retirement (in fact, a vast industry has developed to ensure that we will all "live the dream" [somewhere else] following retirement). In addition to communication and support networks, the development of a global travel infrastructure, along with the decrease in air fares, has made international migration cheaper and more accessible than ever before. These days, anyone with access to a computer and credit card can book a flight online and leave wherever they are.

Alongside the increasing awareness in less-developed countries of a better way of life elsewhere is the deterioration of economic sustainability and livelihoods at home. Structural adjustment policies implemented during the 1980s and 1990s, which were aimed at stimulating the flow of international capital and globalization of the financial markets, have arguably contributed to the existing disparities between poor and rich nations, widening the gap in human welfare, and compounding the effects of rising poverty, unemployment, and population growth rates. However, the decline in social protection and increase in unemployment are not the only components of what has been referred to as the *global economic recession* that developed after 2008. Many of those currently employed in less-developed countries would be more accurately characterized as underemployed, meaning employment is insecure, precarious, unpredictable, or economically unsustainable. Almost 50 percent of the world's 3 billion workers earn less than US$2 per day. In contrast to developed countries experiencing aging populations and declines in birth rates, most underdeveloped nations have growing, youthful populations, further conflating the unemployment issues and increasing overall human insecurity. Migration has shaped the Middle East and North African (MENA) region for thousands of years. And there are a multitude of factors, including demographic and socioeconomic trends, conflict, and in part climate change, that are affecting the circumstances in this region.

Widespread political and social change, also known as the Arab Spring, since 2011 has ensured that migration issues remained in the spotlight. New regimes in Egypt, Libya, and Tunisia, and increasing conflict in Iraq and Syria, have brought these challenges into perspective. Regionally the Arab Spring and its repercussions have also had an impact. Humanitarian problems have been exacerbated with regard to **displaced people**. In Syria, for instance, after several years of conflict, more than 15 million individuals within the county are in need of assistance. As of 2015, Mercy Corps (2015) estimates that there are roughly 7.6 million people who are internally displaced within Syria's borders, with another 4 million forced to flee the country. Many of those who are most acutely affected are women and children, and other vulnerable groups including migrant workers and refugees.

The spillover effects have been no less dramatic. Over 1.7 million Syrians—nearly half children—are displaced and have taken refuge in the five neighboring countries of Egypt, Iraq, Jordan, Lebanon, and Turkey. The demands on these countries' capacities to absorb these displaced people, many of whom are undergoing their own crises, have created fundamental challenges to human security. The levels of conflict and instability coupled with high rates of unemployment and underemployment, particularly among young people, have also helped to push people toward irregular migration, both in the region and on a global scale.

The MENA countries are also transit stations for many on this irregular migration route, and as such act as a conduit and source for exploitation and human rights violations by traffickers. The International Organization for Migration (IOM 2015) provides an example:

> In 2012, a new light was shed on the extortion and mistreatment of migrants along routes that originate from the Horn of Africa and those that either attempt to cross Egypt's southern border with Sudan and extend through the Sinai Peninsula to Israel or attempt to cross the Gulf of Aden via Yemen and onward to Saudi Arabia. In other cases, as their initial resources are depleted, migrants become stranded en route or in-country, with limited access to livelihood, essential services or long-term solutions. Another pressing issue related to migration is the new and continuing internal and cross-border displacement occurring in several countries in the Middle East and North Africa.

The MENA region is also a destination for millions of migrant workers and contract labor, nowhere more so than the oil-rich countries of the Gulf, including the United Arab Emirates, Qatar, and Kuwait, among others.

To give an example, the tiny oil-rich state of Qatar has the highest ratio of migrant workers to the local population in the world. Over 90 percent of the workforce is composed of immigrants, and Qatar anticipates hiring nearly 1.5 million more laborers to build the stadiums, roads, ports, and hotels needed for the highly controversial World Cup tournament it is slated to stage in 2022. Owen Gibson and Pete Pattisson (2014) describe the situation of grave insecurity for many of these workers in an article in *The Guardian*:

> [There are about 400,000 Nepalese workers in Qatar] building the infrastructure to host the 2022 World Cup, [and they] have died at a rate of one every two days in 2014. . . . The Nepalese foreign employment promotion board said 157 of its workers in Qatar had died between January and mid-November [of 2014]—67 of sudden cardiac arrest and eight of heart attacks. Thirty-four deaths

were recorded as workplace accidents. . . . [M]igrant workers from Nepal, India, Sri Lanka and elsewhere are dying in their hundreds. While some are listed as having been killed in workplace accidents, many more are said to have died from sudden, unexplained cardiac arrest.

The massive earthquake that struck Nepal in late April 2015 also had repercussions for Nepalese workers in Qatar. With over 8,000 deaths recorded in the small Himalayan country, the Nepalese workers in Qatar were denied leave to attend the funerals of their loved ones in what was seen as a cruel and callous act of a wealthy state intent on delivering stadiums and infrastructure in time for 2022.

However, this picture is not unique to Qatar. Many of these working conditions and lack of empathy are common among other small, oil-rich states in the Gulf, including the Kingdom of Saudi Arabia, where workers are often mistreated and abused. Historically, migrant labor has been used to sustain private enterprise, providing massive profits with minimal labor costs. Cycles of large-scale unemployment encourage this situation while simultaneously perpetuating exploitative practices like weak or nonexistent labor standards, underpayment, nonpayment, extended working hours, discrimination, sexual harassment, violence, physical abuse, and denial of freedom of association and union rights, among others.

The State and Migrant Security

If we can think of migration as a result of globalization, it should also be seen as a powerful force with the potential to change economic policy in both sending and receiving countries. Heads of states who participate in discussions within the global arena on issues of migrant rights and protection often enforce strict immigration policies and actions to strengthen border controls in response to these situations. Such measures that highlight state sovereignty and security often supersede migrant rights. At the international level, this type of state-centric behavior continually obstructs positive discourse and any progress for achieving equal rights. At a national level, it is seen as the division between "us" and "them" (the other) and reinforces anti-immigration sentiments, discrimination, and hatred.

In times of global fiscal insecurity, negative sentiments tend to worsen, and migrants and immigrants are frequently blamed for unemployment rates, increased crime rates, and even disease, despite their overall positive effects on an economy. An interesting correlation linking heightened migration restrictions in receiving countries with increased rates of occurrence of irregular migration concludes that making fewer legal opportunities available only increases the frequency of trafficking and illegal entrance. For irregular migrants, the passage alone is dangerous and at times life threatening.

Those who succeed and remain unauthorized are at risk of exploitation by employers and landlords who may intimidate migrants with disclosure.

Migrant Rights and Protection: The Case of Southeast Asia

Intraregional labor migration within what is referred to as the Association of Southeast Asian Nations (ASEAN) is steadily rising, with an estimated 1.5 million people migrating for work each year. As a result of disparities in wealth within the ASEAN region it is expected that this trend will continue. Most migrant workers are unskilled or semiskilled and up to 40 percent of the demographic is categorized as irregular.

The division within the migrant population between regular and irregular migrants has produced sets of responses by governments to migration problems. Most ASEAN members use memorandums of understanding and other bilateral agreements to resolve migration issues that arise between them, yet many offer little in support of migrant rights, nor are they binding agreements (IOM 2008). Labor agreements across the ASEAN region appear generally inadequate for both migrants and nationals alike, showing a state-level disregard for labor rights in general. In contrast, anti-trafficking has garnered widespread support within the region, including the adoption and implementation of the UN's International Trafficking Framework to address the issue at the regional level.

The responses taken by ASEAN governments regarding migration and labor policies indicate a clear delineation between political willingness and international diplomacy that characterizes the problem at the global scale. Despite increasingly integrated trade and economic dependency within the ASEAN region, there have been two predominant development trends that have resulted in a regional division of migrant-sending and migrant-receiving countries that infers a division of prosperity. For migrant-sending countries, intraregional migration has eased poverty and unemployment while encouraging foreign exchange and engendering economic growth. However, because the most economically insecure can be correlated with the unskilled or low-skilled labor market (compared to those with trades or higher education), this demographic tends to represent a large portion of the migrant population. Conversely, migrant-receiving countries encourage professionals to renew temporary work permits and encourage permanent immigration while simultaneously increasing stipulations on the unskilled and low-skilled migrants. While temporary or circular migration has accomplished the goal of meeting labor market demands and providing employment to those in need, migrant-receiving countries still have control and therefore any protection felt by the vulnerable has been temporary at best.

In 1990, the United Nations, aided by the ILO, developed what is perhaps the most comprehensive document regarding migrant rights: "International Convention on the Protection of the Rights of All Migrant Workers and Members of Their Families."

This document is a request for all states to pursue nondiscriminatory practices regarding all migrants, legal or irregular; however, it has yet to be ratified by the majority of UN member states. What is obvious is that in the absence of a binding and consensual agreement by the majority of states, migrant rights will continue to be violated. As an example, migrant and refugee rights have been violated fairly harshly in recent times by the Australian state (see the box below).

Stopping the Boats in Australia: Operation Sovereign Borders

In September 2013, in the wake of an election victory, the Australian government implemented **Operation Sovereign Borders (OSB)**. This policy was designed to stop the boats carrying refugees, migrants, and victims of trafficking into Australia. It has been highly controversial and is seen as one of the harshest anti-asylum and anti-immigration policies on a global scale. By summer 2015, this policy had prevented a total of 18 asylum-seeker boats from reaching Australia.

Key Points
- Australia is the eighth-largest recipient of asylum seekers in the industrialized world, many of them coming from Afghanistan, Sri Lanka, Iraq, Iran, or Burma but also more than a few from Indonesia and Vietnam among other Southeast Asian states. It is a question that preoccupies politics at the elite and mass levels.
- The Australian government is convinced that these boats are controlled by ruthless smugglers seeking to maximize exploitation of trafficking victims and create human misery.
- Previous governments introduced "offshore processing," a term used to describe temporary detention camps in Nauru and Papua New Guinea, which were also heavily criticized by rights groups as being woefully inadequate, with poor hygiene, terrible living conditions, and a complete lack of dignity. This policy of transferring arrivals to offshore locations has been seen as inhumane in many ways. This is all the more so given Australia's history as a nation-state of immigrants and multiculturalism.
- Australia receives the world's largest share of "boat people," with more than 20,000 arriving in 2013. The vast majority of these asylum seekers hold legitimate claims.
- In 2014, the Australian government paid $31 million to the government of Cambodia to take in a group of refugees housed at the detention center in Nauru. The government was heavily criticized by NGOs and the UN for outsourcing their international legal obligation toward asylum seekers to a country with a poor human rights record.
- In June 2015, this policy become even more controversial when Indonesia claimed that payments of $31,000 were made to Indonesian crew members to return asylum seekers, emphasizing Australia's "stop the boats" policy at any cost (Phipps 2015).

Should Australia grant refuge to the seemingly never-ending flow of asylum seekers showing up on their shores? This is by no means an easy question given the economic and political implications. On the one hand, many of those arriving are some of the most marginalized and vulnerable people risking their lives at sea for a chance at a better life. Yet they are arriving illegally, since many of them have no other means for making an asylum claim. As Gabrielle Appleby (2015), an associate professor at the University of New South Wales, writes, "Australia's harsh stance is best explained by domestic political expediency."

Indeed, Australia's policymakers struggle with the legitimate challenge of dealing with asylum seekers, a topic that is highly divisive within the country. The government considers it a national security threat, while activists demand that a solution be grounded within a human rights framework. Regardless, Australia's asylum-seeker problem is one that does not originate within its own borders. It stems from a deep sense of human insecurity in far off lands. Until asylum seekers feel safe in their own countries, Australia's refugee crisis will continue.

THE FAILURE OF STATES (AGAIN)

One of the reasons why we have displaced people, transnational crime, and the complex problems of human trafficking is because many of the states where these problems emanate from are either "failed" or failing, where the capacities of the nation-state are so severely compromised they are unable to control their territory and the machinery of government. The failed states argument has been presented in earlier chapters, but what failed states are good at is the ability to offer shelter to criminal and terrorist networks, which typically operate outside the realm of the rule of law and the norms ascribed to communities who have healthy, developed institutions. They provide the dark underbelly of politics and violence with the lifeblood to carry on their nefarious activities.

This makes it easier in many ways for criminal gangs and organizations to operate, whether in Africa, Asia, Eastern Europe, or elsewhere on a global scale. Many of these states have allowed criminals and people on the run to live there and seek succor from the despots, tyrants, or warlords who often inhabit the political space where the state once operated. Many of these states, including Sudan and Pakistan for instance, allowed or provided tacit approval for Osama bin Laden to stay there and conduct operations. Many of these states (especially in Africa) are actually resource rich, and these resources are in turn creating and maintaining the conflicts going on there, such as in parts of Nigeria. For instance, we have conflicts over diamonds in the Congo and Angola, as well as other resources, which have limited the state's ability to control the ever-changing political landscape. In Somalia there are serious piracy problems in the Indian Ocean.

These are criminal activities that these weak states have little control over and indeed may be encouraging and fostering in a climate of lawlessness and corruption.

THE TRAFFICKING PROBLEM

Human trafficking is a modern variant of the slave trade in which people are forced into sexual slavery and various forms of exploitative labor. It represents a grave threat to human security on a global scale. The US Department of State's Trafficking in Persons Report (2012) provides a short definition of human trafficking as follows: "the act of recruiting, harboring, transporting, providing, or obtaining a person for compelled labor or commercial sex acts through the use of force, fraud, or coercion." The 2014 report points out that social scientists estimate that between 25 and 30 million people are victims of trafficking at any given time, though empirical data can only identify a small proportion of the victims (US Department of State 2014). Many of them are vulnerable females; women or girls constitute about 75 percent of those trafficked, and the majority—nearly 60 percent—of the victims are traded into sexual exploitation (United Nations Office on Drugs and Crime 2012). It should be noted that there are differences between human trafficking and **human smuggling**, which are outlined in the box below.

Differences between Human Trafficking and Smuggling

Trafficking	Smuggling
Must contain an element of force, fraud, or coercion (actual, perceived, or implied), unless the person is under 18 years of age and is involved in commercial sex acts	Person is generally cooperating
Forced labor and/or exploitation	No actual or implied coercion
Persons trafficked are victims	Persons smuggled are complicit in the smuggling crime; they are not necessarily victims of the crime of smuggling (though they may become victims depending on the circumstances in which they were smuggled)
Individuals involved are enslaved, subjected to limited movement or isolation, or had their documents confiscated	Persons are free to leave, change jobs, etc.
Need not involve the actual movement of the victim	Facilitates the illegal entry of person(s) from one country into another
No requirement to cross an international border	Always crosses an international border
Person must be involved in labor/services or commercial sex acts; that is, he or she must be "working."	Person must only be in the destination country or attempting to enter illegally

Source: US Department of State 2006.

Every country around the world is affected in one way or another by the scourge of human trafficking, whether as a source country, a transit point, or a destination. The staggering numbers only serve to prevent real socioeconomic development or the mobilization of human capital, and threaten security in various forms at the national, regional, and international levels. Most importantly, though, is that trafficking is a dangerous threat to the security of individuals.

Globalization and Trafficking

Globalization has been seen as the cause of much of the widespread economic, social, and societal development inequities throughout the world. And as we have noted throughout this text, despite its many positive aspects globalization operates as a double-edged sword that also contributes to grave human security issues, including human trafficking and sexual exploitation. The process of globalization emphasizes competitiveness and economic development while being a contributing factor to the violation of human rights of those who are most vulnerable (Nazemi 2012). In the global market of human trafficking, whether through organized criminal networks or domestic familial networks, the economic advantages of trafficking vastly outweigh the risks for traffickers across the globe (Wheaton, Schauer, and Galli 2010).

On a global scale this problem is intensified, not limited to a singular demographic, and crosses many international boundaries. Consider the following statistics compiled by the United Nations Office on Drugs and Crime (2014):

- Women and girls account for roughly 75 percent of the trafficking trade on a global scale.
- In general, traffickers tend to be male nationals of their home country, but not exclusively.
- The trafficking industry is valued per annum at $31.6 billion. The estimated number of people trafficked between Canada and the United States every year is 1,500–2,200. The Middle East region has the highest number of trafficked victims compared to other regions (70 percent).
- Trafficking for sexual exploitation is more common in Europe, Central Asia, and the Americas, whereas forced labor is common in Africa, the Middle East, Southeast Asia, and the Pacific.
- More than half (58 percent) of all trafficking cases involve sexual exploitation, whereas trafficking for forced labor accounts for 36 percent of cases.
- Across 118 countries there were 136 different nationalities defined as victims of trafficking, making this a truly global phenomenon.
- East Asia remains the most prolific transnational source of persons.

- Worldwide, 134 countries have criminalized trafficking by means of a special offense in line with the UN Trafficking in Persons Protocol.
- Convictions for trafficking are generally very low. Nearly 16 percent of identified cases in 132 countries did not result in a single conviction.

Globalization helps to facilitate trafficking through the use of increasingly integrated transportation and communications technologies. Furthermore, when the global center of power shifted in the 1990s, unintentional consequences opened floodgates for traffickers. These criminals exploit porous and transparent borders, political and economic upheaval, and mass migration of those seeking opportunities in established and emerging economies (Clark 2003). Traffickers also use the widespread accessibility afforded by the Internet, along with a variety of other mechanisms of globalization, to capitalize on this lucrative industry (Brewer 2009). It is unlikely that globalization will disappear anytime soon—and arguably nor should it given all of its positive aspects—however, those in political and economic power positions must place a higher recognition on the potential for human rights violations and the spread of human security issues.

Supply and Demand

Human trafficking can take many forms, from sex trafficking to child labor to migrant labor, all of which are modern forms of slavery. While human trafficking is not a new phenomenon, trafficking today is big business that generates extensive profits on an annual basis. In today's world, women and children are increasingly becoming commodities to be purchased, sold, and consumed; trafficking of vulnerable people has reached a level of global crisis and is an ongoing and prevalent human rights and human security catastrophe (Rahman 2011; Nazemi 2012).

An increasingly integrated world economy has enabled the human trafficking industry to thrive. The ILO conducted a recent study that estimated the lucrative criminal profits of human trafficking likely exceeds US$31 billion annually, making it the second-largest source of illicit income throughout the world, behind drug trafficking (Nazemi 2012). Economic globalization is the prime culprit of the facilitation of an exorbitant number of vulnerable trafficking victims worldwide; it has led to the emergence of a segregated population of vulnerable individuals from which victims of human trafficking are increasingly drawn. As the age of globalization booms, one can only expect these numbers to increase as inequalities and economic disparities between the developing and developed nations grow at the present rate.

Human trafficking is a matter of supply and demand, and globalization has increased the interdependence between states for commerce and thus facilitates the transfer of commodities. As humans are now viewed by many as a commodity, the human trafficking market is characterized by product differentiation; a successful trafficker's business model is dynamic and adapts as vulnerable populations change and areas of demand shift (Wheaton et al. 2010). In order to maintain a lucrative business, traffickers use knowledge of vulnerable populations, recruitment tactics, and other criminal connections to further their goals and prey on their victims.

There are various push and pull factors that play a part in human trafficking. These factors are largely associated with human security concerns: Lack of education, low social status, gender, political instability, poor local economy, and globalization, among many other potential factors, act as causal agents in human trafficking. Human trafficking victims often initially seek to relocate because of some of the above-noted push and pull factors, hoping to help their family by contributing financially. Traffickers offer options to these vulnerable individuals by facilitating illegal border crossings, covering the cost of travel and relocation, and promising better job opportunities in more developed nations or cities, all of which turn out to be fake (Rahman 2011; Wheaton et al. 2010).

Ethnic Minorities and Trafficking in Southeast Asia

There is the difficult question of ethnic minorities in terms of migration and human security. Ethnic minorities in Bangladesh, Myanmar, Thailand, and other Southeast Asian countries are at increased risk of human trafficking. Those who are trafficked are victims of human insecurity and often have no options other than to follow the commands of the criminal organizations responsible. The following is a victim's account provided by the United Nations High Commissioner for Refugees:

Nurul and his relative Faisal are among hundreds of persons of concern who have spoken to UNHCR about travelling irregularly by sea in South-East Asia. Their testimony is typical of many who have made the maritime journey from Bangladesh and Myanmar to Thailand and Malaysia.

With no assets in Myanmar to their names, Nurul and Faisal had been unable to afford the passage to Malaysia. So when a human smuggler approached them offering a sharply discounted price of MMK 50,000 (USD 50), they accepted, despite their doubts. One night in September, they were led by smugglers to the seashore, where dozens gathered to wait for a boat. As night passed, frustration grew. When some asked to return home, the smugglers brandished knives. Nurul heard one smuggler call a superior to say that many in the group did not have enough money to pay. "If I beat them," the superior responded, over speakerphone, "The money will come out."

In the morning, a boat arrived with an armed crew from Myanmar and Thailand. Nurul and Faisal and 600 others eventually boarded, including hundreds of passengers who had separately embarked from Bangladesh and a group of fishermen who were intercepted en route and forced onto the boat.

A single cabin above deck housed the crew. The two dozen women and children on board were kept in the open on the upper deck, which had two hatchways providing access to two lower levels otherwise enclosed by the hull. The level immediately below deck was a mezzanine running along the perimeter of the hull that encircled a large open space overlooking the bottom level. Both levels were filled to the edges with passengers.

Below deck, Nurul and Faisal were forced to squat for the length of the journey, brushing up against other men on all sides. A single fan the size of an ordinary table fan serviced the entire hold. They were fed one meal a day, a handful of rice scooped into a plastic bag with two chili peppers. One cup of water was given to each passenger twice daily, as was the opportunity to use one of two latrines on the upper deck.

Those who tried to receive additional rations or use the latrines out of turn were beaten, including with belts; some were kicked down ladders as they tried to climb above deck. Several individuals were beaten to death, and a total of seven people died on board from beatings, starvation, or dehydration. Because the first was someone in Nurul's immediate vicinity, Nurul and three others were made to carry the body above deck and throw it overboard, uncovered except for the clothes worn by the deceased. Nurul was forced to do the same for the six that followed.

After eight days, the boat reached the coast of Thailand, where smaller vessels were sent to ferry passengers to shore. In the rush to disembark, Nurul and Faisal believe five more people died while attempting to cross between boats. All others were taken to a large, forested camp after reaching shore, not to be sent on to Malaysia until they could each pay MYR 6,500 (USD 1,900). Nurul and Faisul were instructed to cry over the phone to their relatives and detail their suffering in order to elicit payment. Until payment was made, each person was beaten—sometimes with a cane—three times a day, in addition to being forced to stand in physically straining positions for hours at a time. One position required Nurul to bend his knees and hold his arms out as if sitting on a motorcycle; another was to bend over and hold his head between his legs. Faisul remembers the sting of chili powder being thrown in his eyes.

Faisul was released after eight days, and Nurul after 15, once their relatives were able to make the payments. They were both brought from the camp to a fence at the Malaysian border that they climbed over using ladders on either side. Each walked for several hours to a road where they were picked up by a vehicle and taken with 5–10 others to a holding house, which they called a "receive" house. From there, Nurul was sent by taxi and bus to relatives in Penang. Faisul was picked up at a nearby mosque by a Malaysian woman hired by a relative. A final MYR 300 (USD 90) was demanded from the woman before Faisul was released.

Source: United Nations High Commission for Refugees 2014.

Addressing the Problem: Cooperative Efforts in Handling Transnational Problems

The growth of globalization and transnational problems have made the meaning of national jurisdiction less clear and sovereign principles and standards less applicable, especially over the issue of human trafficking. The protection of children's rights in Southeast Asian states is one that urgently requires multilateral cooperation, as evidenced by the human trafficking issue. In many parts of the region, social inequality, limited resources for families, and low-quality education have contributed to the high vulnerability of children to trafficking and labor exploitation. A lack of awareness and comprehension of the scope of abuse and exploitation of children makes this problem even more difficult to resolve.

Human security in Southeast Asia is about educating and training people to recognize and respond to trafficking. It is only recently that we have seen growing interdependence and cooperation among these states to curb the production of child pornography, sexual tourism, and child labor. Multilateral cooperation between states in the Mekong subregion, as well as between agencies such as UNICEF, the ILO, and international nongovernmental organizations, has increased over this issue. Part of the problem is that offenders who exploit children receive minor charges and sentences or escape the law entirely, mainly because states seem incapable of enforcing it. Concerned states are incorporating international standards into their domestic laws and are engaging in extensive monitoring of human rights violations and other illegal activities, such as recruiting a person for trafficking or selling a person for prostitution across national borders; these changes might be constructive in the process of developing a regional human rights system.

An increase in undocumented female migrants is particularly important, because they are more vulnerable to exploitative situations due to their lack of legal status. These women, sold as property, are victims of racial discrimination, physical abuse, and prostitution. The number of female migrant workers exported from countries like Bangladesh, Burma, India, Nepal, China, and Pakistan is constantly increasing, and female migrant workers outnumber male migrants in Sri Lanka, Indonesia, and the Philippines. In 1995, the Fourth World Conference on Women held in Beijing, China, was a historic event that raised awareness about women's issues in various respects, including poverty, education, and violence. It also recognized the particular vulnerability of migrant women to abuse and violence. The **Beijing Declaration**, which came out of the conference, argued that governments should take the lead in implementing social change and development. To regulate the flow of migrants and protect the rights of migrant workers, some Asian countries took some initiatives. These included crackdowns on illegal recruiters, providing shelters and counseling for workers, setting up training centers, and regular monitoring of migrants' health. Apart from the accession and ratification of the Migrant Workers Convention, a number of legal policy changes took place in many Asian countries, including the implementation of a new regulation, drafting national law on migrants, and signing a memorandum of understanding.

As we've been arguing, globalization has a significant impact on labor markets and the movement of people toward opportunity and new economic conditions. The consequences of uneven development and fractured and unstable political and social structures contribute to these problems of poor or inadequate earning opportunities. Human trafficking is prevalent in Afghanistan, for instance, but is often overlooked as a cultural issue versus a human rights violation and illegal under the UN Trafficking Protocol (United Nations Office on Drugs and Crime 2003). Afghanistan has a law against human trafficking, but it does not comply with international standards nor do they enforce their own law. Within Afghanistan, both trafficking and smuggling are an issue. Boys and girls are trafficked within the country for forced prostitution or forced begging, and labor in brick kilns, carpet-making factories, and domestic servitude. NGOs report that there is a growing problem of Afghan boys in particular being subjected to sexual exploitation, more commonly called *bacha baazi*, where wealthy men use harems of young boys for social and sexual entertainment. Further, UNICEF found that 43 percent of marriages in Afghanistan were with forced brides under the age of 18 (UN GIFT 2008). This is especially true when it is the powerful elites in Afghanistan that take part in *bacha baazi*.

The nature of globalization has also exacerbated the demand for human trafficking throughout the world. As the world shrinks and evolves toward a global community, the transfer of people, both voluntarily and through coercion, is becoming more prevalent. Human trafficking is one of the dark sides of globalization; it has created an environment where illicit practices flow across borders and human trafficking has become a fast-growing global criminal activity that affects nearly every nation across the globe. In addition to sexual exploitation, which is most commonly thought of when the topic of human trafficking is discussed, it can also include migrant labor and outsourcing. For instance, the United States is increasingly outsourcing production services to countries such as India, China, and Bangladesh for the purpose of cheaper labor, which results in exploitive working conditions for the workers. In this light, forms of slavery and human trafficking are not just outcomes of globalization—they are a part of the globalization process itself (Rahman 2011).

THE RISE OF TRANSNATIONAL CRIME

One of the major problems that has accompanied the rise of globalization is the rise of global **transnational crime**. This has been described in part as the

McDonaldization of crime, or the development of a **McMafia** (Glenny 2008). This network has pervasive roots in local economies and can be seen as responsible for many of the social ills that are interrelated and connected within communities. Such activities include human smuggling, sex trafficking, drug trafficking, corruption, and extortion, among many others. There is little doubt that this insidious development has created a spider-like web of nefarious criminal networks that pose a real threat to human security.

One of the most important books to detail the rise of the global crime network following the end of the Cold War is by Misha Glenny (2008), where he coins the term *McMafia*. It is a pervasive account of the tentacles forged under globalization, and it pays particular attention to globalization and sex trafficking. The following excerpt from the *New York Times* sums up many of Glenny's important points and illustrates how this affects the globalization of human security:

> When the advanced economies opened world markets to their goods but retained protectionist subsidies on their own agricultural sectors, they created a vast army of the dispossessed and the desperate, as well as a lucrative market in prostitution and illegal immigration. The collapse of the Soviet Union also ensured a ready supply of women for Western Europe.... Often the women are recruited by other women, some of them buying their way out of sexual slavery by delivering others to their captors. "The illegality of labor smuggling lies in the illogicality of globalization," Mr. Glenny writes. The European Union has a labor shortage and an aging population that is not being replenished because of low birthrates. But restrictive immigration policies remain in force. The result? An open invitation to far-reaching criminal enterprises. (Grimes 2015)

Mexico's War on Drugs: A Case Study

In this case study we look at the implications of the Mexican drug war on human security. This is not a traditional war but one created and fought by illegal organizations who act outside of the state, and who are now fighting against the state and between themselves. In this sense it is low intensity and asymmetrical with profound consequences for human security. It also involves attempts by the government to end the war, resulting in an increasing cycle of violence and undermining the protection of vulnerable individuals and groups.

Mexico's ex-president Felipe Calderón declared the struggle against the cartels as a war in 2008, referring to his government's battle against illegal narcotics and their purveyors (Diaz 2008). Since the beginning of this conflict under Calderón's presidency, Mexico has seen a death toll of at least 60,000 (the vast majority of them criminals) and unconfirmed reports of 100,000 deaths (including disappearances resulting from infighting among drug cartels and cartel–government violence). Here we examine some of the history behind this conflict, the diverse issues and factors that contribute to it, and the human security dilemma it creates. The key actors in the conflict are described, and finally we look at attempts toward resolution that have taken place, along with the consequences of those attempts. Reviewing this issue is important not only because Mexico is part of the North American Free Trade Agreement, but also because it shares one of the longest borders in the world, a distance of 1,333 miles with the United States, and the violence and consequences have spilled over into these areas.

Drugs and their movement have been a part of Mexican society for a long time, so there is nothing new about this aspect of illegal behavior in Mexico. However, the drug cartels became more prominent and noticeable from 2006 onwards with the decline of the drug-fueled war in Colombia and the demise of the Cali and Medellin cartels, which had overall control at the time. To some extent the decline invigorated the Mexican cartels to build and expand their operations.

The main goal of the Mexican drug cartels (like most cartels) is to control and maintain their supply routes while also expanding their business all the time. Drug trafficking is both extremely lucrative and highly illegal and engenders competition among bandit groups that is accompanied by extreme violence when rivals fight it out. There are estimates of between $14 billion to $50 billion in profits being made from the sale of these illegal drugs in Mexico. It's the intensity of the drug war in Mexico over the last 10 to 15 years that has made it a distinctive conflict in terms of media attention and the fact that there are so many casualties. This has created an image of Mexico as being an unsafe country, in particular for tourists. The violence has been featured widely in the media, prompting books, documentaries, and fictionalized dramas based on aspects of the US–Mexican border. Despite the fact that most ordinary Mexicans are not involved in any kind of drug or cartel business, these civilians are the ones who are highly affected by it, facing the trauma of living in a situation of insecurity. The sheer number of deaths indicates that the conflict is akin to a civil war.

Some writers argue that it is the national policy against the war on drugs undertaken by Mexican President Felipe Calderón after his election in 2006 that is responsible for the upsurge in drug crime–related violence. Some have seen the increase in bloodshed as directly related to the increase in enforcement. Yet various factors and issues contribute to the violent conflict that we see today in the streets of Mexico.

There is no doubt that supply and demand play a large part in the drug war. Most of the drugs in the United States come from Mexico, with the cartels supplying about 90 percent of the cocaine that enters the United States. Mark Kleiman (2011) argues, for instance, that if the illegal importation of drugs into the United States stopped, "Mexico's drug violence would shrink dramatically."

Despite the massive profits from drugs, little of this filters down to the ordinary people at the bottom. A report from the National Council for the Evaluation of Social Development Policy states that the number of poor people in Mexico is up by more than 3 million since 2009, which means that 46.2 percent of the population lives in poverty (Wilkinson 2011). In such economic conditions, drug cartels can offer employment opportunities to impoverished young men that legitimate employment simply can't aspire to. There is fairly easy money to be made for people living in conditions of economic insecurity and who live in the absence of state- or private enterprise–created jobs. Because poverty has increased, the gap between the poor and the rich at the upper and lower ends of the spectrum has also increased. This inequity coupled with a poor educational system that doesn't meet the needs of its populace, major rates of illiteracy, and the creation of an underclass who see no way out apart from turning to crime is helping to fuel the conflict. We see little of this conflict in countries where the income and wealth gap is significantly reduced and where people have access to good education and opportunities.

We can also see that the drug war has actually been fueled by the United States. In 2009, a statement by the US Government Accountability Office's director of international affairs and trade said "many of the firearms fueling Mexican drug violence originated in the United States" (US Government Accountability Office 2009). More than 80 percent of the weapons seized in Mexico can be traced back to the United States, especially to the border states of Arizona, New Mexico, and California. The violence is exceptional. By the beginning of 2014, some estimated that well over 100,000 people had been killed (according to the government, 9 out of 10 of these were criminals or were involved with criminal activity). This compares very unfavorably to 2012, when estimates of those killed were under 20,000 (Council on Foreign Relations 2014).

With reference to armed conflict and wars, we expect to see state armies involved, using necessary force to meet violent threats or uprisings. Typically, in an armed conflict the state controls the monopoly of violence (this is inherent in the notion of a state). The Mexican war on drugs represents an issue around the rule of law: In a country where the rule of law is sound, the various police forces would be the expected response to drug-related crime, preventing it from evolving to a level of violence that would require the military to get involved. In Mexico, however, former president Calderón turned to his military to deploy forces against the drug cartels. In stable, functioning states where human security is much higher, the military would never get involved in such drug-related crimes.

One could question whether resorting to the military was more reflective of the fact that Mexico's local and federal police forces are incompetent and corrupt. Nevertheless,

Stephanie Brophy (2008) writes, the fact that the cartels pursue violence with such impunity indicates a parallel power structure operating outside the rule of law—one that challenges state authority and considers the violent tools of coercion a shared instrument of power.

From a Human Security Perspective

Street fighting and extreme levels of violence represent the greatest risk of the Mexican drug war for all parties concerned. Therefore, it seems reasonable that a shift in strategy to one focused on reducing the violence rather than on arrests and drug seizures would better address the issue from a human security perspective. In deploying the military to combat drugs Calderón perhaps made a mistake with such a heavy-handed approach. The result has been that the military has been accused of human rights violation. On the other hand, it is clear that there is no demarcation of boundaries between one criminal activity and the other, leading to human insecurity. The drug cartels have also been responsible for activities like human trafficking, prostitution, and rape, and as Misha Glenny (2008) has pointed out, these connections are global. Some argue that change is just around the corner. Economic security can and is instrumental in making drugs less attractive by fostering education and jobs.

The Mexico drug war has brought about escalating violent conflict among the cartels and also between the cartels and the state. Factors such as high drug demand in the United States, Mexico's poverty, large economic profits to be gained from supplying drugs, escalating violence, corruption, and arms smuggling into Mexico are all factors responsible for the intractability of the conflict and the increased brutality of the last decade.

CONCLUSION

John Gray, an English philosopher, ponders questions of progress, globalization, and modernization in much of his work. He is also good at citing Thomas Hobbes, who lived through the English Civil War and witnessed the insecurity it brought to the population. The argument can be expanded that it is the failure of the state to really exercise its power against the instigators (criminals who operate in the marketplace) that has created the dilemmas we face under globalization. Gray (2004, 109) argues succinctly:

> In the twentieth century the state was the chief enemy of freedom. Today it is the weakness of the state that most threatens freedom. In many parts of the world, states have collapsed. In others, the state is corroded or corrupt. The result is that billions of people lack the rudimentary conditions of a decent life. Even in many rich countries fear of crime is pervasive.

It is clear that the state and its functions have been eroded at the core, leaving it unable to fulfill many of its tasks, including battling transnational crime networks. Hobbes recognized the need for a strong state that would provide order in times of chaos. Organized crime appears anarchical in the long run, threatening the state and established institutions. It has also become a global phenomenon with its tentacles stretching everywhere.

This is also in part due to the fact that consumers are involved—often without their knowledge—in this world of crime because they benefit from low wages paid to illegal and migrant labor. The costs of food, according to Glenny are lower in places like Europe because of the lower wages paid to the migrant and illegal labor force. And the structural inequities of the global economy have also contributed to the rise in crime. As Glenny (2008, 345) argues:

> It is not globalization in itself that has spurred the spectacular growth of orga-
> nized crime in recent years but global markets that are either insufficiently regu-
> lated, especially in the financial sector, or markets that are too closely regulated,
> as in the labor and agricultural sectors.

Globalization, as we have seen, has its positive and negative aspects. Typically migrants are good for developed and developing economies because they bring skills and ideas into a dynamic relationship. For example, Dubai's economy has grown largely on the backs of unskilled migrant laborers from the Indian subcontinent.

And despite the criticism of low wages and harsh conditions in the Gulf state, many are still making money that they send home to improve the living conditions of their families. The same is true for the vast numbers of Filipinos who work for low wages all over the world to boost their family's income and their home economy immeasurably. There is little doubt, though, that the state could do more to prevent abuse, resolve crime, and decrease the levels of human insecurity that we see around the world.

KEY TERMS

Beijing Declaration; Displaced People; Human Smuggling; Human Trafficking; McMafia; Migrant; Operation Sovereign Borders (OSB); Refugee; Transnational Crime

FURTHER READING

Bhattacharyya, Gargi. 2005. *Traffick: The Illicit Movement of People and Things.* London: Pluto Press.

Brewer, Devin. 2009. "Globalization and Human Trafficking." *Human Rights & Human Welfare:* 46–56. http://www.du.edu/korbel/hrhw/researchdigest/trafficking/Globalization.pdf.

Cholewinski, R., and P. Taran. 2009. "Migration, Governance and Human Rights: Contemporary Dilemmas in the Era of Globalization." *Refugee Survey Quarterly* 28 (4): 1–33. http://dx.doi.org/10.1093/rsq/hdq019.

Clark, Michele A. 2003. "Human Trafficking Casts Shadow on Globalization." *Yale Global Online.* http://yaleglobal.yale.edu/content/human-trafficking-casts-shadow-globalization

Clark, Michele A. 2003. "Trafficking in Persons: An Issue of Human Security." *Journal of Human Development* 4 (2): 247–63. http://dx.doi.org/10.1080/1464988032000087578.

Freeman, R.B. 2006. "People Flows in Globalization." *Journal of Economic Perspectives* 20 (2): 145–70. http://dx.doi.org/10.1257/jep.20.2.145.

Koser, K. 2010. "Introduction: International Migration and Global Governance." *Global Governance* 16 (3): 301–15.

Munck, R. 2008. "Globalisation, Governance and Migration: An Introduction." *Third World Quarterly* 29 (7): 1227–46. http://dx.doi.org/10.1080/01436590802386252.

Nazemi, N. 2012. "How Globalization Facilitates Trafficking in Persons." *Political Communication* 6 (2): 5–14.

Rahman, M. 2011. "Human Trafficking in the Era of Globalization: The Case of Trafficking in the Global Market Economy." *Transcience Journal* 2 (1): 54–71.

Sens, Allen, and Peter Stoett. 2010. *Global Politics: Origins, Currents, Directions,* 4th ed. Toronto: Thomson Nelson.

Shelley, Toby. 2007. *Exploited: Migrant Labour in the New Global Economy.* London: Zed Books.

WEBSITES

Anti-Slavery: www.antislavery.org
Global Modern Slavery Directory: http://globalmodernslavery.org
HumanTrafficking.org: http://humantrafficking.org
Human Trafficking Search: http://humantraffickingsearch.net
Interpol: www.interpol.int
Terrorism, Transnational Crime and Corruption Center (TraCCC):
    http://traccc.gmu.edu
United Nations High Commissioner for Refugees: http://unhcr.org
United Nations Office on Drugs and Crime: www.unodc.org
World Health Organization: http://who.int

CONCLUSION

Understanding conflict in the post–Cold War era requires a new set of tools to navigate the world of human insecurity. The themes of human security, conflict, and development can no longer be considered in isolation and need to be embraced by both scholars and practitioners alike if we are to seriously consider the dynamics of human vulnerability. Globalization and complex interdependency has brought far-away conflicts and collective suffering to our doorsteps. In an age of social media, migration, affordable travel, and trade liberalization, societies are increasingly connected for better or for worse.

Although global interconnectedness has brought much wealth and security to parts of the world, half the planet is still living below poverty thresholds. Violent conflict is prevalent in many societies, while human rights and the rule of law struggle to gain legitimacy in authoritarian societies. Indeed, there are many corners of this world where insecurity reigns and human depravation and misery are a way of life. Yet this is no longer possible to ignore: Suffering in one jurisdiction impacts others. Refugees, migrants, and political violence spread across borders. Infectious diseases and toxic air pollution indiscriminately attack us all. No human can fully escape and avoid such tragedy. Indeed, we all seek freedom from fear and freedom from want.

This book has discussed what we believe are critical themes that cut across borders and need to be seriously considered by those looking to build a better planet. It will require a new approach in thinking, a new *modus operandi*, if you will. But it will also require a multidimensional strategy that can incorporate a diverse range of stakeholders. As we move into the post–Millennium Development Goal era, we wish to point out five key themes that must stay in the foreground of humanitarians and policymakers alike.

First, there is a clear relationship between human security, conflict, and development that can only be solved with a stronger values-based framework that is concerned with empathy. While globalization and social media has made the world smaller, there is a danger that society will only consider these interactions in a superficial manner. The international order is built around competition and profit maximization by encouraging ideologies of self-interest and consumerism. Much of this system depends on the exploitation of weak and marginalized societies. These communities will continue to be vulnerable until there is a stronger effort to narrow the gap of inequality between the North and South. A change in thinking must occur if such communities are to be lifted out of poverty and conflict.

Second, while we make no claim that human security should trump traditional security, we appeal to those working in these areas to consider the various types of human security. We have identified economic, food, health, environmental, community, personal, and political types of security, where each must be considered in an interconnected way and requires a bottom-up development approach. There are also pluralistic approaches to finding solutions to each of these challenges, as seen throughout the diverse cultures found around the world. Notably, the difference between Western and Asian accounts of human security continues to stand out.

Third, we must acknowledge that there are both winners and losers in the era of globalization. With multinational corporations spanning the globe in search of profit, the Global North continues to expand its grip on wealth and resources while the South struggles to compete. While some countries like China are clearly raising their standard of living, others are falling behind, with bottom-billion societies risking the prospect of becoming failed states. Global inequality is on the rise, and without a change of thinking this gap will widen.

Fourth, the rise of new wars in the post-conflict era has exacerbated human security. Civil, ethnic, and identity wars are on the rise, while asymmetrical warfare carried out by nation-states against small-scale insurgencies has altered the traditional security threat. Moreover, the rise of gender violence and internally displaced people has led to breakdowns in human security. This, along with the proliferation in transnational terrorism and a decrease in nationalistic movements, has led to an expansion of the security state as well as protracted conflicts the world over.

Finally, the dysfunctionality of state institutions and the law is contributing to the collapse of human security throughout the developing world. Corrupt governments that are able to manipulate courtrooms, police who conduct investigations using torture as a method of interrogation, as well as bureaucracies that lack the capacity to deliver services are all contributing to human insecurity. Without the rule of law or a functioning government, human rights cannot be respected. Human security cannot exist without human rights.

We remain optimistic even though the short-term prospects for building a more equitable and secure world seem bleak. We are optimists because we see the potential in the human spirit and the continued resilience of even the most marginalized groups. Improved human security will require a change in thinking, especially in how we apply economic and political structures to our societies. This is not to say that the system needs a revolutionary overhaul; rather, a sustained injection of human empathy that cuts across borders could signal the beginning of a better world for all.

GLOSSARY

actor-oriented approach: An approach that focuses on the ability and expertise of civil society groups. Certain approaches to development by NGOs (actors) are seen as superior to others and are therefore promoted as best practice approaches to aid delivery.

aid versus trade debate: A controversial debate that asks if providing aid to developing countries is more effective than promoting free market economic principles. Those who advocate trade over aid claim that no-strings-attached development funding for lower-income countries are in fact perpetuating poverty by creating donor dependency rather than encouraging economic independence through free market principles.

anarchy: The absence of a central government. There is no single system or government that has absolute control over the entire system in international relations.

apartheid: A system of racial segregation in South Africa that existed between 1948 and 1994. The term is an Afrikaans word that translates to "the state of being apart," as it stood as a policy that enforced white segregation from black people. Apartheid was a highly oppressive system that denied basic human rights to South Africa's black population and gave political and economic privilege to the country's white minority.

Asian values: An Eastern version of human rights sponsored mainly by Singapore and Malaysia in the early 1990s. Asian values reflected the rigid, conservative values of certain Asian states, most notably emphasizing that individual, Western-style rights were alien to Asian cultures.

Beijing Declaration: Adopted in 1995, the Beijing Declaration was drafted following two weeks of talks at the Fourth World Conference on Women involving over

17,000 participants. The declaration was endorsed by 189 governments who gave commitments in 12 areas of concern involving the universal rights of women and girls.

best practice: A commercial process and procedure that is considered to be the most successful and responsible method of operation when compared globally.

bottom billion: A term coined by Paul Collier that seeks to identify and explain why the poorest 1 billion humans on the planet are seemingly becoming poorer. According to Collier, there are four traps that can explain this: protracted conflict, weak governance, mismanagement of state resources, and bad geography.

Brahimi Report: Officially referred to as the *Report of the Panel on United Nations Peace Operations*, the Brahimi Report (2000) was a UN-commissioned report lead by Lakhdar Brahimi that set out recommendations of how to reform UN peacekeeping operations.

bribery: An illicit payment or gift that is used to achieve a personal gain by influencing a decision maker in either the private or public sector.

business case: A business argument that demonstrates a clear economic advantage for a new corporate policy or strategy. For example, a business case for labor rights might argue that companies that respect their workers are less likely to be sued in court, thereby minimizing litigation costs.

capabilities approach: A theory developed by Nobel Laureate Amartya Sen that claims human well-being should be measured based on the capability of an individual to reach his or her full potential through access to opportunity. This interdisciplinary concept is often referred to as the *human development approach* in that it seeks to understand the wide-ranging needs (economic, education, health, etc.) of an individual to become "capable" and reach his or her goals.

caste: A hierarchical system where individuals are born into a social grouping and are unable to leave it regardless of wealth, education, or success. The term is often associated with the social class system found in India.

civil society: Individual citizens or groups of people who organize and work outside the realm of government. Civil society actors can include activists, media, business associations, family networks, and other entities who are distinct from government agents.

civil war: A war between one or more groups of combatants who are operating within the same state.

clash of civilizations: Originally suggested as a term by Bernard Lewis, it came to prominence in the work of conservative political scientist Samuel Huntington, who argued that conflicts in the future (following the Cold War) were more likely to be drawn around religious, cultural, and civilizational lines.

collective action: Cooperative efforts made by a group who share a common objective. For example, a group of countries enacting laws to combat climate change.

colonialism: A system based on the physical exploitation of a foreign territory by another state either by military force, through business interests, or from settlers (or the combination of all three).

colonial philanthropy: A term used to describe European paternalistic attitudes of charity during the colonial era. While colonial philanthropists endorsed the abolition of slavery and the protection of Indigenous peoples, they often advocated Christian evangelism and the appointment of land reservations to preserve Indigenous rights in occupied colonial territories.

complex emergency: A serious humanitarian crisis involving political violence, poverty, conflict, and often a natural disaster such as famine, earthquakes, or typhoons.

conflict prevention: A term used to describe the long-term commitment by key stakeholders, including NGOs, government, intergovernmental organizations, and armed nonstate actors, to promote activities such as participatory dialogues, disarmament, peacebuilding, preventative diplomacy, and conflict resolution.

conflict resolution: A term used to describe the facilitation process for ending conflict peacefully. It often involves third-party mediators or negotiators who act in an independent capacity to solve a dispute between conflicting sides. Practitioners of conflict resolution include nonstate actors such as NGOs, high-level preventative diplomats, or local community leaders.

constructivism: A different and distinctive approach to international relations that highlights the social or intersubjective dimension of global politics. It explores the normative influence of institutional structures and the relationship between normative changes and state identity and interests.

corporate complicity: A term used to describe businesses who serve as accomplices when the state violates human rights. For example, a company may ask police to disrupt a labor dispute, only to have officers then harm or kill those protesting.

corporate social responsibility (CSR): A term used to describe the ethical and social responsibility of business. CSR is concerned with the self-compliance of industry, community outreach, as well as legal accountability. Businesses that promote CSR are advocates for human rights, health and safety of workers, as well as the environment.

corruption: Illegal behavior by public or private officials that use deceit to achieve personal gains. Corrupt acts may involve acts of nepotism, patronage, or bribery.

coup d'état: Involves the forced removal of a government and seizure of political power by a branch of the armed forces through either violent or nonviolent means.

crimes against humanity: Often described as ill treatment of civilians during wartime, it was defined at the Nuremberg trials to include "murder, extermination, enslavement, deportation and other inhumane acts against any civilian population" and has been expanded to include crimes such as apartheid in South Africa.

cultural relativism: A concept that argues against the uniform application of the Universal Declaration of Human Rights throughout the world. For cultural relativists, the denial of rights may be legitimate depending on socioeconomic or political circumstances in a jurisdiction. For example, some cultural relativists may argue that not all countries are ready to accept or need democratic rights. These arguments hold strong Westphalian claims that endorse a state's right to decide how it organizes politically since there is no universal model to fit each state.

democratic deficit: An accountability gap that exists between the electorate and a democratically elected government. It occurs when elected officials must make decisions without consulting the electorate, prompting critique from citizen groups left out of the decision-making process.

development: Came into its own as a subject after 1950 when social scientists started to examine causes of poverty and underdevelopment in a systematic and comparative way. Nowadays it focuses on poverty reduction and human development.

displaced people: Individuals who are forced to flee their country on account of persecution, war, or natural disaster.

due diligence: The rigorous investigation of a company to ensure its business operation is legal, moral, and safe. Due diligence can be carried out by independent third parties or in-house compliance officers.

dysfunctional institutions: A term used to describe weak state institutions that are unable to provide public goods and services to its citizens. Dysfunctional institutions may suffer from funding shortages, corruption, or other types of challenges that weaken the organization's overall capacity.

empathy: A term often used to describe how individuals comprehend or feel what another individual is experiencing, especially in times of crisis. Human security considers why empathy may be extended to one group but not to another.

End of History: A concept coined by Francis Fukuyama in 1989 that suggests Western liberal democracy may serve as the final and most effective type of governance model needed for political organization.

epistemic community: A term coined by Peter Haas referring to a group of subject experts who serve as advisers to government and industry. Also referred to as *policy communities*, knowledge is built and shared among the community and with officials who seek expert advice on matters of public policy.

ethnic cleansing: The forcible removal of ethnic minorities from a territory controlled by rival ethnic groups. In some cases there have been plans to systematically exterminate such minority groups. This was used by ethnic Serbians after the breakup of Yugoslavia.

Eurocentrism: The belief in European exceptionalism; the process of spreading European cultural values throughout the world.

failed state: A country that is extremely weak in terms of its political and social infrastructure, typically in either a state of collapse or about to collapse, which leads to anarchy and political violence.

famine: An event that occurs when there is an extensive shortage of food brought on by many factors, including dysfunctional political policies, natural disaster, or conflict, among others.

first-generation rights: Those rights that are considered basic human rights, often associated with the Universal Declaration of Human Rights, and are considered universal, inalienable, and guaranteed. These rights are protected so long as the government refrains from acting against the individual. Sometimes called *civil-political rights* because they outline the protection of political liberties and empowerment.

food security: A concept that asks how people access and use food. It seeks to improve food availability and to ensure healthy nutrition levels in a population.

free rider: An actor who benefits from individual or group action without having to contribute to the act. For example, a country may benefit from the environmental policies of its neighbors without having to enact its own regulations.

functional approach: An approach to civil society that calls for a variety of models to be used in the field depending on circumstances.

gender-based violence: Violence that is primarily directed toward women and girls. It is committed by men who seek to disempower and oppress their victims through physical and mental assault.

genocide: The planned and systematic killing of any large group of persons who are associated with a specific ethnic group.

Gini coefficient: A statistical measurement used by UN agencies to assess how economic inequality compares among societies.

global civil society: An extensive range of nongovernmental actors operating transnationally and within the social space that exists between the state, market, and family. Globalization has dramatically increased the number of such groups, who use technology and networks to organize with one another across borders.

global commons: The space that is shared between all people on the planet, such as natural resources including air, water, and land. Resource depletion is a consequence of the failed efforts to maintain and protect the global commons, which are seen as a public trust to be enjoyed by all life on Earth.

globalization: Refers to the acceleration of activities and processes that increase the reality and opportunities for interdependence on a global scale. It appears to have at least five distinct forms: (1) viewing the world as a single place where borders become irrelevant; (2) the use of communications and technology to break down trade and social barriers; (3) the notion that we are faced with common environmental, political, and social problems (i.e., global warming and terrorism); (4) the shape of cultural globalization resulting in a homogenization or "McDonaldization" of cultures where different countries share similar attributes; and finally, (5) the idea that the sovereign state is being weakened with the rise of extra-state actors (corporations, social movements, and so on, which are having global influence).

Global Reporting Initiative (GRI): An independent standardization organization that assists organizations looking to develop corporate social responsibility reports and measure their sustainability programs.

honor killings: The calculated murder of an individual, usually a woman and usually by members of her own family, based on the perception that she has shamed the family's reputation or dishonored the community.

Human Development Index (HDI): A tool that relies on statistical indicators to assess the overall wealth and health of a country's population.

human rights: Principles developed over hundreds of years that, after World War II, have been codified in a modern fashion through international human rights agreements, including the Universal Human Rights Declaration among others.

human security: A view that security issues revolve around the vulnerability of individual people, whether from political, social, or economic threats, among others.

human smuggling: The transfer of an individual who has paid a fee to a smuggler for the purpose of entering a new jurisdiction illegally.

human trafficking: The transfer of an individual from one jurisdiction to another through force or coercion for the purpose of criminal activities, such as slavery, prostitution, or removal of organs, among many others.

humanitarian intervention: The exercise of force by one state or group of states in another state's territory without the consent of that state based on humanitarian grounds. It was unlawful to do this before 1990.

humanitarian law: International laws governing the rules of war that seek to protect civilians caught up in conflict.

imperialism: The promotion of empire through military force, colonization, and economic policy. During the nineteenth and twentieth centuries, Europe and Japan used imperialist policy to force their authority on other states, thereby dominating them both politically and culturally.

interdisciplinary: A scholarly approach that demands multiple disciplines of study be applied for understanding challenges within the specific field. In human security this may include anthropology, economics, geography, history, sociology, and political science, among many others.

intergovernmental organization (IGO): An organization whose membership is principally made up of sovereign states.

International Commission on Intervention and State Sovereignty (ICISS): An international commission led by Gareth Evans and Mohamed Sahnoun that explored the issue of humanitarian intervention. The group mainstreamed the responsibility to protect (R2P) concept by building a case around the legitimate use of collective force against states who commit mass atrocities against their populations.

International Criminal Court (ICC): An institution brought into being by the Statute of Rome (1998) and based in the Hague, Holland. It is responsible for criminal trials of international war crimes.

interstate conflict: War between at least two governments, where each combatant is engaged in conflict that crosses national boundaries.

intrastate conflict: Conflict that occurs within one country's borders and involves a range of combatant nonstate actors fighting one another, as well as the governing authority.

ISO 26000: Drafted by the International Organization for Standardization in 2010, ISO 26000 is a standardization scheme that seeks to help organizations implement themes of corporate social responsibility into their business operations.

jihad: An Arabic term used to describe a religious and sacred struggle to preserve Islam and serve God's purpose on Earth. Extremists have used the term as a justification for "holy war," though this interpretation has been disputed.

just cause: A term used to describe the rationale behind the legal and moral grounds for armed intervention.

just war theory: A military doctrine that considers the legality and legitimacy of conflict. Historically, the theory was forwarded by Christian theologians who were concerned with the morality of conflict. The theory explores two criteria for justifying armed conflict: (1) the right to go to war (*jus ad bellum*), and

(2) the right conduct in war (*jus in bello*). Recently, a third category has been included in the theory, which is concerned with the responsibility of post-war reconstruction (*jus post bellum*).

Kimberley Process: A scheme designed to monitor the origins of diamonds to ensure they are not connected to conflict. Conflict diamonds, or "blood diamonds," have fueled conflict throughout the world, especially in Africa. The Kimberley Process was mainstreamed through a UN resolution with the help of many stakeholders, including UK-based NGO Global Witness.

kleptocratic regime: An authoritarian regime that steals resources from its citizens for the personal gain of the country's political officials.

last resort: A principle that argues war must be the absolute last resort if all other means of remedying the situation have failed, such as diplomacy.

legitimate authority: A term used to describe and question the legitimacy of a sovereign or government that claims to represent a population.

liberalism: A political belief system that advocates economic freedom and individual human rights. The principles of liberty and equality are core themes within liberal ideology, both of which must be guaranteed within a constitutional framework and protected within a governance system that endorses a strong rule of law.

liberal imperialism: Liberal imperialists justify imperial ventures as a humane goal of foreign policy, delivering progress and democracy through the imposition of their cultural and social values and the use of humanitarian interventionism.

liberty: A term that describes individual freedom from authoritarian control or arbitrary political power. Those who are denied liberty are unable to achieve a basic level of human security.

McDonaldization: A term coined by George Ritzer to explain the scientific management of the fast-food industry to ensure predictable and efficient results that could thus be replicated. Society is thus rationalizing a desire to produce more standard and predictable goods that are creating a low-paid, homogeneous society.

McMafia: A term coined by Misha Glenny to describe the emergence and wealth of post–Cold War transnational crime networks.

mediation: A type of alternative dispute resolution designed to negotiate peace settlements between conflicting groups through dialogue. The goal is to help parties develop empathy and a deeper understanding of one another. Also see *conflict resolution*.

migrant: An individual who chooses to leave one geographical location to permanently live in another for economic, social, or political reasons. This should be differentiated from a *refugee*, who has been forced to leave his or her geographic location on account of political violence.

military intervention: A post-Westphalian military operation that seeks to disrupt the internal affairs of a sovereign state accused of not protecting its citizens from violence.

Millennium Development Project: A project commissioned by the United Nations secretary-general in 2002 to develop a practical action plan on a global basis to achieve the Millennium Development Goals and to reverse the poverty, hunger, and disease affecting billions of people.

modernization: A theory that sees development as a transformative process where states evolve from a traditional type of society to a modern society over a historical period. Modernization theorists explore economic, social, and cultural factors that contribute to a state's development trajectory. Accordingly, modernization is a process that can be planned through technocratic advice found in multilateral institutions, like the World Bank, and international development agencies from the Global North.

Montreal Protocol: Entered into force in 1989, the Montreal Protocol on Substances that Deplete the Ozone Layer is a treaty intended to end the production of materials that deplete the ozone layer. The treaty is an important human security document not only because of its environmental intentions, but also because it signaled a major diplomatic breakthrough, demonstrating an acknowledgment of human interconnectedness and the collective challenge of managing the global commons.

multidimensionality: A term used to describe the dimensions of poverty, including heath, nutrition, and education levels. There is no single method for defining poverty; it may require a monetary approach that considers the financial state of an individual; a participatory approach that calls for local input to identify poverty rather than applying an international standard; a social exclusion view, which considers the marginalization and depravation of certain groups within a society; as well as the capabilities approach, which seeks to understand an individual's capacity to achieve "the good life."

multinational corporation (MNC): A term used to describe a business with multiple operations and offices across the globe. MNCs usually have a headquarters in one home jurisdiction but move their assets and products across borders.

national security: The policy(ies) conducted by a state to counter real or perceived internal and external threats to the state and to ensure the safety of its citizens.

neocolonialism: A system of control where one state dominates others through economic and political policy that forces occupied territories to comply with the controlling power. Also referred to as *imperialism*, this system has been most often associated with European forms of political control over other regions of the world. For example, the "Scramble for Africa" is an example of European political policies that brought the African continent under direct and indirect forms of Western control.

nepotism: When political elites show favoritism to family members and close friends by awarding lucrative government contacts through unfair bidding process.

New World Order: A term used by former American President George Bush and Russian President Mikhail Gorbachev to describe the post–Cold War era following the collapse of the Soviet Union.

nongovernmental organization (NGO): A civil society organization that acts independently of the government or business and which may promote special interests such as human rights or the environment. NGOs may be funded by private individuals, businesses, or governments.

nonstate actors: Agents that operate outside of government yet have the ability to influence the state. These entities may include private military companies, terrorists, nongovernmental organizations, and business.

North–South divide: A term used to describe the socioeconomic gap between wealthy countries in the Northern hemisphere and economically developing states in the Southern hemisphere.

official development assistance (ODA): A term used to describe overseas development aid provided by countries holding membership within the Organisation for Economic Co-operation and Development (OECD).

Operation Sovereign Borders (OSB): A military program adopted by the Australian government to combat illegal migrants arriving by boat off the coast of Australia.

Ottawa Treaty: Officially known as the Convention on the Prohibition of the Use, Stockpiling, Production and Transfer of Anti-Personnel Mines and on their Destruction, this treaty was spearheaded by the Canadian government and the International Campaign to Ban Landmines. Entered into force in 1997, this treaty was a major cornerstone in Canada's foreign policy strategy at the time, which centered on human security. The treaty is also recognized for its innovative multilateral process that involves regular consultation with civil society groups. As of 2015, 162 countries have signed the treaty while 35 have not, including China, India, Russia, and the United States.

patronage: The awarding of government positions and contracts based on political loyalty rather than merit.

peacebuilding: A relatively new concept developed in the 1990s to describe actions that identify and support structures that strengthen and engrain peace to prevent a reoccurrence into conflict.

peacekeeping: Peacekeeping is about having a third party act as an unbiased or impartial mediator to assist in the dispute settlement between two or more parties. There have been more than 50 peacekeeping missions since the end of World War II, and the majority of these were set up following the end of the Cold War, reflecting the move to intrastate rather than interstate wars.

peacemaking: A term used to describe efforts led by the United Nations to persuade hostile groups to reach an accord through diplomacy, mediation, and negotiation.

planners: A term coined by William Easterly to describe bureaucrats working in development agencies that plan aid strategies rather than implement them. Planners may have good intentions, but they have little experience or understanding of how their bureaucratic policies impact communities since they are far removed from the operation where the aid is being implemented.

political violence: External violence that is uncontrolled by the state and which has political motivations.

political will: The political motivation behind the decisions made by government officials.

post-conflict development: A term used to describe the political, economic, and social activities of a range of actors operating in a post-conflict setting. These groups seek to help stabilize the local economy, provide social assistance, and contribute to institution-building. Activities can range from training police officers to building hospitals. The purpose is to establish a sustained peace and higher levels of human security through international assistance.

post-Westphalian sovereignty: An argument that internal governance comes with responsibility, and there is no absolute right to manage the internal affairs of a state, especially when human rights are denied. Foreign states therefore have a responsibility to criticize the internal affairs of governments who commit grave rights abuses against their citizens.

poverty: There are three classifications for poverty. *Absolute poverty* can be defined as those living on less than $1.25 per day, *moderate poverty* considers those living on less than $2.00 per day, while *relative poverty* compares levels of inequality between groups within the same jurisdiction. Also see *multidimensionality*.

poverty line: Also referred to as the *poverty threshold*, it identifies the minimum level of required income by an individual to be considered as living above poverty. The World Bank has placed its poverty threshold at US$1.25 per day, adjusted to purchasing power parity to account for the economic jurisdiction of the individual.

poverty trap: A term used by development economists to describe states that are unable to escape poverty. Paul Collier has written extensively on poverty traps while identifying protracted conflict, weak governance, and the "resource curse" as explanations for bottom-billion countries that are unable to reach higher levels of development.

precautionary principle: A principle that instructs business to reject operations that could damage the environment or cause human harm.

prisoner's dilemma: A thought experiment used in game theory that seeks to test how individuals perceive their self-interests.

private military company (PMC): A business organization that employs security contractors who work in conflict zones for economic gain. Also known as *mercenaries*, these business actors are generally not bound by international humanitarian law. They offer a controversial yet cost-effective alternative for governments looking to reduce their military budget.

proportional means: Military doctrine that demands the minimum use of force when engaging in an armed intervention to ensure the protection of noncombatants.

public–private partnership (PPP): A joint venture partnership between government and the private sector.

race to the bottom: A socioeconomic occurrence where businesses compete for the lowest possible price for materials throughout their supply chain to ensure a lower price for their customers. Paradoxically, a lower price requires that suppliers cut corners by paying lower wages and ignoring environmental standards.

realism: The name of a descriptive and prescriptive theoretical approach to international relations. It involves a perpetual competition for power and security among states.

reasonable prospect: A concept that argues military intervention must not be approved if the result will cause more harm than good. Therefore, the decision maker must consider the long-term impact of armed intervention on the society in conflict.

refugee: According to the UN convention of 1951, individuals who have a well-founded fear of being persecuted for their religion, race, nationality, or membership of a social group or political persuasion and seek the protection of another foreign state. The key difference between a refugee and a migrant is the involuntary nature of the refugee and political persecution, whereas migrants tend to be motivated by money and better opportunities for life.

regionalism: The economic, political, and cultural administration of policy by actors residing in the same geographic region who share similar interests and objectives. For example, the European Union enacts policy for its members, which are only based in Europe.

rent-seeking: The act of manipulating a political system to enhance personal wealth by receiving economic gains on account of state policy decisions.

residential school policy: A policy administered by the government of Canada that saw the forced removal of over 150,000 Indigenous children from their parents and communities. The purpose was to assimilate First Nations, Inuit, and Métis children into Euro-Canadian culture through mandatory religious education. Thousands of children were abused and died in these schools, while generations of Indigenous youth lost total contact with their parents. It was not until 1996 that the last school closed its doors.

responsibility to protect (R2P): A normative concept that rejects the idea that sovereignty is an absolute right. Advocates of R2P call for military intervention against governments who are committing mass atrocities against their populations, such as genocide, war crimes, and crimes against humanity.

restorative justice: A strategy that seeks to remedy an injustice through a collaborative process that involves victims, perpetrators, and the community. It seeks to repair harm through healing and forgiveness rather than punishment.

right intention: A term used to describe the moral motivation behind a state's desire to engage in armed conflict.

rule of law: A legal principle that demands all individuals residing within a state be governed by that nation's laws. The law must be administered impartially, demonstrate judicial independence, and ensure equality. Many of these themes may be enshrined in a constitution and must ensure that no individual may act above the law.

Scramble for Africa: A period that lasted from 1881 to 1914 where European governments split and divided territory throughout the content of Africa in their pursuit for resources and imperialist ambitions.

second-generation rights: Those rights that are seen as entitlements and are not universally accepted, such as the right to maternity leave or the right to employment insurance. These rights require the government to implement policy to ensure these rights are allocated, and support for them is often ideologically divisive and can differ greatly between communities and states.

slavery: A term used to describe forced labor where one individual acts as the owner of another human being. There are different types of slavery, including a mode of production where the slave is forced to work. Tribute, or in-kind, slavery is a modern form of debt-bondage where the slave works to pay debt without any specified time frame of ending the slavery. Indentured slavery is similar to debt-bondage, but the worker is unpaid by contract until the debt has been cleared.

social contract theory: A theoretical contact that establishes rules for governing the relationship between individuals and the sovereign. A social contract may set limits on individual rights in exchange for protection from the state, whose subjects acknowledge the sovereign's legitimacy and right to rule.

social Darwinism: A belief that biology could be used to explain the strengths and weaknesses of different racial groups. Social Darwinists advocated a philosophy of natural selection and survival of the fittest, which was used to rationalize the exertion of power over certain groups based on their ethnicity. Social Darwinism is often associated with racist beliefs in North America and Western Europe that were used to help justify colonial occupation and imperialist expansionism.

sovereignty: The principle that states should enjoy legal autonomy and have exclusive rights to conduct their affairs within their state borders, independently of external actors.

sphere of influence: The space in which business actors operate with authority and have the ability to influence other actors who operate in the same space, such as government. Businesses may leverage their power to influence the state on certain social, economic, or environmental issues. For example, business has the ability to ask government agencies to ensure they are respecting human rights.

sphere of responsibility: The direct area of operations where business actors have a responsibility to promote social, economic, and environmental issues. For example, business has the responsibility to ensure that its employees are paid on time and work in a safe environment.

stakeholder engagement: An initiative where an organization or government consults actors who hold influence over the entity's decision-making process. Direct stakeholders may include shareholders, employees, and customers, while indirect stakeholders might include community members, activists, and academics.

state of nature: A concept used to describe the hypothetical setting of human relations before governments and societies existed.

structural adjustment programs: Economic recovery policies drafted by the World Bank and International Monetary Fund for countries experiencing financial crisis. The policies offer loans in exchange for the government's commitment to restructure its economy, often involving liberalization policies and austerity measures.

supply chain: A mode of production involving vast networks of suppliers who send goods and material to one point of assembly where the final product is created. For example, a supply chain of a T-shirt may involve cotton, dyes, buttons, and thread. Each of these components also has their own supply chain, making it difficult for managers to trace all the material throughout the chain.

sustainable development: A practical form of development that incorporates (1) supporting human life and ecological processes, (2) using resources in a sustainable way so they can be regenerated, and (3) making sure future generations have these resources available to them.

technocrat: An individual who provides expert or technical advice to governments or an intergovernmental organization.

technology transfer: The transfer of cutting-edge technology from wealthy nations to less-developed states for the purpose of skills training, environmental protection, as well as improved health and safety, among other goals.

terrorism: The act of using violence by nonstate actors to achieve political ends. It can include suicide bombing, kidnapping, or hijacking, and sometimes it is even practiced by states to achieve their goals. It relies on securing a disproportionate response following an act of terror from the government and media it is targeting as an audience.

third-generation rights: Those rights that are considered collective rights. They are more controversial, since they focus less on the individual. An example of a collective right is the right to clean air.

torture: The infliction of physical or mental abuse against a person in custody by an agent by the state for the purpose of extracting information or to punish the individual in custody.

trade liberalization: The removal of regulatory (duty and surcharges) and nontariff barriers (quotas, licensing rules) to ensure the free movement of goods and services across borders.

transnational crime: Organized crime that spreads across borders and impacts the international community. Such organizations are often involved in narcotics, human trafficking, terrorism, and other illicit activities that require a multilateral response by states.

triangular trade: A colonial trading system that saw the British Empire transport roughly 6 million slaves to the Americas from Africa. Trading ships would then carry raw goods from the Americas back to Europe before the traders would continue on to Africa where the boats would bring weapons and cloth.

triple bottom line: A term coined by John Elkington, who argued against the profit-maximization principle. Rather, the triple bottom line demands that business takes a more holistic approach to sustainability and pursues social, economic, and environmental goals.

truth commissions: Commissions that seek to end conflict through restorative justice. For example, the South African Truth and Reconciliation Commission sought to heal those who suffered under apartheid. Some perpetrators where given amnesty in exchange for testimony that would go on the public record. While controversial, the commission saw it as a critical healing process that could help the nation move forward.

underdeveloped: A state that has yet to achieve high levels of economic wealth. This is contrary to developed states, which have reached high levels of economic prosperity.

United Nations Global Compact (UNGC): A UN initiative designed to help the business community report and implement strategies of corporate social responsibility. The UNGC's main focus is human rights, the environment, labor, and anti-corruption.

United Nations Peacebuilding Commission (PBC): Established in 2005 along with the Peacebuilding Fund and the Peacebuilding Support Office, the commission consolidates the United Nations peacebuilding activities while serving as an intergovernmental advisory body for states needing post-conflict development assistance.

Universal Declaration of Human Rights: Drafted by the United Nations General Assembly on 10 December 1948, the UDHR is the first global statement that all individuals are entitled to basic human rights. The UDHR was drafted following World War II and the Holocaust, which had horrified Europe. The UDHR set a basic framework for drafting dozens of human rights treaties that would be worked into international law for years to come.

universalism: A theory that argues human rights are an undeniable truth that cannot be rejected based on political beliefs or socioeconomic circumstances. Universalists argue that the Universal Declaration of Human Rights must be equality enforced in all communities throughout the world regardless of cultural beliefs.

war crimes: Acts committed during war by any combatant that violate the Geneva Conventions or international law.

War on Terror: A term used to describe the international military campaign to minimize and disrupt terrorism. The term was frequently used by the media and the George W. Bush administration after 9/11.

wealth gap: The economic gap that exists between rich and poor countries.

Westphalian sovereignty: The belief that no country has the right to interfere with the internal governance matters of sovereign states. The concept endorses a version of sovereignty that has been forwarded since the Peace of Westphalia, where governments were guaranteed the absolute right to self-determination.

REFERENCES

Acharya, Amitav. 2001. "Human Security: East versus West." *International Journal:* 442–60.

Ackerman, Robert W. 1973. "How Companies Respond to Social Demands." *Harvard Business Review* 51 (4): 88–98.

Adetunji, Jo. 2001. "Forty-Eight Women Raped Every Hour in Congo, Study Finds." *The Guardian*, May 12. http://www.theguardian.com/world/2011/may/12/48-women-raped-hour-congo.

African Commission on Human and Peoples' Rights. 1986. African Charter on Human and Peoples' Rights. http://www.achpr.org/instruments/achpr.

African Renewal Online. 2010. "Darfur: An Experiment in African Peacekeeping." http://www.un.org/africarenewal/magazine/december-2010/darfur-experiment-african-peacekeeping.

Alberdi, Inés. 2008. "Rape as an Act of War: An Issue for the U.N." *New York Times*, June 19. http://www.nytimes.com/2008/06/19/opinion/lweb19kristof.html?_r=o.

Alesina, Alberto F., Stelios Michalopoulos, and Elias Papaioannou. 2012. Ethnic Inequality. http://www.nber.org/papers/w18512. http://dx.doi.org/10.2139/ssrn.2169485.

Alexander, Ruth. 2012. "Is Apple Really Worth More than Poland?" *BBC News*, March 13. http://www.bbc.com/news/magazine-17344386.

Alves, J. L. 2000. "The Declaration of Human Rights in Postmodernity." *Human Rights Quarterly* 22 (2): 478–500. http://dx.doi.org/10.1353/hrq.2000.0018.

Ammann, Theresa. 2014. "Ebola in Liberia: A Threat to Human Security and Peace." *Fieldsights—Hot Spots, Cultural Anthropology*, http://www.culanth.org/fieldsights/597-ebola-in-liberia-a-threat-to-human-security-and-peace.

Anderson, Siwan, and Debraj Ray. 2010. "Missing Women: Age and Disease." *Review of Economic Studies* 77 (4): 1262–300. http://dx.doi.org/10.1111/j.1467-937X.2010.00609.x.

Anheier, Helmut, Marlies Glasius, and Mary Kaldor, eds. 2001. *Global Civil Society*. New York: Oxford University Press.

Annan, Kofi. 2000a. "The Politics of Globalization." In *Globalization and the Challenges of a New Century: A Reader*, edited by Patrick O Meara, Howard D. Mehlinger, and Matthew Krain. Bloomington: Indiana Press.

———. 2000b. "We the Peoples: The Role of the United Nations in the 21st Century." In *Millennium Report*. New York: United Nations.

————. 2001. *Definitions of Human Security: Global Development.* http://www.gdrc.org/sustdev/husec/Definitions.pdf.

Appleby, Gabrielle. 2015. "Australia's Rigid Immigration Barrier." *New York Times*, May 7. http://www.nytimes.com/2015/05/08/opinion/australias-rigid-immigration-barrier.html?_r=0.

Arnold, Denis G. 2010. "Transnational Corporations and the Duty to Respect Basic Human Rights." *Business Ethics Quarterly* 20 (3): 372–76.

Asian Human Rights Commission. 2015. "The Practice of Honour Killings." Accessed July 31. http://www.humanrights.asia/resources/journals-magazines/hrschool/lesson-series-35-the-practice-of-honour-killings.

Asian Legal Resource Centre. 2011. "WORLD: The MDG-HR Nexus—Need to Understand Deprivation of Civil Rights as a Cause of Poverty." http://www.humanrights.asia/news/alrc-news/ALRC-ART-001-2011.

Associated Press. 2014. "Indian Officials Order Coca-Cola Plant to Close for Using too Much Water." *The Guardian*, June 18. http://www.theguardian.com/environment/2014/jun/18/indian-officals-coca-cola-plant-water-mehdiganj.

Ban Ki-moon. 2012. "Secretary-General's Address to the General Assembly." http://www.un.org/sg/statements/index.asp?nid=6312.

Barber, Benjamin. 1996. *Jihad vs. McWorld.* New York: Ballantine Books.

Barnett, Jon, and W. Neil Adger. 2007. "Climate Change, Human Security and Violent Conflict." *Political Geography* 26 (6): 639–655. http://dx.doi.org/10.1016/j.polgeo.2007.03.003.

Barnett, Michael N. 2011. *Empire of Humanity: A History of Humanitarianism.* New York: Cornell University Press.

Barnett, Michael and Christopher Zürcher. 2009. "The Peacebuilder's Contract: How External Statebuilding Reinforces Weak Statehood." In *The Dilemmas of Statebuilding: Confronting the Contradictions of Postwar Peace Operations*, edited by Roland Paris and Timothy Sisk. New York: Routledge.

Barry, J., and B. Doherty. 2001. "The Greens and Social Policy: Movements, Politics and Practice." *Social Policy and Administration* 35 (5): 587–607. http://dx.doi.org/10.1111/1467-9515.00255.

BBC News. 2011. "Q&A: East Africa Hunger Crisis." July 22. http://www.bbc.com/news/world-africa-14249733.

Beaucar Vlahos, Kelley. 2014. "'Windfalls of War': Companies with Spotty Records Making Billions off Afghanistan." *FOX News*, February 20. http://www.foxnews.com/politics/2014/02/20/windfalls-war-contractors-with-spotty-records-made-billions-off-afghanistan/.

Bellamy, Alex J. 2008a. "Conflict Prevention and the Responsibility to Protect." *Global Governance* 14 (2): 135–56.

————. 2008b. "The Responsibility to Protect and the Problem of Military Intervention." *International Affairs* 84 (4): 615–39. http://dx.doi.org/10.1111/j.1468-2346.2008.00729.x.

Bellamy, Alex J., and Paul Williams. 2009. "The West and Contemporary Peace Operations." *Journal of Peace Research* 46 (1): 39–57.

Bellamy, Alex J., Paul Williams, and Stuart Griffin. 2010. *Understanding Peacekeeping.* Cambridge: Polity Press.

Benenson, Peter. 1961. "The Forgotten Prisoners." http://www.amnestyusa.org/about-us/amnesty-50-years/peter-benenson-remembered/the-forgotten-prisoners-by-peter-benenson.

Bennett, Juliette. 2001. "Business in Zones of Conflict—The Role of the Multinationals." *Promoting Regional Stability.* http://capacity-training-international.com/2011/12/31/business-in-zones-of-conflict-the-role-of-the-multinationals-in-promoting-regional-stability/.

Berman, Sheri. 1997. "Civil Society and the Collapse of the Weimar Republic." *World Politics* 49 (3): 401–29. http://dx.doi.org/10.1353/wp.1997.0008.

Blanton, Robert G., and Shannon L. Blanton. 2007. "Human Rights and Trade: Beyond the Spotlight." *International Interactions* 33 (2): 97–117. http://dx.doi.org/10.1080/03050620701268300.

Blowfield, M., and A. Murray. 2008. *Corporate Responsibility: A Critical Interdiction.* Hong Kong: Oxford University Press.

Bowen, Howard R. (1953) 2013. *Social Responsibilities of the Businessman.* Iowa City: University of Iowa Press.

Brahm, Eric. 2003. "Latent Conflict Stage." Beyond Intractability. http://www.beyondintractability.org/essay/latent-conflict.

Brewer, Devin. 2009. "Globalization and Human Trafficking." *Human Rights & Human Welfare:* 46–56. http://www.du.edu/korbel/hrhw/researchdigest/trafficking/Globalization.pdf.

Brophy, Stephanie. 2008. "Mexico: Cartels, Corruption, and Cocaine: A Profile of the Gulf Cartel." *Global Crime* 9 (3): 248–61.

Brundtland, Gro Harlem. 1987. Report of the World Commission on Environment and Development: Our Common Future. http://www.un-documents.net/our-common-future.pdf.

Buhaug, Halvard. 2015. Climate–Conflict Research: Some Reflections on the Way Forward. *WIREs Climate Change.* http://www.hbuhaug.com/wp-content/uploads/2015/03/Buhaug_WIREsCC_2015.pdf.

Burgess, Heidi, and Guy Burgess. 2003. "What Are Intractable Conflicts?" Beyond Intractability. http://www.beyondintractability.org/essay/meaning-intractability.

Burke, Jason. 2013. "Delhi Rape: How India's Other Half Lives." *The Guardian,* September 10. http://www.theguardian.com/world/2013/sep/10/delhi-gang-rape-india-women.

Business and Human Rights Resource Centre. 2013. "Philippine Typhoon Haiyan/Yolanda: Company Contributions to Humanitarian Aid." http://business-humanrights.org/en/documents/philippine-typhoon-haiyanyolanda-%E2%80%93-company-contributions-to-humanitarian-aid-nov-2013.

———. 2015a. "Business and Human Rights—A Brief Introduction." Accessed July 31. http://www.business-humanrights.org/GettingStartedPortal/Intro.

———. 2015b. "UN 'Protect, Respect and Remedy' Framework and Guiding Principles." http://business-humanrights.org/en/un-secretary-generals-special-representative-on-business-human-rights/un-protect-respect-and-remedy-framework-and-guiding-principles.

Caiden, Gerald E. 2009. "Concluding Remarks: Toward Cleaner Governance?" In *Preventing Corruption in Asia: Institutional Design and Policy Capacity,* edited by Ting Gong and Stephen K. Ma, 222–38. New York: Routledge.

Campion, Mukti Jain. 2011. "Bribery in India: A Website for Whistleblowers." *BBC News,* June 6. http://www.bbc.com/news/world-south-asia-13616123.

Carothers, Thomas. 1999. "Civil Society." *Foreign Policy* 117: 18–29. http://dx.doi.org/10.2307/1149558.

Carroll, Archie B. 1979. "A Three-Dimensional Conceptual Model of Corporate Performance." *Academy of Management Review* 4 (4): 497–505.

Center for Justice and Accountability. 2014. "Timor-Leste (East Timor): Crimes against Humanity under the Indonesian Occupation. http://www.cja.org/article.php?list=type&type=198.

Chandler, David. 2004. "The Responsibility to Protect? Imposing the 'Liberal Peace.'" *International Peacekeeping* 11 (1): 59–81.

Chomsky, Noam. 2006. *Failed States: The Abuse of Power and the Assault on Democracy.* New York: Henry Holt & Company.

Chua, Amy. 2004. *World on Fire: How Exporting Free Market Democracy Breeds Ethnic Hatred and Global Instability.* Toronto: Anchor Press.

Clark, Michele A. 2003. "Human Trafficking Casts Shadow on Globalization." *Yale Global Online.* http://yaleglobal.yale.edu/content/human-trafficking-casts-shadow-globalization.

Clinton, Bill. 1998. "Remarks to the People of Rwanda." March 25. http://millercenter.org/president/speeches/speech-4602.

Collier, Paul. 2008. *The Bottom Billion: Why the Poorest Countries Are Failing and What Can Be Done about It.* Oxford: Oxford University Press.

Council on Foreign Relations. 2014. "Mexico's Drug War." http://www.cfr.org/mexico/mexicos-drug-war/p13689.

Dallaire, Romeo. 2003. *Shake Hands with the Devil: The Failure of Humanity in Rwanda.* Toronto: Random House.

David, Saul. 2011. "Slavery and 'the Scramble for Africa.'" BBC. http://www.bbc.co.uk/history/british/abolition/scramble_for_africa_article_01.shtml.

David, Steven. 1997. "Internal War: Causes and Cures." *World Politics* 49 (4): 552–76. http://dx.doi.org/10.1017/S0043887100008054.

Davies, J.B., S. Sandström, A. Shorrocks, and E. Wolff. 2009. "The Global Pattern of Household Wealth." *Journal of International Development* 21 (8): 1111–24. http://dx.doi.org/10.1002/jid.1648.

Dawson, Stella. 2012. "Dirty Money Costs Developing World $6 Trillion, Led by China: Report." Reuters, December 17. http://www.reuters.com/article/2012/12/18/us-funds-global-illicit-idUSBRE8BH00220121218.

De Haan, A. 2009. *How the Aid Industry Works: An Introduction to International Development.* Boulder, CO: Kumarian Press.

The Democracy Center. 2000. "Bolivia's War over Water." http://democracyctr.org/bolivia/investigations/bolivia-investigations-the-water-revolt/bolivias-war-over-water/.

Deng, Francis M. 2011. "Idealism and Realism: Negotiating Sovereignty in Divided Nations." Lecture given at Uppsala University, Uppsala, Sweden, September 10, 2010.

Diaz, Lizbeth. 2008. "Four People Killed in Mexico Drug-Smuggling Area." Reuters, May 19. http://www.reuters.com/article/2008/05/19/us-mexico-drugs-americans-idUSN1954747020080519.

Dine, Janet. 2005. *Companies, International Trade and Human Rights.* Melbourne: Cambridge. http://dx.doi.org/10.1017/CBO9780511660139.

Doctors Without Borders. 2015. "History and Principles." http://www.doctorswithoutborders.org/about-us/history-principles.

Domashneva, Helena. 2013. "NGOs in Cambodia: It's Complicated." *The Diplomat,* December 3. http://thediplomat.com/2013/12/ngos-in-cambodia-its-complicated/.

Donnelly, Jack. 2013. *Universal Human Rights in Theory and Practice.* 3rd ed. Ithaca: Cornell University Press.

Drezner, Daniel W. 2000. "Bottom Feeders." *Foreign Policy* 121: 64–70. http://dx.doi.org/10.2307/1149620.

Duffield, Mark. 2007. "Development, Territories, and People: Consolidating the External Sovereign Frontier." *Global, Local, Political* 32 (2): 225–46. http://dx.doi.org/10.1177/030437540703200204.

Dunne, Tim, and Marianne Hanson. 2009. "Human Rights in International Relations." In *Human Rights: Politics and Practice*, edited by Michael Goodhart, 61–76. Oxford: Oxford University Press.

Durden, T. 2013. "It's a '0.6%' World: Who Owns What of the $223 Trillion in Global Wealth." Zerohedge. http://www.zerohedge.com/news/2013-06-02/its-1-world-who-owns-what-223-trillion-global-wealth.

Easterly, W. 2006. *The White Man's Burden: Why the West's Efforts to Aid the Rest Have Done So Much Ill and So Little Good*. London: Penguin.

Edkins, Jenny. 2000. *Whose Hunger? Concepts of Famine, Practices of Aid*, vol. 17. Minneapolis: University of Minnesota Press.

Elder, Miriam. 2013. "Russia Passes Law Banning Gay 'Propaganda.'" *The Guardian*, June 11. http://www.theguardian.com/world/2013/jun/11/russia-law-banning-gay-propaganda.

Elkington, John. 1997. *Cannibals with Forks: The Triple Bottom Line of 21st Century*. Oxford: Capstone Publishing Ltd.

Engle, Karen. 2011. "On Fragile Architecture: The UN Declaration on the Rights of Indigenous Peoples in the Context of Human Rights." *European Journal of International Law* 22 (1): 141–63. http://dx.doi.org/10.1093/ejil/chr019.

Escobar, A. 2011. *Encountering Development: The Making and Unmaking of the Third World*. Princeton, NJ: Princeton University Press.

Evans, Alex. 2010. "Resource Scarcity, Climate Change and the Risk of Violent Conflict." *World Development Report 2011*. http://web.worldbank.org/archive/website01306/web/pdf/wdr%20background%20paper_evans_0.pdf.

Evans, G.J., and M. Sahnoun. 2001. *The Responsibility to Protect: Report of the International Commission on Intervention and State Sovereignty*. International Development Research Centre.

Evans, Paul M. 2004. "Human Security and East Asia: In the Beginning." *Journal of East Asian Studies* 4 (2): 263–84.

Falk, Richard. 2005. "Legality and Legitimacy: The Quest for Principled Flexibility and Restraint." *Review of International Studies* 31 (1): 33–50.

———. 2014. *(Re)Imagining Humane Global Governance*. New York: Routledge.

Fenn, Mark. 2014. "Tense Times in Thailand." *The Diplomat*, June 5. http://thediplomat.com/2014/06/tense-times-in-thailand/.

Ferreiro, M. 2012. "Blurring of Lines in Complex Emergencies: Consequences for the Humanitarian Community." *Journal of Humanitarian Assistance*. http://sites.tufts.edu/jha/archives/1625.

Food and Agriculture Organization. 2013. "Drought." http://www.fao.org/docrep/017/aq191e/aq191e.pdf.

Friedman, Milton. 2002. *Capitalism and Freedom*. 3rd ed. Chicago: University of Chicago Press. http://dx.doi.org/10.7208/chicago/9780226264189.001.0001.

Fukuda-Parr, Sakiko. 2004. "Gender, Globalization and the New Threats to Human Security." *Peace Review* 16 (1): 35–42. http://dx.doi.org/10.1080/1040265042000210139.

Fukuyama, F. 2006. *The End of History and the Last Man*. New York: Free Press.

Fund for Peace. 2015. The Fragile States Index 2015. http://library.fundforpeace.org/library/fragilestatesindex-2015.pdf.

Galtung, Johan. 1969. "Violence, Peace, and Peace Research." *Journal of Peace Research* 6 (3): 167–91. http://dx.doi.org/10.1177/002234336900600301.

Garwood, Paul. 2006. "Coca-Cola Plant Opens in Afghan Capital." *Washington Post*, September 11. http://www.washingtonpost.com/wp-dyn/content/article/2006/09/11/AR2006091100073.html.

Gasper, D. 2005. "Securing Humanity: Situating 'Human Security' as Concept and Discourse." *Journal of Human Development* 6 (2): 221–45. http://dx.doi.org/10.1080/14649880500120558.

Geneva Academy. 2013. "The International Code of Conduct for Private Security Service Providers." http://www.geneva-academy.ch/docs/publications/briefing4_web_final.pdf.

Geneva Declaration on Armed Violence and Development. 2006. "How Does It Work?" Accessed June 28. http://www.genevadeclaration.org/the-geneva-declaration/how-does-it-work.html.

Gibson, Owen, and Pete Pattisson. 2014. "Death Toll among Qatar's 2022 World Cup Workers Revealed." *The Guardian*, December 23. http://www.theguardian.com/world/2014/dec/23/qatar-nepal-workers-world-cup-2022-death-toll-doha.

Giddens, Anthony. 1991. *Modernity and Self-Identity: Self and Society in the Late Modern Age*. Cambridge: Polity.

Glenny, Misha. 2008. *McMafia: A Journey through the Global Underworld*. Toronto: House of Anansi.

Global Partnership for the Prevention of Armed Conflict. 2015. "Our Work." http://www.gppac.net/our-work.

Global Policy Forum. 2005. Failed States. https://www.globalpolicy.org/nations-a-states/failed-states.html.

Global Security. 2015. "Forces Democratiques de Liberation du Rwanda (FDLR) (Democratic Liberation Forces of Rwanda)." http://www.globalsecurity.org/military/world/para/fdlr.htm.

Global Witness. 2013. "The Kimberley Process." https://www.globalwitness.org/en/campaigns/conflict-diamonds/kimberley-process/.

Government of Eritrea. 2013. "Eritrea Rejects Amnesty International's Wild Accusations." http://www.tesfanews.net/wp-content/uploads/eritrea-rejects-amnesty-international-wild-accusations.pdf.

Gray, Colin. 2005. "How Has War Changed since the End of the Cold War?" *Parameters* 35 (1): 14–26. http://www.offnews.info/downloads/2020war_changed.pdf.

Gray, John. 2004. *Heresies*. London: Granta Books.

Grimes, William. 2015. "Wiseguys and Fall Guys, Welcome to Globalization." *New York Times*, April 11. http://www.nytimes.com/2008/04/11/books/11book.html?_r=0.

Haas, Peter. 1992. "Introduction: Epistemic Communities and International Policy Coordination." In *Knowledge, Power, and International Policy Coordination*, edited by Peter Haas, 1–35. Columbia: University of South Carolina Press.

Hammarskjold, Dag. 2014. "The Pursuit of Peace." http://www.canadianperescenterforpeace.com/The-Pursuit-of-Peace.php.

Hampson, Fen Osler, and Jean Daudelin. 2002. *Madness in the Multitude: Human Security and World Disorder*. Toronto: Oxford University Press.

Hanlon, Robert, and Stephen Frost. 2013. "Teaching Corporate Social Responsibility, Human Rights and Corruption: A Survey of 343 Faculty at the Top 20 Business Schools in the *Financial Times* Global MBA Rankings." *Journal of Business Ethics Education* 10: 1–35.

Hehir, Aidan. 2013. *Humanitarian Intervention: An Introduction*. London: Palgrave Macmillan.

Hehir, Aidan, and Robert Murray. 2015. "The Need for Post-R2P Humanitarianism." OpenCanada.org, March 17. http://opencanada.org/features/the-need-for-post-r2p-humanitarianism/.

Hills, J., and R. Welford. 2005. "Coca-Cola and Water in India." *Corporate Social Responsibility and Environmental Management* 12 (3): 168–77. http://dx.doi.org/10.1002/csr.97.

Hobbes, Michael. 2014. "Stop Trying to Save the World: Big Ideas Are Destroying International Development." *New Republic*, November 17. http://www.newrepublic.com/article/120178/problem-international-development-and-plan-fix-it.

Hobsbawm, Eric. 1996. *The Age of Extremes: A History of the World, 1914–1991*. London: Vintage Books.

Hopgood, Stephen. 2013. "Human Rights: Past Their Sell-By Date." https://www.opendemocracy.net/openglobalrights/stephen-hopgood/human-rights-past-their-sell-by-date.

Hopkins, Michael. 2012. *Corporate Social Responsibility and International Development: Is Business the Solution?* London: Earthscan.

Howard-Hassmann, Rhoda. 2012. "Human Security: Undermining Human Rights." *Human Rights Quarterly* 34 (1): 88–112. http://dx.doi.org/10.1353/hrq.2012.0004.

Human Rights Watch. 2011. "Gold's Costly Dividend: Human Rights Impacts of Papua New Guinea's Porgera Gold Mine." https://www.hrw.org/report/2011/02/01/golds-costly-dividend/human-rights-impacts-papua-new-guineas-porgera-gold-mine.

Huntington, Samuel. 1996. *The Clash of Civilizations: The Remaking of the World Order*. New York: Simon and Schuster.

ICB Japan. 2015. "Outline of the Report of the Commission on Human Security." Accessed August 4. http://www.icbjapan.org/humansecurity_outline.pdf.

International Alert. 2010. "The Programming Framework for International Alert: Design, Monitoring, Evaluation." http://intl.staging.winonaesolutions.net/sites/default/files/publications/201001ProgrammingFramework.pdf.

International Alert. 2015. "Our Corporate Engagement Principles." http://www.international-alert.org/how-we-work-companies.

International Bridges to Justice. 2015. "Burundi." http://www.ibj.org/where-we-work/burundi/.

International Center for Not-for-Profit Law. 2015. "NGO Law Monitor: Rwanda." http://www.icnl.org/research/monitor/rwanda.html.

International Committee of the Red Cross. 2015. "Rule 93. Rape and Other Forms of Sexual Violence." https://www.icrc.org/customary-ihl/eng/docs/v1_rul_rule93.

International Criminal Court. 1998. "Rome Statute of the International Criminal Court."

International Crisis Group. 2006. "Pakistan: Political Impact of the Earthquake." http://www.crisisgroup.org/en/regions/asia/south-asia/pakistan/B046-pakistan-political-impact-of-the-earthquake.aspx.

International Organization for Migration. 2008. "Situation Report on International Migration in East and South-East Asia: Regional Thematic Working Group on International Migration including Human Trafficking." http://publications.iom.int/books/situation-report-international-migration-east-and-south-east-asia.

———. 2015. "Where We Work: Middle East and North Africa." https://www.iom.int/cms/en/sites/iom/home/where-we-work/africa-and-the-middle-east/middle-east-and-north-africa.html.

Islamic Relief. 2016. "Syria Appeal." http://www.islamic-relief.com.au/1210/syria-appeal/.

Jarroud, Marianela. 2013. "Mining and Logging Companies 'Leaving All of Chile Without Water.'" *The Guardian*, April 24. http://www.theguardian.com/global-development/2013/apr/24/mining-logging-chile-without-water.

Jenkins, Rob. 2013. *Peacebuilding: From Concept to Commission*, vol. 72. New York: Routledge.

Job, Brian. 2004. "The UN, Regional Organizations, and Regional Conflict: Is There a Viable Role for the UN?" In *The United Nations and Global Security*, edited by Mark Zacher and Richard Price. New York: Palgrave-St. Martin's Press.

Jones, Pete. 2013 "Congo: We Did Whatever We Wanted, Says Soldier Who Raped 53 Women." *The Guardian*, April 11. http://www.theguardian.com/world/2013/apr/11/congo-rapes-g8-soldier.

Jones, Sam. 2015. "UN: 15-Year Push Ends Extreme Poverty for a Billion People." *The Guardian*, July 6. http://www.theguardian.com/global-development/2015/jul/06/united-nations-extreme-poverty-millennium-development-goals.

Kaldor, Mary. 2007. *Human Security*. Cambridge: Polity Press.

———. 2013. *New and Old Wars: Organized Violence in a Global Era*. New York: John Wiley & Sons.

Kaplan, Robert. 1994. "The Coming Anarchy." *Atlantic Monthly*. http://www.theatlantic.com/magazine/archive/1994/02/the-coming-anarchy/304670/.

Kapoor, Ilan. 2012. *Celebrity Humanitarianism: The Ideology of Global Charity*. New York: Routledge.

Kinsman, Jeremy. 2015. "Harper's Foreign Policy: Hard Realism or Empty Posturing?" OpenCanada.com, January 5. https://www.opencanada.org/features/harpers-foreign-policy-hard-nosed-realism-or-empty-posturing/.

Kleiman, Mark. 2011. "Surgical Strikes in the Drug Wars: Smarter Policies for Both Sides of the Border." *Foreign Affairs* 90 (5): 89–101.

Kostovicova, Denisa, and Marlies Glasius. 2011. "Introduction: Agency in Bottom-up Politics." In *Bottom-Up Politics: An Agency-Centred Approach to Globalization*, 1–17. Basingstoke: Palgrave Macmillan. http://dx.doi.org/10.1057/9780230357075.0007.

Laderchi, Caterina R., Ruhi Saith, and Francis Stewart. 2003. "Does It Matter That We Do Not Agree on the Definition of Poverty? A Comparison of Four Approaches." *Oxford Development Studies* 31 (3): 243–74. http://dx.doi.org/10.1080/1360081032000111698.

Lambert, David, and Alan Lester. 2004. "Geographies of Colonial Philanthropy." *Progress in Human Geography* 28 (3): 320–41. http://dx.doi.org/10.1191/0309132504ph489oa.

Larrain, J. 2013. *Theories of Development: Capitalism, Colonialism and Dependency*. New York: John Wiley & Sons.

Lipschutz, Ronnie D. 1992. "Reconstructing World Politics: The Emergence of Global Civil Society." *Millennium* 21 (3): 389–420. http://dx.doi.org/10.1177/03058298920210031001.

MacDonald, Shawn. 2013. *Peacebuilding and the Private Sector: Integrated Peacebuilding; Innovative Approaches to Transforming Conflict*. Boulder, CO: Westview Press.

MacFarquhar, Neil. 2010. "U.N. Poverty Goals Face Accountability Questions." *New York Times*, September 18. http://www.nytimes.com/2010/09/19/world/19nations.html.

Marshall University. 1977. "The Sullivan Principles." http://www.marshall.edu/revleonsullivan/principles.html.

Mason, Simon, and Sandra Rychard. 2005. "Conflict Analysis Tools." http://www.css.ethz.ch/publications/pdfs/Conflict-Analysis-Tools.pdf.

Massingham, Eve. 2009. "Military Intervention for Humanitarian Purposes: Does the Responsibility to Protect Doctrine Advance the Legality of the Use of Force for Humanitarian Ends?" *International Review of the Red Cross* 91 (876): 803–831. http://dx.doi.org/10.1017/S1816383110000068.

McBeth, Adam. 2014. "Crushed by an Anvil: A Case Study on Responsibility for Human Rights in the Extractive Sector." *Yale Human Rights and Development Journal* 11 (1): Article 8. http://digitalcommons.law.yale.edu/yhrdlj/vol11/iss1/8.

McGreal, Chris. 2008. "Tutsi Rebels in Congo Accused of Murdering Civilians." *The Guardian*, November 7. http://www.theguardian.com/world/2008/nov/07/congo-tutsi-hutus-kiwanja-rwanda.

Meadows, Donella H., Dennis L. Meadows, Jorgen Randers, and William W. Behrens III. 1972. *The Limits to Growth: A Report for the Club of Rome's Project on the Predicament of Mankind.* New York: Universe Books.

Mercy Corps. 2015. "Quick Facts: What You Need to Know About the Syria Crisis." http://www.mercycorps.org/articles/iraq-jordan-lebanon-syria-turkey/quick-facts-what-you-need-know-about-syria-crisis.

Ministry of Foreign Affairs of Japan. 2014. "Submission of Report by Commission on Human Security to Secretary-General of the United Nations Kofi Annan." http://www.mofa.go.jp/policy/human_secu/commission/report0305.html.

Moran, Mary, and Daniel Hoffman. 2014. "Introduction: Ebola in Perspective." *Fieldsights—Hot Spots, Cultural Anthropology*, http://www.culanth.org/fieldsights/586-introduction-ebola-in-perspective.

Morelle, Rebecca. 2013. "Rise in Violence Linked to Climate Change." *BBC News*, August 2. http://www.bbc.com/news/science-environment-23538771.

Morton, Eddie. 2014. "Civil Pay Increase Questioned." *Phnom Penh Post*, April 8. http://www.phnompenhpost.com/business/civil-pay-increase-questioned.

Nagan, Winston P., and Haddad, Aitza M. 2011. "Sovereignty in Theory and Practice." *San Diego International Law Journal* 13: 429–520.

Nazemi, N. 2012. "How Globalization Facilitates Trafficking in Persons." *Political Communication* 6 (2): 5–14.

Neate, Rupert. 2015. "Apple Soon to Be Worth More Than $1tn, Financial Analysts Predict." *The Guardian*, March 23. http://www.theguardian.com/technology/2015/mar/23/apple-company-worth-1tn-market-value.

Neu, D.E., and R. Therrien. 2003. *Accounting for Genocide: Canada's Bureaucratic Assault on Aboriginal People.* Toronto: Fernwood Books.

Oetzel, J., M. Westermann-Behaylo, C. Koerber, T. Fort, and J. Rivera. 2010. "Business and Peace: Sketching the Terrain." *Journal of Business Ethics* 89 (4): 351–73.

Ohmae, Kenichi. 1999. *The Borderless World: Power and Strategy in the Interlinked Economy: Management Lessons in the New Logic of the Global Marketplace.* New York: Harper Business.

Open Society Justice Initiative and MUHURI. 2013. "'We're Tired of Taking You to the Court': Human Rights Abuses by Kenya's Anti-Terrorism Policy Unit." Open Society Foundations. https://www.opensocietyfoundations.org/sites/default/files/human-rights-abuses-by-kenya-atpu-20140220.pdf.

Owen, Taylor. 2004. "Human Security: Conflict, Critique, and Consensus: Colloquium Remarks and a Proposal for a Threshold-Based Definition." *Security Dialogue* 35 (3): 373–87.

Oxfam. 2005. "Exploring the Links between International Business and Poverty Reduction: A Case Study of Unilever in Indonesia." http://policy-practice.oxfam.org.uk/publications/exploring-the-links-between-international-business-and-poverty-reduction-a-case-112492.

———. 2014. "Case Study 3—ANZ and Phnom Penh Sugar." https://www.oxfam.org.au/grow/files/2014/06/anz-report.pdf.

Oxfam International. 2015. "Wealth: Having It All and Wanting More." http://policy-practice.oxfam.org.uk/publications/wealth-having-it-all-and-wanting-more-338125.

Paffenholz, T., ed. 2010. *Civil Society & Peacebuilding: A Critical Assessment.* London: Lynne Rienner Publishers.

Page, Edward, and Michael Redclift, eds. 2002. *Human Security and the Environment: International Comparisons.* Cheltenham, UK: Edward Elgar Publishing Limited.

Paris, Roland. 2001. "Human Security: Paradigm Shift or Hot Air?" *International Security* 26 (2): 87–102.

———. 2010. "Saving Liberal Peacebuilding." *Review of International Studies* 36 (2): 337–65. http://dx.doi.org/10.1017/S0260210510000057.

Parliament of Canada. 2000. "The New NATO and the Evolution of Peacekeeping: Implications for Canada." *Report of the Standing Committee on Foreign Affairs.* http://www.parl.gc.ca/Content/SEN/Committee/362/fore/rep/rep07apr00-e.htm.

Perrin, Benjamin, ed. 2012. *Modern Warfare: Armed Groups, Private Militaries, Humanitarian Organizations, and the Law.* Vancouver: University of British Columbia Press.

Phipps, Claire. 2015. "Did Australia Pay People-Smugglers to Turn Back Asylum Seekers?" *The Guardian,* June 17. http://www.theguardian.com/world/2015/jun/17/did-australia-pay-people-smugglers-to-turn-back-boats.

Phipps, Claire, David Hills, and Bryan Armen Graham. 2015. "FIFA in Crisis Amid Corruption Arrests and World Cup Voting Inquiry—As It Happened." *The Guardian,* May 27. http://www.theguardian.com/football/live/2015/may/27/fifa-officials-arrested-on-corruption-charges-live.

Pingeot, Lou, and Wolfgang Obenland. 2014. *In Whose Name? A Critical View on the Responsibility to Protect.* New York: Global Policy Forum and Rosa Luxemburg Stiftung.

Pinker, Steven. 2011. *The Better Angels of Our Nature: The Decline of Violence in History and Its Causes.* London: Penguin.

Princen, Thomas. 2001. "Joseph Elder: Quiet Peacemaking in a Civil War." In *When Talk Works: Profiles of Mediators,* edited by Deborah M. Kolb, 427–58. San Francisco: Jossey-Bass.

Project Ploughshares. 2015. "Research and Action for Peace: Vision." http://.ploughshares.ca.

Pupavac, Vanessa. 2005. "Human Security and the Rise of Global Therapeutic Governance." *Conflict Security and Development* 5 (2): 161–81. http://dx.doi.org/10.1080/14678800500170076.

Rahman, M. 2011. "Human Trafficking in the Era of Globalization: The Case of Trafficking in the Global Market Economy." *Transcience Journal* 2 (1): 54–71.

Ramcharan, Bertrand G. 2008. *Preventive Diplomacy at the UN.* Bloomington: Indiana University Press.

Ramsbotham, Oliver, Hugh Miall, and Tom Woodhouse. 2011. *Contemporary Conflict Resolution.* Cambridge: Polity Press.

Rawls, John. 2009. *A Theory of Justice.* Cambridge, MA: Harvard University Press.

Remembering Srebrenica. 2014. "Sudbin Musić—Trnopolje Camp, Prijedor." http://www.srebrenica.org.uk/survivor-stories/sudbin-music/.

Renan, Ernest. 1990. "What Is a Nation?" *Nation and Narration* 11: 8–22.

Reuters. 2011. "China Paper Warns of 'Sound of Cannons' in Sea Disputes." October 25. http://www.reuters.com/article/2011/10/25/us-china-seas-idUSTRE7901MV20111025.

Rice, Susan. 2008. U.S. Foreign Assistance and Failed States. Brookings Policy Brief. Washington: Brookings.

Roach, Stephen C., Martin Griffiths, and Terry O'Callaghan. 2014. *International Relations: The Key Concepts.* Toronto: Routledge.

Robbins, James. 2014. "How Syria Sank into All Out Civil War." *BBC News*, January 17. http://www.bbc.co.uk/news/world-middle-east-25755987.

Robinson, Mary. 2003 "Foreward." In *Business and Human Rights: Dilemmas and Solutions*, edited by Rory Sullivan. Sheffield: Greenleaf.

Roosevelt, F.D. 1941. "The Four Freedoms". Speech, Washington, DC, January 6. Retrieved from http://www.fdrlibrary.marist.edu/pdfs/fftext.pdf.

Sachs, Jeffrey. 2006. *The End of Poverty: Economic Possibilities for Our Time.* New York: Penguin.

Salehyan, Idean. 2008. *From Climate Change to Conflict: No Consensus Yet.* Bloomington: Indiana University Press.

Schrage, Elliot J. 2003a. "Emerging Threat: Human Rights Claims." *Harvard Business Review.* https://hbr.org/2003/08/emerging-threat-human-rights-claims.

———. 2003b. "Judging Corporate Accountability in the Global Economy." *Columbia Journal of Transnational Law* 42: 153–76.

Sen, Amartya. 2005. "Human Rights and Capabilities." *Journal of Human Development* 6 (2): 151–66. http://dx.doi.org/10.1080/14649880500120491.

Shell. 2015. "Climate Change." http://www.shell.com/global/environment-society/environment/climate-change.html.

Shiffman, John, and Daniel Trotta. 2013. "Patriot or Traitor, Snowden Driven by Fear of Government Intrusion." Reuters, June 11. http://www.reuters.com/article/2013/06/11/us-usa-security-snowden-idUSBRE95A0TH20130611.

Smith, Steve. 2005. "The Contested Concept of Security." *Critical Security Studies and World Politics*: 27–62.

Snowdon, Karon. 2014. "ANZ Bank Dumps Cambodia Customer PP Sugar." Radio Australia, July 9. http://www.radioaustralia.net.au/international/radio/program/asia-pacific/anz-bank-dumps-cambodia-customer-pp-sugar/1340362.

Sorokin, P.A. 1962. *Social and Cultural Dynamics.* Vol. 1. New Jersey: Transaction Publishers.

Spurk, C. 2010. *Understanding Civil Society: Civil Society and Peacebuilding: A Critical Assessment.* Boulder, CO: Lynne Reinner Publishers.

Stanford Encyclopedia of Philosophy. 2011. "Hugo Grotius." http://plato.stanford.edu/entries/grotius/.

Steger, Manfred. 2013. *Globalization: A Very Short Introduction.* Toronto: Oxford University Press. http://dx.doi.org/10.1093/actrade/9780199662661.001.0001.

Stern, Nicholas. 2006. "Stern Review: The Economics of Climate Change." http://mudancasclimaticas.cptec.inpe.br/~rmclima/pdfs/destaques/sternreview_report_complete.pdf.

Sullivan, Rory, and Nina Seppala. 2003. "From the Inside Looking Out: A Management Perspective on Human Rights." *Business and Human Rights*, edited by Rory Sullivan. Sheffield: Greenleaf. http://dx.doi.org/10.9774/GLEAF.978-1-909493-38-4_9.

Suu Kyi, Aung San. 1995. "Opening Address for NGO Forum on Women." http://gos.sbc. edu/k/kyi.html.

———. 2010. *Freedom from Fear: And Other Writings*. London: Penguin.

Thakur, Ramesh. 2006. *The United Nations, Peace and Security: From Collective Security to the Responsibility to Protect*. Cambridge: Cambridge University Press. http://dx.doi.org/10.1017/CBO9780511755996.

———. 2014. "The United Nations and the Elusive Quest for Peace." Speech given at the University of Melbourne. http://ssps.unimelb.edu.au/video/united-nations-and-elusive-quest-peace.

Thomas, Caroline. 2001. "Global Governance, Development and Human Security: Exploring the Links." *Third World Quarterly* 22 (2): 159–75.

Thomas, Caroline, and Peter Wilkin, eds. 1999. *Globalization, Human Security, and the African Experience*. Boulder, CO: Lynne Rienner Publishers.

Thürer, Daniel. 1999. "The 'Failed State' and International Law." Global Policy Forum. https://www.globalpolicy.org/component/content/article/173/30464.html.

Tisdall, Simon. 2011. "US–Pakistan Relations Facing Biggest Crisis Since 9/11, Officials Say." *The Guardian*, April 12. http://www.theguardian.com/world/2011/apr/12/us-pakistan-relations-crisis.

Transparency International. 2015. "About." http://blog.transparency.org/about/.

UN Action Against Sexual Violence in Conflict. 2015. "Stop Rape Now." Accessed June 26. http://www.stoprapenow.org/uploads/aboutdownloads/1282162584.pdf.

United Nations. 1948. "Universal Declaration of Human Rights." http://www.un.org/en/documents/udhr/.

———. 2000. "Brahimi Report: Report of the Panel on United Nations Peace Operations." http://www.un.org/en/events/pastevents/brahimi_report.shtml.

———. 2008. "Security Council Demands Immediate and Complete Halt to Acts of Sexual Violence against Civilians in Conflict Zones, Unanimously Adopting Resolution 1820 (2008)." Press release, June 19. http://www.un.org/press/en/2008/sc9364.doc.htm.

———. 2013. "Inequality Matters: Report of the World Social Situation 2013." http://www.un.org/esa/socdev/documents/reports/InequalityMatters.pdf.

———. 2015. "Background: Cambodia Peacekeeping Missions." Accessed August 6. http://www.un.org/en/peacekeeping/missions/past/untacbackgr2.html.

United Nations Development Programme. 1994. *Human Development Report 1994*. http://hdr.undp.org/sites/default/files/reports/255/hdr_1994_en_complete_nostats.pdf.

———. 2002. "Human Development Report: Deepening Democracy in a Fragmented World." http://hdr.undp.org/sites/default/files/reports/263/hdr_2002_en_complete.pdf.

———. 2013. "Human Development Report 2013: The Rise of the South: Human Progress in a Diverse World." http://hdr.undp.org/sites/default/files/reports/14/hdr2013_en_complete.pdf.

———. 2014. "Public–Private Partnership Publications." http://www.undp.ro/publications/ppp.php.

———. 2015. "Frequently Asked Questions." http://www.undp.org/content/undp/en/home/operations/about_us/frequently_askedquestions.html.

United Nations Foundation. 2002. "Understanding Public-Private Partnership." http://www.globalproblems-globalsolutions-files.org/unf_website/PDF/understand_public_private_partner.pdf.

―――. 2013. "Nelson Mandela Quotes We Love." http://www.unfoundation.org/blog/nelson-mandela-quotes-we-love.html.

United Nations General Assembly. 1999. "Report of the Secretary-General Pursuant to General Assembly Resolution 53/35: The Fall of Srebrenica." http://www.un.org/en/ga/search/view_doc.asp?symbol=A/54/549.

United Nations GIFT. 2008. "The Vienna Forum Report: A Way Forward to Combat Human Trafficking." http://www.ungift.org/docs/ungift/pdf/vf/ebook2.pdf.

United Nations Global Compact. 2015. "The Ten Principles." http://www.unglobalcompact.org/AboutTheGC/TheTenPrinciples/index.html.

United Nations High Commission for Refugees. 2014. "Irregular Maritime Movements." http://www.unhcr.org/53f1c5fc9.pdf.

United Nations International Children's Emergency Fund. 2013. "Protection, Care and Support for Children Affected by HIV and AIDS." http://www.unicef.org/protection/.

United Nations News Centre. 2016. "Solutions Needed to Stem Global Refugee Crisis, Says New UN Agency Chief." January 7. http://www.un.org/apps/news/story.asp?NewsID=52955#.Vo_Y8xUrJXh.

United Nations Office on Drugs and Crime. 2003. "United Nations Convention against Transnational Organized Crime and Its Protocols on Trafficking in Persons and Migrant Smuggling." http://www.unodc.org/unodc/en/human-trafficking/index.htm/.

―――. 2012. "Country Profile Americas: Canada." In *Global Report on Trafficking in Persons*, 8–13. New York: United Nations Publications.

―――. 2014. "Global Report on Trafficking in Persons." http://www.unodc.org/documents/data-and-analysis/glotip/Trafficking_in_Persons_2012_web.pdf.

United Nations Peacebuilding Commission. 2015a. "Mandate of the Peacebuilding Commission." Accessed July 25. http://www.un.org/en/peacebuilding/mandate.shtml.

―――. 2015b. "What Is Peacebuilding?" Accessed August 6. http://www.un.org/en/peacebuilding/pbso/pbun.shtml.

United Nations Peacebuilding Fund. 2011. "What Is Peacebuilding? Definitions and Policy Development." http://www.unpbf.org/application-guidelines/what-is-peacebuilding/.

United States Agency for International Development. 2005. "Fragile States Strategy." http://www.au.af.mil/au/awc/awcgate/usaid/2005_fragile_states_strategy.pdf.

University of Minnesota Human Rights Library. 2015. "Global Sullivan Principles." Accessed July 25. http://www1.umn.edu/humanrts/links/sullivanprinciples.html.

Uppsala University. 2015. *UCDP Conflict Encyclopedia.* http://www.ucdp.uu.se/gpdatabase/search.php.

US Department of State. 2006. "Fact Sheet: Distinctions between Human Smuggling and Human Trafficking 2006." http://www.state.gov/m/ds/hstcenter/90434.htm.

―――. 2012. "Trafficking in Persons Report 2012." http://www.state.gov/j/tip/rls/tiprpt/2012/192352.htm.

―――. 2014. "Trafficking in Persons Report 2014." http://www.state.gov/j/tip/rls/tiprpt/2014.

US Government Accountability Office. 2009. "Firearms Trafficking: U.S. Efforts to Combat Arms Trafficking to Mexico Face Planning and Coordination Challenges." http://www.gao.gov/products/GAO-09-781T.

Verdeja, Ernesto. 2013. "Transitional Justice and Genocide." In *Genocide Matters: Ongoing Issues and Emerging Perspectives*, edited by Joyce Apsel and Ernesto Verdeja, 172–94. New York: Routledge.

Vike-Freiberga, Veira. 2005. "Secretary-General's Message to the Third Summit of the Council of Europe." http://www.un.org/sg/STATEMENTS/index.asp?nid=1451.

von Einsiedel, Sebastian, and Rahul Chandran. 2015. *The High-Level Panel and the Prospects for Reform of UN Peace Operations*. United Nations University: Center for Policy Research.

Walker, J.W.S.G., and A.S. Thompson, eds. 2008. *Critical Mass: The Emergence of Global Civil Society*, vol. 5. Waterloo, ON: Wilfrid Laurier University Press.

Washington State Department of Ecology. 2012. "What Is Climate Change?" http://www.ecy.wa.gov/climatechange/whatis.htm.

Weiss, Thomas G. 2013. *Humanitarian Business*. Cambridge: Polity Press.

Weiss, Thomas G., and Rorden Wilkinson. 2013. *International Organization and Global Governance*. New York: Routledge.

Whalan, Jeni. 2013. *How Peace Operations Work: Power, Legitimacy, and Effectiveness*. Oxford: Oxford University Press. http://dx.doi.org/10.1093/acprof:oso/9780199672189.001.0001.

Wheaton, E.M., E.J. Schauer, and T.V. Galli. 2010. "Economics of Human Trafficking." *International Migration* 48 (4): 114–41. http://dx.doi.org/10.1111/j.1468-2435.2009.00592.x.

Wilkinson, Tracy. 2011. "Poverty Grew in Mexico to Nearly Half the Population, Study Finds." *Los Angeles Times*, July 29. http://articles.latimes.com/2011/jul/29/world/la-fg-mexico-poverty-20110730.

Windsor, Duane. 2006. "Corporate Social Responsibility: Three Key Approaches." *Journal of Management Studies* 43 (1): 93–114. http://dx.doi.org/10.1111/j.1467-6486.2006.00584.x.

Women's International League for Peace and Freedom. 2014. "Peace Quotes." http://wilpf.org/peace-quotes/.

World Bank. 2015a. "Mobilizing the Billions and Trillions for Climate Finance." http://www.worldbank.org/en/news/feature/2015/04/18/raising-trillions-for-climate-finance.

———. 2015b. "Overview." http://www.worldbank.org/en/topic/poverty/overview.

World Business Council for Sustainable Development. 2015. "Corporate Social Responsibility." http://www.wbcsd.org/work-program/business-role/previous-work/corporate-social-responsibility.aspx.

World Food Programme. 2014. "Bangladesh." http://www.wfp.org/countries/bangladesh/overview.

———. 2015. "What Causes Hunger?" http://www.wfp.org/hunger/causes.

World Health Organization. 2015a. "Complex Emergencies." http://www.who.int/environmental_health_emergencies/complex_emergencies/en/.

———. 2015b. "Food Security." http://www.who.int/trade/glossary/story028/en/.

World Vision. 2013. "World Vision US: 2013 Annual Review." http://www.worldvision.org/sites/default/files/2013-annual-report-brochure-new.pdf.

Zelizer, Craig. 2013. *Integrated Peacebuilding: Innovative Approaches to Transforming Conflict*. Boulder: Westview Press.

Zelizer, Craig, and Valerie Oliphant. 2013. "Introduction to Integrated Peacebuilding." In *Integrated Peacebuilding: Innovating Approaches to Transforming Conflict*, edited by Craig Zelizer, 3–30. Boulder, CO: Westview Press.

INDEX

democratic deficit, 82–83
democratic institutions, 176
Democratic Republic of Congo (DRC), 10,
    24, 32, 74, 89, 185, 213
    intractable conflict, 35–36
    intrastate conflicts, 23
    rape as a weapon of war, 38, 99
democratic rights, 90
democratization, 25–26, 105
demographic pressures, 15
Deng, Francis, 86
Department for Peacekeeping Operations
    (DPKO), 96
deregulation, 207
detention, 30, 72
developing world, 13, 17, 45, 67
development, xi–xii, 4, 11, 62, 75, 97, 118
    "as freedom," 5
    globalization and, 162–63
    human social and economic, 5
    meaning of, 162
development studies, 40, 181
diamond sector, 184, 213
diplomacy, xii, 102
disarmament, 101, 134
disease, 5, 15, 17, 88, 194
    infectious diseases, 227
    migrants and immigrants blamed for, 210
    reducing spread of AIDS, HN1, or
      Ebola, 12
displaced people, 208, 228
Ditchley Formula, 87
Djibouti, 172
do-no-harm principle, 183
Donnelly, Jack, 53–54, 59
drought, 170, 172
drug trafficking, 15, 165, 221–23
due diligence, 183, 187, 189, 202–3
Dunant, Henry, *A Memory of Solferino*, 117
duty to protect. *See* responsibility to
    protect (R2P)
dysfunctional state institutions, 62, 228. *See
    also* failed states
    civil society push against, 128
    corruption, 66

human insecurity, 53, 65–70
    political interference, 67
dysfunctionality of governments, 166,
    174

Earth Summit in Rio de Janeiro, 42, 198
earthquake (Japan 2011), 8
earthquake (Nepal 2015), 210
East Asian Miracle, 8
East Timor, 94–95, 101
    Australian-led intervention in, 136
    genocide, 24
Ebola crisis, 129–30
ecological security, 42
economic crisis (2008–09), 3, 7, 208
economic development. *See* development
economic security, 7, 21
economics, 29
education, 55, 63, 90, 153
Egypt, 208–9
empathy, 4, 12, 28, 228–29
"End of History," 26
environment, 29, 90
    conflict, 40–44
    degradation, 50, 182
    disasters, 5, 12, 88, 171, 205
    as global theme, 25
    protection, 159, 180
    rights centered on, 56
    security, 8, 42
    sustainability, 181, 192. (*See also*
      sustainable development)
environmental movements, 41
Equator Principles, 82, 182, 195, 201
Ethiopia, 172
ethnic-based groups, 50, 161
ethnicity
    cleansing tied to, 57, 100, 140–41, 145
    conflicts, 30, 33–35, 124, 137, 145, 205
    (*See also* identity politics)
    minorities, 8, 10
    politics of, 26 and social class, 15, 25
    violence based on, 24, 35, 120
Eurocentrism, 116
European Union (EU), 84

modern variant on slave trade, 214, 216

sex trafficking, 221

humanitarian crises, 79, 88. *See also* genocide; Syrian civil war

humanitarian intervention, xi, 115, 120, 134–35

military intervention, 145

multilateral participation in, 144

national interests and, 136

rationale for, 142–45

six criteria for, 141

humanitarian law, 117

humanitarian NGOs, 102, 129

humanitarianism, 13, 114, 116–18

distrust for, 112

as instrument of war, 119

politicization of, 120

transnational humanitarian aid workers, 111

Huntington, Samuel, 26–27

Hussein, Saddam, 94

ICISS (International Commission on Intervention and State Sovereignty), 140–42

identity politics, 26, 34–35, 205. *See also* wars of identity

impartiality, 92, 95, 106, 117, 119

imperial humanitarianism, 116–18

imperialism, 114, 116

India, 43, 46, 219–20

NGOs, 121, 127

nuclear weapons, 19

public distrust of government, 128

refusal to acknowledge ICC, 101

Indian Ocean tsunami (2004), 88

Indigenous peoples, 56, 115

cultures, 116

rights, 55

individual human beings, 5, 10, 57

individual rights, 69

Indonesia, 219

inequalities between and within nation-states, 15–16, 29, 162, 216, 228. *See also* wealth gap

insurgents, 29–30

intergovernmental organizations (IGOs), 81–82, 84, 111, 159, 219

internal conflicts. *See* intrastate conflicts

international "aid" policies, 163

International AIDS Vaccine Initiative, 194

International Alert, 126–27

International Bridges to Justice, 126

International Code of Conduct for Private Security Service Providers (ICoC), 187

International Committee of the Red Cross (ICRC), 116–19

International Conference of the American States, 87

"International Convention on the Protection of the Rights of All Migrant Workers," 211

International Criminal Court (ICC), 9–10, 101

International Criminal Tribunal for Rwanda, 100, 138

International Criminal Tribunal (former Yugoslavia), 10, 38, 100

international human rights

law, 55

movement, 53–55, 57, 88

treaties, 60, 62

international humanitarian law (IHL), 117

International Labour Organization (ILO), 79, 153, 195, 203, 211, 216, 219

international law, xi–xii, 85, 87, 110

international mining industry, 184

International Monetary Fund (IMF), 71, 160–61, 164, 177

international NGOs, 82, 88, 102, 111, 121, 125

International Organization for Migration, 209

International Organization for Standardization, 189, 193

international organizations, 79, 81, 83, 103

International Panel on Climate Change (IPCC), 44

Internet, 24

civil society use, 125

political elites, 80

political interference, 66–67

political will, 53, 62, 81, 96, 137, 173, 206, 211

population growth rates, 208

positive liberty, 63

positive rights, 56

post-conflict
development, 135
reconciliation activities, 28, 43
reconstruction agenda, 95, 102

post-2015 development agenda, 159, 175

post-Westphalian sovereignty, 87

post–Cold War era, 3–4, 13, 20–21, 81, 110
casualties, 36
changing nature of conflict, 10, 23–50, 90, 187, 227
corporate policy around human security themes, 181
human security, 30, 46
humanitarianism, 119–20, 136
increasing use of children in conflict and as victims, 153
influence of NGOs, 125
meaning of the state, 25
multilateral regulatory initiatives, 189
new conceptualizations of sovereignty, 86
peacebuilding, 102–6, 135
peacekeeping, 98
push for democratization, 25
religious resurgence, 17
security threats, 23
transparency and accountability within financial sector, 195

post–Millennium Development Goal era, 227

post–9/11, 8, 17, 24, 46, 120
"new" world order following, 48
security threats, 23

poverty, xii, 3, 5, 11, 16–17, 29, 50, 55, 62, 66–67, 90, 159–61, 163–64, 208, 224, 227
absolute poverty, 166–67
global poverty as threat to human security, 166

moderate poverty, 166

multidimensionality, 167

relative poverty, 166–67

solutions to, 176–77

structural roots of, 168

poverty alleviation, 181

poverty line, 167

poverty traps, 61, 174–75

precautionary principle, 183

preventative diplomacy, 97

prisoner's dilemma, 98

private military companies (PMC), 183, 187

private sector, 70, 72–74. *See also* business
corporate complicity in human rights violations, 185
human rights as a business issue, 200
promoting environmental protection, 202

private-sector development in post-conflict societies, 183

Prodi Report, 91

progress, 162–63, 224

Project Ploughshares, 27

"protect, respect, remedy," 192

protection, 4
of journalists and activist citizens, 125

public-private partnerships (PPPs), 193
business case, 194

Public–Private Partnerships for Service Delivery (PPPSD) program, 194

race to the bottom, 15, 189, 202

racism, 113, 115

rape, 38, 74, 89, 100
gang rape in India, 39
as weapon of war, 30, 38–39, 99, 137

Rawls, John, 63–64

realist doctrine, 11–12, 48, 63

reconciliation, 135

refugees, 5, 11, 172, 206, 208, 227
as global theme, 25
from Rwanda, 137
War on Terror and, 48
women and children, 28